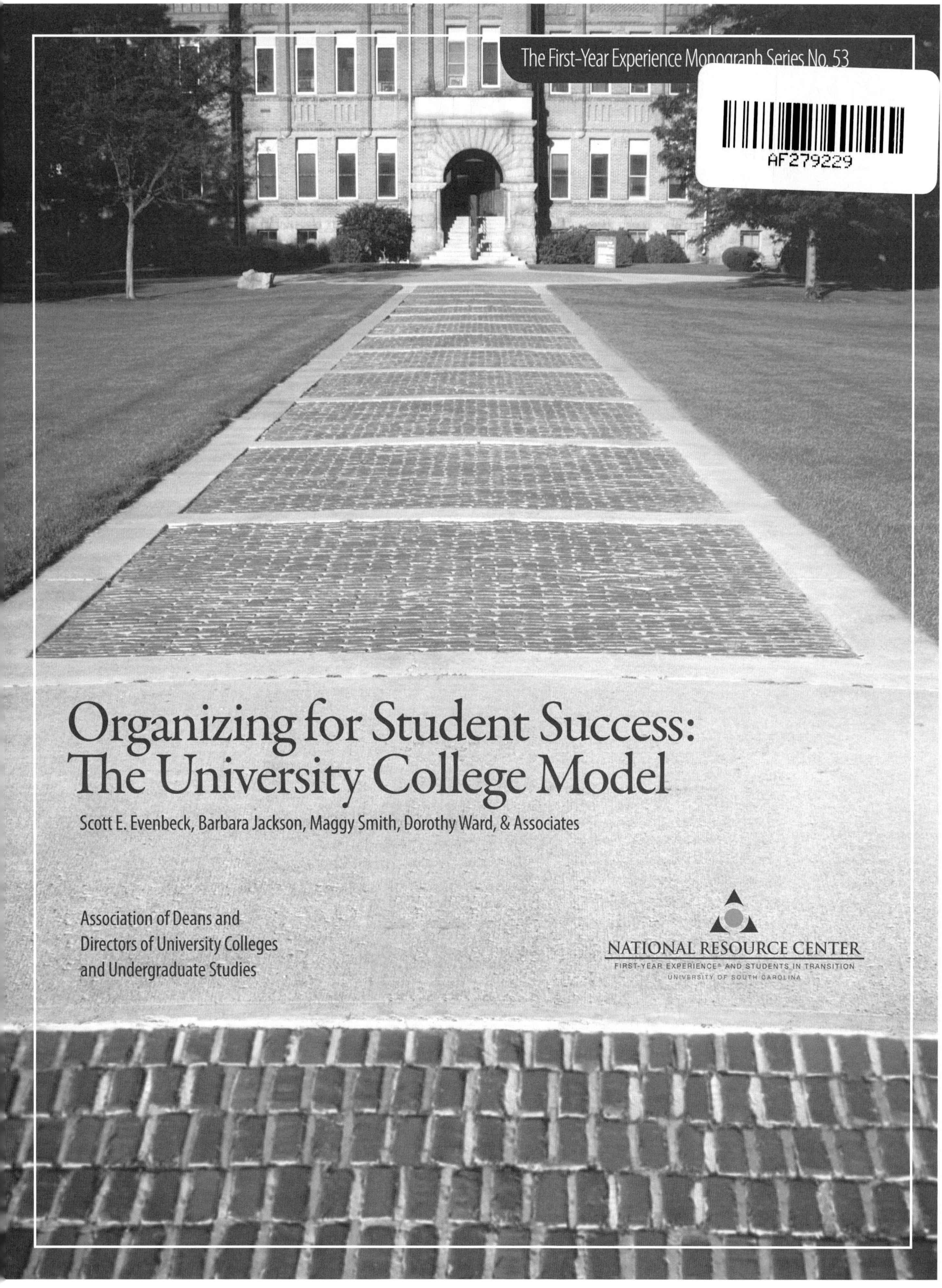

AF279229

Organizing for Student Success:
The University College Model

Scott E. Evenbeck, Barbara Jackson, Maggy Smith, Dorothy Ward, & Associates

Association of Deans and
Directors of University Colleges
and Undergraduate Studies

Cite as:

Evenbeck, S. E., Jackson, B., Smith, M., Ward, D., & Associates. (2010). *Organizing for student success: The university college model* (Monograph No. 53). Columbia, SC: University of South Carolina, National Resource Center for The First-Year Experience and Students in Transition.

Sample chapter citation:

Swing, R. L., & Alexander-Hamilton, J. S. (2010). University colleges: Flexible structures for serving undergraduate students. In S. E. Evenbeck, B. Jackson, M. Smith, D. Ward, & Associates, *Organizing for student success: The university college model* (Monograph No. 53, pp. 1-23). Columbia, SC: University of South Carolina, National Resource Center for The First-Year Experience and Students in Transition.

ISBN 978-1-889-27170-5

Production Staff for the National Resource Center:

Project Manager	Tracy L. Skipper, Assistant Director for Publications
Project Editor	Toni Vakos, Editor
Design and Production	Melody Taylor, Graphic Artist

Additional copies of this monograph may be obtained from the National Resource Center for The First-Year Experience and Students in Transition, University of South Carolina, 1728 College Street, Columbia, SC 29208. Telephone (803) 777-6229. Fax (803) 777-4699.

Library of Congress Cataloging-in-Publication Data

Organizing for student success : the university college model / by Scott E. Evenbeck ... [et al.].
    p. cm. -- (The first-year experience monograph series ; no. 53)
  Includes bibliographical references.
  ISBN 978-1-889271-70-5
  1. College student development programs--United States--Case studies. 2. College freshmen--United States--Case studies. I. Evenbeck, Scott E.
  LB2343.4.O74 2010
  378.1'98--dc22
                        2010024124

Contents

List of Tables and Figures

Preface

Jennifer R. Keup & Carter Hammett-McGarry

In the 17 years since the release of the previous monograph on university colleges, *Portals of Entry: University Colleges and Undergraduate Divisions*, many trends in higher education have continued, including diversification of the undergraduate student population, demands for assessment and accountability, and the focus on enhancing student success and retention. These very issues gave rise to the need for the university college to address undergraduate student issues and concerns and continue to give this model a strong place in American higher education today. This energy and advancement with respect to university colleges is exciting and provides purpose for ongoing scholarship on this topic; validates for the tireless efforts of deans, directors, and other campus staff to the development and success of university colleges; and solidifies the importance of these structures within the first-year experience and students in transition network.

Throughout the development of this book, collaboration emerged as a connecting value between the current volume and the previous one as well as the thread between the history of university college models and their future successes. The contributors to this monograph frequently highlight the importance of collaboration and often reference university colleges as a *community of practice*. As such, we are quite proud that the publication of this monograph represents a partnership between two communities of practice in the field of higher education: the National Resource Center for The First-Year Experience and Students in Transition and the Association of Deans and Directors of University Colleges and Undergraduate Studies. Much like university colleges, the history of both of these organizations is deeply rooted in communities of professionals whose commitment gave rise to more formalized higher education organizations and, thus, represent other examples of the power of collaboration in the field of higher education.

The work of the National Resource Center actually represents a movement in higher education to understand and address the first-year experience (FYE) and students in transition and then to formalize it as a specialization in higher education. Although elements of first-year courses, advising, and services can be found as early as the 18th century, what we recognize as the modern-day movement was initiated at the University of South Carolina in 1972. It began with the introduction of a first-year seminar course on that campus, the success of which can be attributed to the dedicated community of campus professionals who were led by John N. Gardner. Ten years later, this institutional program had emerged as a standard for best practice with respect to the transition, adjustment, and success of first-year students and regularly generated inquiry from other colleges and universities across the country. As such, the time was ripe to broaden the scope of the FYE community of practice by holding a meeting to discuss first-year seminars and other critical student adjustment issues. Although only 75 colleagues were expected to attend, the first meeting drew well over 150 individuals interested in the topic of student success during the first year, and a national movement was born. In order to fully support the growing interest in the first-year experience on a national scale, the National Resource Center for The First-Year Experience and Students in Transition was established in 1986 at the University of South Carolina. Since that time, the Center has served as a leader of the first-year experience movement; supported a growing national and international community of professionals; and advanced research and practice dedicated to student transitions and success through conferences, research, and publications. The body of scholarship and international community of practice that these efforts have generated have forged a foundation of evidence, theory, and collaboration to inform the direction of the first-year experience and students in transition movement and to achieve the Center's mission to "support and advance efforts to improve student learning and transitions into and through higher education."

In a similar example of the evolution of a community of practice into a national presence in American higher education, the Association of Deans and Directors of University Colleges and Undergraduate Studies was founded in 1990 following four years of informal meetings of individuals who were charged with improving student learning and success on their campuses. The group first gathered in Newport, Rhode Island, to discuss common challenges and issues and to resource one another for problem solving and sharing program expansion strategies. Those who attended represented a diverse group of institutions, including private liberal arts colleges, comprehensive regional universities, state universities, and research-intensive institutions. The representatives gained so much from those few days of honest soul searching and creative thinking that they decided to meet annually for roundtable discussions on topics of common interests. There was a definite decision not to follow the model of conferences with keynote speakers and, to this day, the Association of Deans and Directors has held firm to this think-tank format. Individuals who attended the first meeting agreed to seek out colleagues at other institutions who were leading similar efforts and units and invite them to become a member of the association.

Over the past 25 years, the number of colleges and universities holding membership in the association has grown to 120 and maintained the diversity of institutions. Professionals who started the association were leaders of units, such as orientation, academic advising, college transition services and courses, Supplemental Instruction, and learning assistance programs. Over the years, as high-impact student success practices have been designed and implemented across the nation, many units (e.g., learning communities, service-learning, undergraduate research) have found their place and gained support in university colleges and units with similar missions. Furthermore, general education, liberal studies, and interdisciplinary degree programs have found a natural home in a limited number of university colleges across the United States. The Association of Deans and Directors believes that the various units represented in the current membership attest to the necessity for adaptation and flexibility in the design and support of student-centered efforts among varied institutional types and missions. As such, the Association of Deans and Directors of University Colleges and Undergraduate Studies is the modern day guild for people who work in student-centered units and who care about promoting excellence.

We are so pleased to have the expertise of members of our respective organizations and from our unified community of practice represented in this monograph. Many of them have contributed to the meetings of the Association of Deans and Directors of University Colleges and Undergraduate Studies as well as the National Resource Center for The First-Year Experience and Students in Transition. Their input at those events and expertise in our field help provide a plan for addressing difficult situations, innovative ideas for new and existing services, and proven experience upon which we can rely for guidance on projects and to address our concerns. These authors also represent a variety of roles and perspectives in higher education—campus administrators, assessment professionals, national researchers, and educational leaders—and are from a range of institutions. Further, they contributed both topical content as well as institutional case studies of university college models to this publication effort. As such, the content of this monograph provides a broad interpretation and application of the university college model and addresses issues unique to specific campus contexts. We invite readers to explore the breadth of information on strategies and models presented in the monograph for launching and sustaining a centralized effort to improve undergraduate education on their own campuses, comparing and contrasting their campus cultures with those of the institutions represented in the case studies. Readers are also encouraged to examine the services that are provided and the rationale for their inclusion in the units and to identify processes and collaborations that have been useful in strategically embedding the work of these units across campus communities.

We are dedicated to expanding the community of practice that surrounds university colleges both on campuses and nationally, and readers of this monograph are members of that community. Whether readers work on a campus with a longstanding university college or are exploring the model for the first time, we are confident that the content of this monograph will provide history, knowledge, and guidance to help educators address challenges and leverage opportunities to support undergraduate learning and success. We welcome readers to membership in this community of practice and look forward to continuing the dialogue on this topic.

Jennifer R. Keup
Director
National Resource Center for The First-Year Experience and Students in Transition
University of South Carolina

Carter Hammett-McGarry
2009-2010 President
Association of Deans and Directors of University Colleges and Undergraduate Studies
Director of General Education
Appalachian State University

Foreword

Betsy O. Barefoot & John N. Gardner

What is the best way to organize university functions and administrative systems to support beginning students? While there may be more than one answer to this question depending on institutional size and overall mission, an organizational structure that has shown itself to be especially effective in both large and mid-size universities is the university college. University colleges are sometimes known by other names, such as general college, first-year college, or division of undergraduate studies. Regardless of what they are called, there are no better sources for information on the various ways these units operate than the team of authors who have written this monograph: Scott Evenbeck, Barbara Jackson, Maggy Smith, Dorothy Ward, and their colleagues.

A university college can bring needed order to the haphazard way that many institutions provide services to new students and can respond to a central problem of the first year, and that is, who, if anyone, is in charge. A university college is also an effective way to provide an administrative home for new students where they are the highest priority. In fact, it can be argued that there are no other organizational units in postsecondary institutions where first-year students, the perennial underclass of the academy, will have higher status. And while university colleges are generally in charge of the first year, they will frequently administer programs and services for sophomores and transfer students.

In addition to providing programs and services, university colleges enable what are perhaps the most important aspects of a successful organizational structure—communication and collaboration. In today's large universities, the simple act of interacting across unit and division lines can become an elusive goal. It is often easier for any individual or unit to operate as a "lone ranger" than to collaborate with others who are working on related initiatives. This absence of essential interaction results in gaps in service as well as redundancy. But a university college facilitates and depends on close collaboration between its own subunits as well as other faculty and staff members, and through that collaboration the college can reduce both gaps and duplication of effort.

This monograph is a needed update of one produced in 1993 by the National Resource Center and authored by Diane Strommer, *Portals of Entry: University Colleges and Undergraduate Divisions*. In turn, that monograph was an outgrowth of a single article by Strommer published in 1989 in the first volume of the Center's refereed *Journal of The Freshman Year Experience*. That article was one of the earliest sources for information on this unique organizational structure, and we felt then, as we believe now, that the university college concept deserves greater prominence and, hopefully, replication. Some university colleges featured in the 1989 article and 1993 monograph no longer exist, but many others have been born, several of which are featured in this current volume.

Through the years, university colleges have evolved and adapted to the changing needs of students and institutions. And as this monograph describes, today's university colleges exhibit many different characteristics. Some are focused exclusively on the first year, while others serve students until such time as they formally declare a major. Some are primarily centralized advising units, while others oversee components of the curriculum. University colleges sometimes administer first-year seminars, learning communities, developmental education, and honors programs. They also help organize relevant communities of practice within a large institution and sponsor faculty and staff development activities. Almost all university colleges have some relationship to general education. The nature of that relationship may include tenured faculty lines within the college for those who teach general education courses or, more commonly, collaboration between the college and other academic units for the delivery of special programs, student support, and faculty development related to general education.

But, as the authors acknowledge, one of the primary and most unique roles of university colleges is as an institutional change agent. By their very nature, these units take a central position between academic and student affairs. From that vantage point, the university college can be alert to possibilities for synergy between units and departments and can sponsor innovation on behalf of beginning students—innovation that involves multiple institutional constituencies. We would maintain university colleges have truly become the experimental colleges of the modern university.

The monograph authors are to be congratulated for a job well done. They have gathered information about an often-overlooked component of institutional excellence, and that is how organizational structure can be intentionally designed to support an institution's mission and its educational goals while simultaneously providing an administrative home for new students. The ideas and strategies contained in these pages may seem more relevant to universities; however, there are valuable lessons for institutions of any size that wish to investigate centralized models for organizing the first year. It could also be argued that smaller public or private institutions that do not attempt to address in their own appropriate ways the same needs, to which university colleges are a response, will ignore these central educational questions at their own peril.

We commend this monograph, and especially its case studies, to all readers. We are confident that there is much in these pages that will be useful to anyone who seeks greater efficiency and effectiveness in providing needed services to beginning college students.

Betsy O. Barefoot
Vice President and Senior Scholar

John N. Gardner
President
John N. Gardner Institute for Excellence in Undergraduate Education
Brevard, NC

Introduction

Scott E. Evenbeck & Dorothy Ward

For decades, colleges and universities have paid increasing attention to entering students because their success has a profound effect on the bottom line. Simply stated, entering students who receive such targeted attention are more likely to succeed academically and persist in education. The focus on entering students is also the result of external mandates to increase retention and graduation rates. In the United States, research confirms the relationship between the number of baccalaureate degree holders and the vitality of regions (Cortright, n.d.). As such, leaders in the United States and from around the world are calling for increasing the number of citizens with college degrees. In the United Kingdom, a key goal has been widening participation in higher education. In Japan, population trends mandate increased participation in higher education and enhanced success for those who do matriculate in college. Rather than focus only on educating the financially or intellectually elite minority of students who traditionally have had access to higher education, campuses now serve students with diverse ethnic, racial, and cultural backgrounds; secondary school experiences; and goals for postsecondary education.

This widening participation in higher education has resulted in attention to transitions for students moving through the educational system, and much of this attention has focused on the transition of entering students. Few movements in higher education have had more success with colleges and universities around the world than that of the first-year experience, which advocates putting first-year seminars and other curricular innovations in place to serve entering students. Coupled with the learning community movement and with evolving understandings of general education, the first-year experience is now seen as foundational for transforming campuses from sink-or-swim environments for entering students to environments where increasingly diverse students will be successful.

As campuses have adopted such programs to serve entering students, faculty, administrators, and staff have come up with varying strategies for conducting this work, from highly organized structures to loosely connected working groups. This has most often been new work for campuses, and identifying the locus for that work has been an evolving process since many campus units have responsibility for entering students. The admissions office serves as the point of initial contact for new students, who on many campuses are then handed off to the orientation office, which serves students before they attend their first classes. Academic advisors are generally the first people with whom entering students have meaningful conversations and sort out their options for beginning study. On some campuses, faculty who work with students enrolled in developmental courses have special relationships with and/or knowledge of entering students. And, where the first-year seminar, learning communities, or other components of the first-year experience are in place, someone has responsibility and authority for those initiatives. Often, that someone is an assistant provost or director of undergraduate studies or other faculty member with administrative responsibility for developing, implementing, and assessing these efforts to serve entering students. On an increasing number of campuses, the university college model has been adopted to bring all these offices and individuals under a single roof and to provide a coherent context for supporting the success of entering students.

The University College Model

Wenger, McDermott, and Snyder (2002) describe communities of practice as "groups of people who share a concern, a set of problems, or a passion about a topic, and who deepen their knowledge and expertise in this area by interacting on an ongoing basis" (p. 4). On campuses, there are many communities of practice. Persons within admissions offices or English departments share common assumptions about their work. Central to the definition of a university college is this concept of a community of practice. It is persons with authority and responsibility for serving entering students gathered together in an organizational structure to do this work. These structures, with at least minimal resources, offer students an academic home or an organizational unit to provide services and to advocate for their benefit. Such a unit, over time, becomes a community of practice, articulating its assumptions and best practices for serving entering students.

In *Portals of Entry,* Strommer (1993) argued that "administrative structures matter" (p. 5). We agree, especially as these structures provide the context within which communities of practice emerge. To that end, we present the following principles as undergirding our understanding of the university college model:

1. Entering students warrant contexts (i.e., policies and programs) that will enhance their academic success and persistence.
2. All entering students have the capacity for success, and the articulation and support of high expectations are central to the success of entering students.
3. A structure that will make a difference is necessary for the work with entering students. The university college is often a catalyst for creating institutional change, a place grounded in teaching and learning where the institution provides focus on students and their success in ways that impact the entire campus.
4. Students are always changing, as is society. The faculty and staff of the transitional unit serving entering students must live out the call to be reflective practitioners, supporting students in the development of successful habits and helping them move on to their majors and graduation. As a result, work with entering students mandates continual assessment and improvement.
5. Large-scale collaboration is required to impact student success. Yet, if this is not someone's work, then it is no one's work. A university college structure provides institutional ownership for work with entering students, ensuring that someone takes responsibility for student success on the campus.

Student Outcomes Driving the University College Model

A university college model provides a context for the campus to organize its work to serve students in an era where there are accelerating changes in the culture and among incoming students. Rather than seeking to increase student performance simply by recruiting better-prepared students, as is the approach taken by too many colleges and universities, many campuses adopt the university college model to organize their work and to improve the institution so that students succeed. Conley's (2008) research, while focused on the supports students need to make the transition to successful university study, suggests four key areas for institutional improvement:

◇ *Key cognitive strategies.* These range from problem formation and problem solving to interpretation. Conley states that these "are at the heart of the intellectual endeavor of the university . . . [and] necessary to discern truth and meaning as well as to pursue them" (p. 25).

◇ *Key content knowledge.* This includes foundational knowledge in English, mathematics, science, social studies, world languages, and the arts.
◇ *Academic behaviors.* These include self-awareness, self-monitoring, and self-control of processes and actions necessary for academic success, including study skills and time management.
◇ *Contextual skills and knowledge.* Students need information to apply for college and financial aid and then the ability to interact "with a diverse cross-section of academicians and peers" (p. 26).

By linking faculty, academic advisors, and student affairs professionals in a unit with responsibility for entering students, the university college model provides a context that would not otherwise exist to serve new students. Moreover, the university college provides a catalyst for institutional improvement in the key areas identified by Conley. For example, support for the intellectual development of entering students has historically been the province of the faculty who are seen as commanding the concepts and having the unique ability to demystify the college ethos for entering students. Yet, a university college model offers a framework that acknowledges the teaching and learning expertise of other campus professionals and encourages faculty to collaborate with those professionals to develop service-learning and other intentional, experiential learning opportunities that encourage student reflection and enhance student capacity. Foundational knowledge for college is largely impacted by the students' secondary experiences and the articulation of learning across high school to college. As the gateway to university study, the university college helps bridge these educational experiences for entering students.

In terms of the key areas for improvement, academic behaviors and contextual skills and knowledge are the spheres where campuses have the most work to do, particularly in assisting low-income and first-generation students. First-year programming, through first-year seminars, learning communities, and other initiatives, has been helpful in supporting such students in these areas. Yet, too often, services, policies, and programs are not consistent or are implemented only in pockets of the campus. Consolidating efforts for entering students in one unit brings coherence and intentionality to the work. The university college model provides a structure for faculty, advisors, student affairs professionals, students, and others to plan, implement, and assess an inclusive approach, drawing from across the institution to support entering students.

While first-year programs frequently address personal development and self-regulation, the fourth area—contextual skills and knowledge—is perhaps the least understood and least effectively addressed by colleges and universities. Many students bring little social capital and have very limited ability to navigate our systems. Campuses often announce that students are adults and therefore responsible for figuring this out, but what if their strengths do not include these skills? Rather than pronouncing them adults who will have to live with the consequences of their behavior, the university college model provides a structure to help students gain the necessary skills and knowledge to navigate the institution. The university college introduces students to the roles and purposes of higher education and establishes their membership in this community.

Organization of the Monograph

In *Portals of Entry*, Strommer (1993) provided a portrait of the university college model as it was emerging in the last century. This monograph reports on the evolution of that model, using case studies from a variety of institutions to illustrate how the university college structure serves as an administrative home for innovative programs and effective collaborations that support the success of entering students.

Yet, at the start of the monograph project, the editors recognized the absence of comprehensive, systematic data on institutions practicing the university college model. At that point, data were anecdotal and collected informally by administrators discussing common goals and practices at gatherings such as the Annual Conference on The First-Year Experience and the annual meeting of the Association of Deans and Directors of University Colleges and Undergraduate Studies. The monograph editors wanted empirical data on both the number and type of institutions developing university colleges as well as the range of variation in implementing this model.

As a result, the editors began work on this project by asking campuses to report on their structures for serving entering students. The first step was a broadly cast survey to all two- and four-year institutions on the American Council on Education mailing list of chief academic officers. The initial survey was sent to 3,941 administrators under the sponsorship of John Gardner, executive director of the Policy Center on the First Year of College (now the John N. Gardner Institute for Excellence in Undergraduate Education) and simply asked each administrator to identify the type of structure the institution used to serve first-year students. The choices included

◇ *Comprehensive Single Unit/Administrative Structure*—provides campus-wide oversight and alignment of first-year efforts, also appears on the campus organizational chart, has a director, and has a reoccurring operational budget
◇ *Single Unit/Administrative Structure*—meets some, but not all, of the conditions listed above
◇ *Formal Coordinating Body*—oversees a broad range of first-year efforts and has institutional authority for oversight and alignment of first-year initiatives; usually structure is a standing committee that provides campus-wide oversight for elements of the first year but does not provide daily administrative leadership to any one component
◇ *Multiple Administrative Structures*—cooperates to administer and align first-year policies, practices, and programs
◇ *Discrete Structures*—individually provides oversight for the distinct aspects of the first year (e.g., retention, orientation, advising, first-year seminars), but there is limited or no coordination among these structures

The next step of data collection was to gather more detailed information on programs, resources, and structures of institutions clearly committed to a comprehensive approach to first-year student success. A second instrument was sent to all respondents of the first survey who had indicated their institution had a comprehensive single unit or a single administrative structure. The second instrument resulted in 58 institutions being selected for analysis due to their intentional first-year initiatives, structures, and programming. A special effort was also made to secure information from all members of the Association of Deans and Directors of University Colleges and Undergraduate Studies because these institutions clearly self-identified with the philosophy and approach of a comprehensive model.

The model that has emerged contains a number of essential features, including collaboration among and within units serving entering students; strong links to the undergraduate curriculum; holistic support for student learning and development; and a commitment to assessment. The chapters of this monograph describe these essential features. Yet, each of these features is uniquely defined within the contexts of individual campuses. Just as there is no single iteration for the units making up a liberal arts college or the college of science and math, there is no one definition or operationalization of the university college. As such, the examples offered here should be seen as possibilities, not prescriptions for organizing the university college.

The monograph opens in chapter 1 with a discussion of the findings from the two surveys described above. Components that are "usual suspects" for being included in a university college are orientation, academic advising, academic support, first-year curriculum, first-year seminars, learning communities, and general education. These are common programs on nearly all campuses, and providing a sustained focus for such programs is generally the impetus for forming a university college or similar unit. Institutional history and context mandate that the university college be tailored to the circumstances on a particular campus. As a result, there does not appear to be a single model for serving entering students that incorporates all these elements.

Chapters 2 through 5 focus on the essential elements of the university college model. Following each chapter is a series of case studies that illustrate some aspect of the element that is the focus of the chapter. Each case study offers a description of the institution and its students, an overview of the university college model with an emphasis on a unique feature of that model. Where applicable, case study authors describe efforts to assess specific elements of the university college and lessons learned. Together, these case studies offer a rich and compelling portrait of strategies for organizing the entering college experience.

Collaboration, which is explored in chapter 2, is central to the university college model. If a university college comes to be a place apart or a silo, it will not succeed. It exists to move students from matriculation to success in the major and graduation. For many students, their primary engagement with the campus is in the classroom. As such, the university college unit should be a primary unit on campus celebrating a focus on learning (Barr & Tagg, 1995). Yet, collaboration across campus, especially in cocurricular experiences that support entering student engagement, is also critical. The characteristics of successful collaborations and the benefits of those collaborations for entering students and for the institutions that serve them are described. Case studies in this chapter describe student and academic affairs partnerships and collaborations between the university college and local feeder institutions to ensure student success.

The curriculum for entering students is the focus of much work of the university college. Chapter 3 documents institutional commitment to a particular set of practices in the undergraduate curriculum that create productive and sustainable bridges to engage faculty in first-year student learning. These include first-year seminars, learning communities, developmental education, and general education. Successful strategies and the necessary resources for faculty engagement and development are also examined. Case studies describe general education reform, first-year seminars, learning communities, and residential learning initiatives.

Chapter 4 examines how university colleges work to increase student learning through holistic support that addresses the academic and personal development of the student. Through the connection of curricular and cocurricular, enhancement of instructional support, and development of students as teachers and learners, university colleges work to increase students' opportunities for academic success, personal growth, and learning that extends beyond the classroom. Case studies offer descriptions of academic advising initiatives, leadership development programs, peer-led academic support, and the infusion of technology in a first-year seminar.

University colleges, often the youngest academic unit on a campus, are sometimes vulnerable to attacks from other campus departments, especially during periods of financial crises. Comprehensive assessment data on first-year programs can play a critical role in protecting university colleges from budget cuts during such times. Most importantly, collecting assessment data on an ongoing basis and distributing the results widely will ensure continuous improvement of entering student initiatives. Chapter 5 describes a three-pronged strategy for effective assessment focused on needs, processes, and outcomes. Case studies approach assessment from a variety of angles, including comprehensive program review, a multimodal assessment plan, formative and summative assessment strategies, and a self-study model.

As noted above, assessment data are often used to justify existing resources or to lobby for additional resources. Chapter 6 describes the range of resources needed to support the university college, including physical space, technology infrastructure, and staffing. The chapter also examines strategies for managing the resources of the university college along with potential internal and external sources of income.

We conclude the monograph in chapter 7 by arguing that the university college is more than a framework for organizing programs and services for entering students. Through its emphasis on collaboration, the undergraduate curriculum, holistic support for students, and assessment, the university college serves as a catalyst for change on many campuses.

Conclusion

Most campuses offer orientation, first-year seminars, bridge programs, learning communities, academic advising, and a host of other programs designed to support entering college students and ensure their success. However, it is our contention that such programs are most effective in achieving their goals when they are intentionally designed and administered through a single administrative unit. The university college—an administrative unit defined by collaboration, connection to the undergraduate curriculum, attention to holistic student support, and assessment for improvement—is the ideal structure for organizing and delivering these programs for entering students. That said, the design and administration of a university college is most effective when it responds to its unique institutional context. This monograph offers readers a range of options for designing or refining university college structures, and we invite readers to consider how they might best adapt these to fit the needs of their students and the cultures of their institutions.

References

Barr, R. B., & Tagg, J. (1995, November/December). From teaching to learning: A new paradigm for undergraduate education. *Change, 27*(6), 12–25.

Conley, D. T. (2008). Rethinking college readiness. *New England Journal of Higher Education, 22*(5), 24–26.

Cortright, J. (n.d.). City dividends: Gains from improving metropolitan performance. Chicago, IL: CEOs for Cities.

Strommer, D. W. (Ed.). (1993). *Portals of entry: University colleges and undergraduate divisions* (Monograph No. 12). Columbia, SC: University of South Carolina, National Resource Center for The Freshman-Year Experience.

Wenger, E., McDermott, R. A., & Snyder, W. N. (2002). *Cultivating communities of practice: A guide to managing knowledge*. Cambridge, MA: Harvard Business School.

Chapter 1

University Colleges: Flexible Structures for Serving Undergraduate Students

Randy L. Swing & Julie S. Alexander-Hamilton

In the years since the publication of *Portals of Entry: University Colleges and Undergraduate Divisions,* little empirical data have been collected to evaluate how institutions of higher education are organized to serve new students. The changing needs and expectations of new students and families, technological advances, external demands for transparency and accountability, and the constant call to increase retention and graduation rates make this an important topic of conversation and for action.

In order to update the knowledge base about what colleges and universities are doing to support new students, the monograph authors conducted a survey to collect information about current practices in university colleges. Because institutions use a variety of titles for the internal administrative units that have oversight for the first year of college and because they use a variety of organizational arrangements to do so, the survey effort had to (a) identify institutions that have a university college and (b) develop a way to classify different organizational arrangements.

The monograph authors used a combination of techniques to find institutions that have university colleges or similar structures. In Phase I (September, 2006), chief academic officers were surveyed to identify both the organizational structure for the first year of college and a key person who could provide detailed information about that structure. This first phase was the equivalent of an open call for participation in the study. In Phase II (March, 2007), the authors contacted the key individuals named in Phase I and used personal contacts to actively seek participation from colleagues at institutions with well-organized first-year programs.

Institutional representatives were asked to report the first-year organizational structure (FYOS) used to administratively organize the various programs that comprise the first year of college. A five-category typology (based on one originally created by the staff of the Policy Center on the First Year of College, now the John N. Gardner Institute for Excellence in Undergraduate Education, Figure 1.1) was used to standardize reporting of organizational arrangements. The typology can be considered to have two layers: (a) single administrative units and (b) multiple administrative structures, either cooperating or working discretely. These are described below.

Single Administrative Unit Structures

1. A single administrative unit exists that provides campus-wide oversight and alignment of first-year efforts, appears on the campus organizational chart, has a director/senior leader, and has a recurring operational budget. This type of unit was considered to be *comprehensive single unit* (or *comprehensive*).
2. A unit that meets some but not all of the above descriptors was considered to be a *single unit,* but not comprehensive.

Multiple Administrative Units

3. Multiple administrative structures exist that are coordinated by a standing committee or other formal coordinating body.
4. Multiple administrative structures exist that intentionally, but informally, cooperate in providing services during the first college year.
5. Multiple administrative structures operate as discrete structures with limited coordination across units.

From intentional, centralized to loosely administered through a network of discrete programs, the typology provides a standardized set of descriptions that define the administrative connections between various programs comprising the first year of college on a particular campus.

A Comprehensive Single Unit/Administrative Structure provides campus-wide oversight and alignment of first-year efforts. This structure (a) appears on the campus organizational chart, (b) has a director, and (c) has a reoccurring operational budget.

Such units may operate under a variety of names including University College, Freshman Division, General College, or First-Year Studies. These units/structures exist primarily to serve first-year students, but many will have oversight for functions, such as general education, which also serve other undergraduates. All have responsibilities beyond administering a single course, such as a first-year seminar/freshman seminar/new student orientation course. The key distinguishing feature is that a majority of the unit's efforts are focused on most/all of the policies, practices, and programs that define the first college year and at least some delivery of instruction to first-year students. As such, a chief academic affairs or chief student affairs office with broad responsibilities for all undergraduates would not meet this criterion.

A Single Unit/Administrative Structure exists that meets some, but not all, of the conditions listed above.

A Formal Coordinating Body oversees a broad range of first-year efforts and has institutional authority for oversight and alignment of first-year initiatives.

Usually such a structure is a standing committee that provides campus-wide oversight for elements of the first year but does not provide daily administrative leadership to any component of the first-year. Committees with a narrow or single focus would not meet this criterion.

Multiple Administrative Structures cooperate to administer and align first-year policies, practices, and programs.

Key to this configuration is the existence of an effective structure for multiple administrative units (each with responsibility for particular aspects of the first year) to regularly communicate and coordinate efforts to align first-year policies, practices, and programs.

Discrete Structures exist that individually provide oversight for distinct aspects of the first year (e.g., retention, orientation, advising, first-year seminars), but there is limited or no coordination among these structures.

Discrete structures may operate independently on campus-wide, first-year issues or may be highly coordinated efforts within a single college/unit. The key identifying characteristic is the lack of a formalized structure for communication and cooperation among the discrete structures.

Figure 1.1. Typology of first-year organizing structures. This typology was developed by Randy L. Swing, Betsy O. Barefoot, and John N. Gardner for use in the Foundations of Excellence® in the First College Year Self-Study by the Policy Center on the First Year of College (now John N. Gardner Institute for Excellence in Undergraduate Education).

Using the open call as well as personal invitations, a set of 58 institutions was identified that serve new students through intentional structures. The selected institutions were identified by the authors as true peers as a result of responses to the survey questionnaire and their personal knowledge of the institutions. Many were identified because of their participation in the Association of Deans and Directors of University Colleges. Each of the 58 selected institutions had an intentional design for managing the first year of college that was considered to be useful in adding to the knowledge base about first-year organizing structures and university colleges, in particular.

While the monograph authors were primarily interested in institutions that used a single administrative unit to organize the first year, selection was not restricted to that type of FYOS. Of the 58 selected institutions (see Appendix A), 32 (55%) reported using a comprehensive single unit model, 19 (33%) used a single unit model, and 7 (12%) used a model that consisted of multiple or discrete administrative units.

In traditional research methodology, the process that underlies this effort might be considered a convenience sample, but the open call for participation assured that a wide array of institutions were invited to contribute to the knowledge base. The resulting sample is adequate for an exploratory investigation, even if it does not meet the requirements of a randomized study. As such, the reported findings apply to this particular collection of institutions and should be generalized to others only with caution. Interviews and case study approaches are used throughout the various chapters of this monograph to provide depth and breadth beyond the scope of the exploratory study described in this chapter.

Research Design

A representative from each of the 58 selected institutions completed an online survey about the FYOS's history, mission, resources, and scope of work (Appendix B). The data provide a rich overview of how these institutions serve first-year students. Two views of these data will be presented. In section one, the responses of the 58 institutions will be considered as an overview of the practices reported by this group. In section two, the practices will be disaggregated to explore how variations in unit names and organizing structures are aligned with differences in campus services, resources, and the title of the senior administrative leader.

Section One: Overview of First-Year Practices of 58 Institutions

Unit Names

Of the 58 institutions in the study, 26 (45%) reported that their FYOS unit was named University College. The remaining 32 used 18 other unit names for their FYOS. The second most commonly used name was Undergraduate Studies/Division/Program, used by 8 institutions. First-Year Programs/Office was used by 5 institutions (see Table 1.1).

While there is considerable inconsistency in the use of the name University College, that name does not automatically mean that the unit is a comprehensive FYOS. Of the 26 units known as University Colleges, more than 70% self-identified with the set of characteristics listed under the comprehensive single unit definition in the FYOS typology, and just over one third considered themselves to be single units.

Table 1.1

First-Year Organizational Structure Names (N = 58)

Name	Frequency
University College	26
Undergraduate Studies/Division/Program	8
First-Year Programs/Office	5
Unreported	2
Office of Vice President of Instruction/Academic Dean	2
Academic Achievement Center	1
Academic Services	1
Center for Learning & Student Development	1
College of Freshman Studies	1
Developmental Education Program	1
Enrollment Services	1
First-Year Experience	1
General Studies	1
General Studies, Orientation & Academic Advising Center	1
Instructional Support Services & Retention	1
Office of Academic Services	1
Student Development & Enrollment Services	1
Student Success Center	1
Undergraduate Academic Programs	1
Undergraduate Advising Center	1

Similarly, not all comprehensive single unit FYOSs are named University College. Of the 32 institutions that reported using a comprehensive FYOS, only 59% were named University College. Clearly, all units that carry the name University College cannot be assumed to be a comprehensive single unit FYOS or vice versa. In practice, it can be concluded that university colleges are likely to conform to most, but not all, of the following structural components included in the typology for a comprehensive FYOS:

- ◇ Provide campus-wide oversight and alignment of first-year efforts
- ◇ Appear on the campus organizational chart
- ◇ Have a director/senior leader
- ◇ Have a reoccurring operational budget

Section two of this chapter will examine organizational differences by unit name.

History

To gain a better understanding of why these types of first-year organizing structures have become a part of the higher education landscape, participating institutions were asked to identify not only the functions of their FYOS but also to briefly describe in a narrative format, the impetus for establishing the structure, when it was founded, and how it changed over time.

One responding institution traced its origins to 1935 when it was founded as an entry point for all students except those seeking an associate's degree. Another institution traced its unit history to 1945 when services were developed to help meet the academic needs of returning World War II veterans. At the opposite end of the timeline are units that have been developed within the past five years and provide a comprehensive set of student services. A common evolutionary path for units that have been in existence since the early 1980s seems to be a change in how they are identified, moving from general college to university college.

Academic success indicators, such as poor retention and graduation rates, followed by the need to provide centralized student support services, were the most commonly reported reasons for developing FYOSs, such as general colleges and university colleges. Strategic planning, self-study recommendations to focus more directly on first-year students, and the availability of Title III grant funding were also reported as being catalysts for developing campus-wide oversight and alignment of first-year efforts. A smaller number of institutions stated that their FYOS was developed in order to support specific student populations, such as undeclared students, underprepared students, and first-generation students. Many of the units have grown since their founding to incorporate a wide variety of services and programs that go well beyond academic advising and first-year seminars.

Mission

To further understand the purpose, central goals, direction, and individuals served by these structures, participating institutions were asked to briefly describe the mission of their FYOS. Providing services to support student transitions in and out of the classroom, followed by encouraging academic success and skill building, were the central themes of the FYOS mission statements. In order to provide comprehensive services, close collaboration between academic affairs and student affairs was often reported as a component of unit missions (see chapter 2 for a discussion of this as a central element of university colleges). Another common component was provision of a structured set of events that constitute a common experience for all new students. Several respondents named institution-specific goals, such as encouraging students' personal development in keeping with religious convictions and serving as a home to interdisciplinary and international studies. Students and their well-being, both social and academic, were at the core of these mission statements. From helping students identify their personal educational goals to assisting them in making friends, the primary mission of university college models around the country is providing a structured and coherent experience for new students.

Services Provided by Level of Responsibility

Respondents were asked to report their level of responsibility for a variety of services they could provide to students (i.e., primary campus responsibility, responsibility shared with other units, very limited responsibility, no responsibility). Respondents were also able to indicate if the service was not applicable to their context or if they did not know the university college's level of responsibility for that service. The following discussion provides highlights from the survey. Readers may find the full set of survey results in Table 1.2.

Table 1.2

Services Provided by Level of Responsibility (Alphabetical Order)

	Number	**Percentage**
Academic advising services		
Primary campus responsibility	20	34%
Responsibility shared with others	35	60%
Very limited responsibility	3	5%
No responsibility	0	0%
No response/NA	0	0%
Academic support for athletes		
Primary campus responsibility	18	31%
Responsibility shared with others	17	29%
Very limited responsibility	12	21%
No responsibility	10	17%
No response/NA	1	2%
Academic support/learning center		
Primary campus responsibility	35	60%
Responsibility shared with others	15	26%
Very limited responsibility	4	7%
No responsibility	4	7%
No response/NA	0	0%
Admissions functions		
Primary campus responsibility	4	7%
Responsibility shared with others	5	9%
Very limited responsibility	15	26%
No responsibility	32	55%
No response/NA	2	3%
Assessment/institutional effectiveness studies		
Primary campus responsibility	2	3%
Responsibility shared with others	21	36%
Very limited responsibility	25	43%
No responsibility	10	17%
No response/NA	0	0%

Table 1.2 continued

	Number	Percentage
Bursar functions		
Primary campus responsibility	0	0%
Responsibility shared with others	1	2%
Very limited responsibility	9	16%
No responsibility	46	79%
No response/NA	2	3%
Career exploration/planning services		
Primary campus responsibility	7	12%
Responsibility shared with others	23	40%
Very limited responsibility	15	26%
No responsibility	11	19%
No response/NA	2	3%
Developmental mathematics courses		
Primary campus responsibility	19	33%
Responsibility shared with others	9	16%
Very limited responsibility	7	12%
No responsibility	23	40%
No response/NA	0	0%
Developmental reading courses		
Primary campus responsibility	18	31%
Responsibility shared with others	8	14%
Very limited responsibility	7	12%
No responsibility	22	38%
No response/NA	3	5%
Developmental writing courses		
Primary campus responsibility	18	31%
Responsibility shared with others	9	16%
Very limited responsibility	9	16%
No responsibility	22	38%
No response/NA	0	0%

Table 1.2 continued on p. 8

Table 1.2 continued

	Number	Percentage
English as a second language courses		
Primary campus responsibility	3	5%
Responsibility shared with others	5	9%
Very limited responsibility	5	9%
No responsibility	39	67%
No response/NA	6	10%
Faculty development programming		
Primary campus responsibility	2	3%
Responsibility shared with others	14	24%
Very limited responsibility	18	31%
No responsibility	22	38%
No response/NA	2	3%
Faculty/student mentoring program		
Primary campus responsibility	7	12%
Responsibility shared with others	21	36%
Very limited responsibility	12	21%
No responsibility	13	22%
No response/NA	5	9%
Financial aid services		
Primary campus responsibility	4	7%
Responsibility shared with others	1	2%
Very limited responsibility	5	9%
No responsibility	44	76%
No response/NA	4	7%
First-year seminar/FYE courses		
Primary campus responsibility	43	74%
Responsibility shared with others	10	17%
Very limited responsibility	1	2%
No responsibility	3	5%
No response/NA	1	2%

Table 1.2 continued

	Number	Percentage
General Education Courses		
Primary Campus Responsibility	4	7%
Responsibility Shared with Others	21	36%
Very Limited Responsibility	9	16%
No Responsibility	24	41%
No Response/NA	0	0%
Honors Program		
Primary Campus Responsibility	18	31%
Responsibility Shared with Others	5	9%
Very Limited Responsibility	6	10%
No Responsibility	25	43%
No Response/NA	4	7%
Instructional Technology Services		
Primary Campus Responsibility	1	2%
Responsibility Shared with Others	5	9%
Very Limited Responsibility	10	17%
No Responsibility	39	67%
No Response/NA	3	5%
Interdisciplinary Studies Degrees		
Primary Campus Responsibility	10	17%
Responsibility Shared with Others	7	12%
Very Limited Responsibility	6	10%
No Responsibility	29	50%
No Response/NA	6	10%
Learning Communities		
Primary Campus Responsibility	22	38%
Responsibility Shared with Others	20	34%
Very Limited Responsibility	6	10%
No Responsibility	7	12%
No Response/NA	3	5%

Table 1.2 continued on p. 10

Table 1.2 continued

	Number	Percentage
Mathematics tutoring/support services		
Primary campus responsibility	21	36%
Responsibility shared with others	25	43%
Very limited responsibility	2	3%
No responsibility	10	17%
No response/NA	0	0%
New student orientation		
Primary campus responsibility	24	41%
Responsibility shared with others	27	47%
Very limited responsibility	6	10%
No responsibility	1	2%
No response/NA	0	0%
Online courses		
Primary campus responsibility	0	0%
Responsibility shared with others	4	7%
Very limited responsibility	13	22%
No responsibility	36	62%
No response/NA	5	9%
Parent/family support programs		
Primary campus responsibility	9	16%
Responsibility shared with others	14	24%
Very limited responsibility	17	29%
No responsibility	14	24%
No response/NA	4	7%
P-16 college readiness programs		
Primary campus responsibility	6	10%
Responsibility shared with others	5	9%
Very limited responsibility	13	22%
No responsibility	26	45%
No response/NA	8	14%

Table 1.2 continued

	Number	Percentage
Peer advising		
Primary campus responsibility	18	31%
Responsibility shared with others	14	24%
Very limited responsibility	7	12%
No responsibility	12	21%
No response/NA	7	12%
Placement testing		
Primary campus responsibility	23	40%
Responsibility shared with others	15	26%
Very limited responsibility	6	10%
No responsibility	12	21%
No response/NA	2	3%
Registrar functions		
Primary campus responsibility	7	12%
Responsibility shared with others	3	5%
Very limited responsibility	8	14%
No responsibility	39	67%
No response/NA	1	2%
Service-learning		
Primary campus responsibility	4	7%
Responsibility shared with others	13	22%
Very limited responsibility	21	36%
No responsibility	18	31%
No response/NA	2	3%
Stop-out programs		
Primary campus responsibility	5	9%
Responsibility shared with others	9	16%
Very limited responsibility	8	14%
No responsibility	22	38%
No response/NA	14	24%

Table 1.2 continued on p. 12

Table 1.2 continued

	Number	Percentage
Student leadership development		
Primary campus responsibility	2	3%
Responsibility shared with others	19	33%
Very limited responsibility	16	28%
No responsibility	20	34%
No response/NA	1	2%
Student life/student affairs		
Primary campus responsibility	1	2%
Responsibility shared with others	12	21%
Very limited responsibility	18	31%
No responsibility	26	45%
No response/NA	1	2%
Study skills workshops/instruction		
Primary campus responsibility	24	41%
Responsibility shared with others	23	40%
Very limited responsibility	4	7%
No responsibility	5	9%
No response/NA	2	3%
Supplemental Instruction		
Primary campus responsibility	24	41%
Responsibility shared with others	14	24%
Very limited responsibility	8	14%
No responsibility	7	12%
No response/NA	5	9%
TRIO programs		
Primary campus responsibility	11	19%
Responsibility shared with others	4	7%
Very limited responsibility	8	14%
No responsibility	21	36%
No response/NA	14	24%

Table 1.2 continued

	Number	Percentage
Tutoring/mentoring		
Primary campus responsibility	24	41%
Responsibility shared with others	22	38%
Very limited responsibility	5	9%
No responsibility	7	12%
No response/NA	0	0%
Writing tutoring/support services		
Primary campus responsibility	17	29%
Responsibility shared with others	16	28%
Very limited responsibility	13	22%
No responsibility	12	21%
No response/NA	0	0%

Academic advising, peer advising, and placement testing. Academic advising is the cornerstone of the responsibilities of these 58 respondents. About one third (34%) have primary campus responsibility for this service, and 60% more share the responsibility with other units combining to account for the vast majority (94%) of respondents. None of the institutions surveyed reported having no responsibility for academic advising.

A majority (55%) use peer advisors in the delivery of services with 31% reporting primary responsibility and 24% sharing responsibility with other units. Only 12% reported that peer advising was not applicable to the unit.

Another component of advising, placement testing, is also a function of a majority (66%) of the respondents with 40% reporting primary responsibility for placement testing and an additional 26% reporting a shared responsibility. While a significant service for a majority of respondents, 31% report that they have very limited or no responsibility for placement testing.

First-year seminars and learning communities. A majority (91%) of respondents have oversight for first-year seminars. Because 74% have primary responsibility for these courses, it could be said that oversight for first-year seminars is the most frequent activity of the respondents. Only 17% reported sharing responsibility for the course with other units. Similarly, a majority (72%) have oversight for learning communities, with 38% reporting that it is their primary responsibility and 34% indicating that it is a shared responsibility.

New student orientation. A majority (88%) of respondents claim oversight for new student orientation. Forty-one percent report having primary responsibility for new student orientation and 47% share responsibilities with other units.

Study skills instruction, Supplemental Instruction, tutoring, and mentoring. Oversight of a variety of student support programs is a mainstay of the respondents. A majority (81%) have primary (41%) or shared (40%) responsibility for study skills workshops and instruction. Likewise, a majority (79%)

have primary (41%) or shared (38%) responsibility for tutoring programs. More specifically, more than half (57%) of the respondents have primary or shared responsibility for tutoring in writing, while 79% reported primary or shared responsibility for mathematics tutoring. Additional academic support is offered through Supplemental Instruction programs on 65% of responding campuses, with 41% reporting primary responsibility and 24% indicating shared responsibility.

Related to these academic support services are faculty/student mentoring programs, which were the primary responsibility of 12% of respondents. An additional 36% shared responsibilities for these programs with other units. These, and other services, were most frequently provided via an academic support/learning center. A majority (86%) reported either primary (60%) or shared (26%) responsibility for the administration of an academic support/learning center.

Developmental courses. About a third of respondents report having primary responsibility for developmental courses in mathematics (33%), reading (31%), and writing (31%). When primary and shared responsibilities are combined, these totals show significant engagement by nearly half of respondents in remedial education functions (mathematics, 49%; reading, 45%; and writing, 47%).

Other services. Other services provided by respondents include primary responsibility (31%) for academic support for student athletes and honors programs. A wide range of services were reported to be the primary responsibility by only a few respondents but were shared responsibilities of at least a quarter of respondents. These second-tier services are important functions of respondents, even if they seldom have primary responsibility for them. For example (combining primary and shared responsibility), respondents report engagement with assessment (39%), career planning (52%), general education (43%), parent/family support (40%), service-learning (29%), Interdisciplinary Studies degrees (29%), and TRIO programs (26%).

Respondents were asked to gauge their level of responsibility for services that traditionally were assigned to offices such as registrar, financial aid, instructional technology, faculty development, bursar, and admissions. Generally FYOSs have no or very limited responsibility for these office functions.

Sole or Shared Responsibilities for Student Services

Another important way that FYOSs vary is in the type of student served. While the earlier section identified whether services were part of the unit's portfolio, the following data show the degree to which the unit serves particular groups of students (Table 1.3). Survey respondents were presented a list of student populations and asked to indicate if they served all, most, some, or none for each group of students. In addition, respondents could note that the category was not applicable at their institution.

Table 1.3

Students Served by the First-Year Organizational Structure

	Number	Percentage
Declared majors		
Serves all	15	26%
Serves most	6	10%
Serves some	33	57%
Serves none	3	5%
No response/NA	1	2%
First-year students		
Serves all	35	60%
Serves most	14	24%
Serves some	8	14%
Serves none	0	0%
No response/NA	1	2%
Honors students		
Serves all	25	43%
Serves most	4	7%
Serves some	16	28%
Serves none	9	16%
No response/NA	4	7%
International students		
Serves all	14	24%
Serves most	5	9%
Serves some	29	50%
Serves none	4	7%
No response/NA	6	10%
New transfers		
Serves all	15	26%
Serves most	22	38%
Serves some	17	29%
Serves none	2	3%
No response/NA	2	3%

Table 1.3 continued on p. 16

Table 1.3 continued

	Number	Percentage
Probation students		
Serves all	14	24%
Serves most	10	17%
Serves some	29	50%
Serves none	2	3%
No response/NA	3	5%
Provisionally admitted students		
Serves all	27	47%
Serves most	7	12%
Serves some	10	17%
Serves none	4	7%
No response/NA	10	17%
Undeclared students		
Serves all	47	81%
Serves most	8	14%
Serves some	2	3%
Serves none	0	0%
No response/NA	1	2%

Undeclared students are most frequently served by these 58 institutions. The vast majority (81%) report serving all undeclared students, and an additional 14% report serving most undeclared students. Of the 58 institutions, only one reported having no responsibility for this population, and another reported that the category was not applicable for their situation. Clearly, service to undeclared students is a major focus of the FYOS units in this group of institutions.

On the other hand, less than 40% of these institutions have a clear mandate to serve students once they have declared a major, with 26% serving all declared majors and 10% serving most. A majority continue to have responsibility for serving some declared students (57%), with only 7% reporting that they provide no service to declared majors. These findings suggest that most of the units target services toward undeclared majors but continue to provide some services that likely cannot be provided by upper-division colleges and academic departments that provide a majority of services to declared majors.

A majority (60%) report serving all first-year students and an additional 24% serve most first-year students. While there would certainly be overlap between the first-year and undeclared populations, the high percentage of units charged with serving all or most first-year students indicates that services extend beyond the process of selecting a major.

Many FYOSs have special responsibility for one particular group of first-year students with nearly half (47%) of these units serving all provisionally admitted new students. While 17% or the reporting institutions did not provisionally admit students, of the 48 institutions that accommodated provisional admits, 71% of these units are charged with serving this group.

Just under half of these units serve all honors students (43%). About a third serve most or some honor students (35%). Over a quarter have no engagement with honors students in that 16% report no service to honors students and an additional 7% report that the category is not applicable to their campus.

About a quarter of the units provide services to all students who are on probation (24%), new transfer students (26%), or international students (24%). While the units are less likely to serve all students in the aforementioned categories, they still have significant contact with students in these three groups. Combining the responses of *serves all*, *most*, and *some* shows the degree of engagement to be high with all three categories of students (i.e., probation, 91%; new transfers, 93%; and international students, 83%).

Resources

Respondents were asked to provide information about the physical location of their offices, summary data about their staff, and financial resources in terms of salary and nonsalary fiscal resources. Not surprisingly, the responses show a wide array of resource allocations to support these FYOSs.

Over half of the 58 respondents operate mostly from a single campus building. A minority have a dedicated building (9%), while nearly half (48%) are located in a single building that is shared with other functions. A third (33%) operates in multiple buildings, which are all shared with other functions.

Regardless of whether a unit was the primary occupant of a dedicated campus building or shared physical space, most reported that they were located in the heart of campus and easily accessible to both students and faculty. Apart from the unit's physical setting on campus, participating institutions were asked to describe other major resources of the unit. The most commonly reported resource was computer labs for testing purposes and student use, followed by dedicated classroom space for first-year seminars and developmental courses. Other resources included special equipment for accommodating students with disabilities, small offices for peer advisors, and unique lounges for first-year students, honors students, and English-as-second-language students (see chapter 6 for a broader discussion of resources connected to the university college).

The major cost of a FYOS is salary. Of the 41 units reporting salary budgets, they spent a combined total of $66 million. In comparison, they reported nonsalary budgets of $36 million. Salary funds are used to staff the FYOS with administrators, faculty members, clerical support staff, and student employees (See Table 1.4). The reliance of first-year organizing structures on student employees is a key finding, which suggests the units play an important educational role in undergraduate life in providing paraprofessional work opportunities for students in human development and technical fields.

Table 1.4

First-Year Organizational Structure Staff

Faculty/staff category	Number of positions reported
Senior-level administrator	1
Second-level administrators	2
Third-level administrators	8
Tenure-track faculty	4
Nontenure-track faculty	15
Nonfaculty support staff/clerical staff	11
Student employees	44

Fiscal resources were not predictive of the unit's name or structure. University colleges reported salary budgets ranging from $60,000 to $6.1 million, with an average (based on data from only 19 of the 27 institutions) of $1.4 million. Units not titled university college ranged from $450,000 to $5.7 million with an average (based on 22 of 31 institutions) of $1.9 million. On average, units with deans reported 1.9 million in salary dollars compared to 1.4 million for unit heads with other titles.

Section Two: Differences Across the 58 Institutions

As shown in section one, interesting differences in names, histories, missions, and scale of service exist within this group of 58 institutions. The following section focuses on differences by two grouping variables: (a) unit name and (b) unit organizing structure. Institutions that are named University College will be compared to those that use other names. In addition, institutions that identify their FYOS as a comprehensive single unit (i.e., include campus-wide oversight and alignment of first-year efforts, appear on the campus organizational chart, are led by a director/senior leader, and have a recurring operational budget) will be compared to institutions with single units that are not comprehensive in scope (i.e., lack one or more of the abovementioned characteristics).

Unit Name: University College Versus Other Names

Slightly more than half of units named University College (52%) serve all first-year students with an additional 30% serving most first-year students. These data indicate that nearly half of university colleges in this study use something other than a total intake model, which assigns all first-year students, at least initially, to the university college. Among these respondents, responsibility for first-year students is more likely to be shared by a university college than by a FYOS known by another name.

Table 1.5

Students Served by the First-Year Organizational Structure by Unit Name and Structure

	University College (*n* = 27)		Other unit name (*n* = 31)		Comprehensive (*n* = 32)		Single (*n* = 19)	
	Number	**%**	**Number**	**%**	**Number**	**%**	**Number**	**%**
Declared majors								
Serves all	3	11%	12	39%	8	25%	5	26%
Serves most	3	11%	3	10%	4	13%	12	63%
Serves some	18	67%	15	48%	17	53%	1	5%
Serves none	2	7%	1	3%	1	3%	1	5%
No response/NA	1	4%	0	0%	2	6%	0	0%
First-year students								
Serves all	14	52%	21	68%	23	72%	10	53%
Serves most	8	30%	6	19%	6	19%	5	26%
Serves some	4	15%	4	13%	2	6%	4	21%
Serves none	0	0%	0	0%	0	0%	0	0%
No response/NA	1	4%	0	0%	1	3%	0	0%
Honors students								
Serves all	14	52%	11	35%	13	41%	7	37%
Serves most	2	7%	2	6%	2	6%	2	11%
Serves some	5	19%	11	35%	9	28%	5	26%
Serves none	5	19%	4	13%	5	16%	3	16%
No response/NA	1	4%	3	10%	2	6%	2	11%
International students								
Serves all	6	22%	8	26%	7	22%	7	37%
Serves most	3	11%	2	6%	5	16%	0	0%
Serves some	15	56%	14	45%	16	50%	10	53%
Serves none	2	7%	2	6%	1	3%	1	5%
No response/NA	1	4%	5	16%	3	9%	1	5%

Table 1.5 continued on p. 20

Table 1.5 continued

	University College (n = 27)		Other unit name (n = 31)		Comprehensive (n = 32)		Single (n = 19)	
	Number	%	Number	%	Number	%	Number	%
New transfers								
Serves all	4	15%	11	35%	6	19%	6	32%
Serves most	16	59%	6	19%	10	31%	2	11%
Serves some	7	26%	10	32%	13	41%	10	53%
Serves none	0	0%	2	6%	1	3%	1	5%
No response/NA	0	0%	2	6%	2	6%	0	0%
Probation students								
Serves all	3	11%	11	35%	5	16%	6	32%
Serves most	7	26%	3	10%	7	22%	2	11%
Serves some	16	59%	13	42%	16	50%	10	53%
Serves none	1	4%	1	3%	2	6%	0	0%
No response/NA	0	0%	3	10%	2	6%	1	5%
Provisionally admitted students								
Serves all	11	41%	16	52%	14	44%	10	53%
Serves most	3	11%	4	13%	5	16%	0	0%
Serves some	6	22%	4	13%	6	19%	3	16%
Serves none	2	7%	2	6%	2	6%	2	11%
No response/NA	5	19%	5	16%	5	16%	4	21%
Undeclared students								
Serves all	23	85%	24	77%	28	88%	14	74%
Serves most	2	7%	6	19%	3	9%	3	16%
Serves some	2	7%	0	0%	1	3%	1	5%
Serves none	0	0%	0	0%	0	0%	1	5%
No response/NA	0	0%	1	3%	0	0%	0	0%

University colleges appear to lose their mandates to serve all declared majors to a larger extent than units with other names. While only 11% of university colleges serve all students who have declared a major, 39% of units with other names serve all declared majors.

A smaller percentage of university colleges (15%) than units with other names (35%) serve all new transfer students. While university colleges are less likely to serve all new transfers, a fuller picture is visible if the reporting categories of *all* and *most* are combined. When combined, 74% of university colleges report serving all or most new transfer students compared to 54% of units with other names.

More than one third of university colleges (37%) and fewer than half (45%) of units with other names provide services to all or most students on probation. Still service to probation students is part of the mission of the vast majority of these units in that 96% of university colleges and 87% of other units report providing services to all, most, or some students on probation.

Differences were found in service to honor students and provisionally admitted students. A majority of university colleges serve all or most honors students (59%) and provisionally admitted students (52%). A smaller percentage of units with other names serve all or most honor students (41%), while a larger percentage of them serve provisionally admitted students (65%). The data may suggest that additional academic creditability, at least in terms of engagement with honors students, comes with the university college name for the FYOS.

Scale of Service to First-Year Students: Comprehensive Versus Single Units

Comprehensive units are more likely to serve all first-year students (see Table 1.3). Seventy-two percent of comprehensive units, compared to 53% of single units, reported serving all first-year students. However, comprehensive units appear to lose their mandates to serve all students at the point that students declare a major. Only 25% of comprehensive units serve all students once they have declared a major, compared to 88% that serve all undeclared students. A similar percent of single units (26%) serve all students once they have declared a major, but a majority of these (63%) report that they continue to serve most declared majors, compared to 13% of comprehensive units. So while 89% of single units report serving all or most declared students, only 38% of comprehensive units report the same. The current research does not clearly explain why these two organizing structures offer different levels of support to declared majors, but this is one of the striking differences in the two forms.

Fewer than half of comprehensive (38%) and single units (43%) provide services to all or most students on probation, but a clear majority engages in some connection with probation students. Combining the response categories of all, most, and some shows that 88% of comprehensive units and 96% of single units provide services to at least some probation students.

Service to new transfers is similar for both comprehensive and single units. Half of the comprehensive units report serving all or most new transfer students, and slightly fewer (43%) single units report the same. In addition, 41% of comprehensive units and 53% of single units report serving at least some new transfers showing that more than 90% of these units had engagement with at least some new transfer students.

The two FYOSs were essentially the same in their service to provisionally admitted, honors, and international students. About half of both comprehensive and single unit FYOSs (comprehensives, 44%; single units, 53%) serve all provisionally admitted students. Slightly less than half serve all or most honor students (comprehensives, 47%; single units, 48%), and about one third serve all or most international students (comprehensives, 38%; single units, 37%).

Title of the Senior Leader

Of the 58 institutions in the study, 27 (47%) use the title of *dean* for the unit's senior manager, 8 more (14%) use *vice/associate/assistant provost/president*, 11 (19%) use *directors*, and 12 (21%) use various other administrative titles. Units named University College were far more likely to be led by a dean (65%) than by a director (19%). However, the title of dean was not exclusive to university colleges. Of the units that were not named University Colleges, 31% were led by a dean rather than a director (19%).

Perhaps one of the manifestations of unit histories noted above is the variation of titles for the senior leaders of these FYOSs. The majority of comprehensive units are led by a dean (59%) or associate provost/vice provost (13%). These two titles, combined, account for 72% of the comprehensive units. In comparison, 19% of these units are led by a director or some other title (8%).

No clear pattern can be discerned for the title of the leaders of the single units that are not comprehensive in scope. A similar percent of these leaders carried the title of dean (32%), assistant/associate vice provost/president (31%), or director (26%).

Survey respondents were asked to compare the title of the leader of the FYOS to the leaders of other campus units. A majority (60%) of all respondents felt the FYOS title was about equal to the titles of other leaders equally positioned on the campus. A notable minority (34%) reported that the FYOS title was *generally lower* than titles for similar leadership positions on the campus. This finding suggests that there may be some truth in the widely held belief that close association with first-year students equates to lower status on some campuses.

Summary and Conclusion

Institutions selected for this survey all have significant investments in a FYOS. A majority qualify as a comprehensive single organizing structure with campus-wide oversight and alignment of first-year efforts. These units (a) appear on the campus organizational chart, (b) have a director, and (c) have a recurring operational budget. They have oversight for more than a single first-year course and exist primarily to serve first-year students. Others in this study approach the full array of conditions described above but vary in at least one significant way so that they do not fully meet the definition of comprehensive.

As such, all 58 campuses in this study would be recognized by a campus' faculty and staff as a major unit with clear responsibility for organizing the first year of college and for many other aspects of the undergraduate experience outside of traditional disciplinary majors.

While recognizable, there remains considerable variance among the group with each reflecting a unique set of services, focus on specific student populations, and set of resources available to carry out their missions. University colleges tend to be led by a dean, have faculty lines assigned, and serve as the official home for students. While it is not possible to state that university colleges always have more resources and a wider portfolio of initiatives, they often represent the most structured and well-situated of the various FYOSs explored in this research.

Of course, the intention of this chapter is simply to describe the structures higher education uses to organize and deliver the first year of college. We cannot offer data about the effectiveness or efficiencies of these structures. We hypothesize that, like everything else about this topic, a wide variation exists. The use of case studies, as provided in this monograph, should be helpful in answering questions of cost/benefit for the various arrangements.

It is possible to conclude from these data that a number of American colleges and universities have elected to use significant resources to provide comprehensive organizational structures to assure continuity of services to new students. These data provide a roadmap for the sets of services that could be part of a comprehensive structure for organizing the first year of college. As the case studies in the monograph indicate, there are many ways to organize the first year of college and many stories of successfully doing so.

These data also suggest that FYOSs take on a wide array of activities, which could easily lead them to be spreading their attention and resources too thin. Particularly noteworthy is the long list of activities that the respondents reported as being part of their portfolio but for which they are not the unit with primary responsibility. A positive review might suggest that FYOSs often share and "play well with others," but an alternative view might suggest a lack of focus on what matters most to these units.

Likewise, the range of students served virtually requires these units to be generalists and to work with large numbers of students. While most focus heavily on first-year students, many carry loads via service to sophomores and other continuing students. Of particular interest is the category we labeled *serves some* students. It is likely that greater efficiencies can be reached when *serving all* or at least *serving most* students in specific groups. Further research could shed light on the conditions that undergird the noted patterns and question the efficiency of retaining services that serve only a few students.

Chapter 2

Collaborations for Entering Student Success

Frank E. Ross & Maggy Smith

The need for collaboration in higher education can be traced to the rise of the research university and increasing disciplinary specialization. Kellogg (1999) notes, "In the colonial colleges, the faculty was responsible for the intellectual, social, and spiritual development of students" (p. 2). Yet, "as faculty found less time to focus on the social and personal development of their students, student affairs professionals emerged to fulfill that need" (p. 2). As time went on, increased specialization and bifurcation of responsibility for student learning led to the creation of silos within higher education. Kellogg suggests that "the need for integration of these roles, and an attempt to change from separatist to seamless, has been a recent focus of higher education administrators" (p. 3). Evidence of this is seen in calls for the creation of seamless learning environments by leading professional organizations. *The Student Learning Imperative* (ACPA, 1994) described critical higher education collaborations and reminded educators that "students benefit from many varied experiences during college and . . . learning and personal development are cumulative, mutually shaping processes that occur over an extended period of time in many different settings" (p. 3). More recently, *Learning Reconsidered* (Keeling, 2004) underscored the importance of collaboration in the academy and argued for the integrated use of all of higher education's resources to educate the whole student.

The literature related to collaboration in higher education, particularly between academic affairs and student affairs, illustrates the importance of campus partnerships in enhancing student learning (Martin & Murphy, 2000; O'Halloran, 2007; Schuh, 1999). Yet, some research (Kolins, 1999; O'Halloran, 2005) suggests that enhancing academic performance and increasing persistence are often driving forces behind such partnerships.

University colleges are an example of a substantial collaborative effort, providing initiatives that have a significant impact on entering students in their transition to the college environment. When institutions are able to set aside reporting structures and put the student as the focus of the conversation, they create optimal conditions for collaboration that allow everyone to concentrate on student learning and success. In the seminal monograph on university colleges, *Portals of Entry*, Strommer (1993) speaks of the institution-wide perspective fundamental to this approach for serving first-year students. While few university college units structurally encompass all the personnel and services that support entering students (i.e., from admissions to faculty who teach general education), the data in chapter 1 make clear that university colleges frequently play a role in most services and initiatives geared toward entering students. As a result, they assume a responsibility for creating collaborations for student success among faculty, staff, administrators, and students. For example, 34% of respondents to our survey share responsibility for learning communities; 40% share responsibility for study skills, and 24% for Supplemental Instruction. Other areas for collaboration that will be described in the case studies throughout this monograph include first-year seminars, student leadership development and employment, P–20 working relationships, campus-based advisory councils, first-year convocations, service-learning, civic engagement initiatives, and dual-credit programs and early college high schools. These collaborations are realized through resource sharing, joint personnel appointments, and coordination of services and programs.

With the increasing price of higher education and with the greater outreach to prospective student populations that once would have been ignored, there has been a marked rise in the diversity and flexibility of curricular structures. As a result, collaboration often extends beyond the campus to include other higher education institutions, secondary institutions, local businesses and civic organizations, state bureaucracies, national organizations, and international partners. For example, university colleges may collaborate with local school districts in development of early college high schools or dual-enrollment programs.

Students are also earning college credit in diverse ways. With the aggressive growth in distance education, students are increasingly accumulating credit from a variety of institutions. Military personnel are especially encouraged to pursue distance education while they are on active duty. Also, student veterans and their families are attending postsecondary institutions at increasingly higher rates (Coll, Oh, Joyce, & Coll, 2009; U.S. Department of Veterans Affairs, 2009), which makes the need for effective collaborations more paramount. University colleges provide the critical network of campus and community partners to aid and support these students during their active duty and in the transition to campus life through specialized orientation programs, learning communities, mentoring, and social support for veteran students.

Essential collaborations, coupled with a strong emphasis on student success, make university colleges *the* nexus for academic and social development of entering college students. This chapter examines significant strategies for university college collaborations with both campus and external partners to support entering student success. Readers will find details regarding successful collaborations in and with university colleges, including characteristics of effective collaborations and benefits of collaboration.

Characteristics of Effective Collaboration

Faculty and administrators in higher education are being challenged to improve student learning through increased student-centeredness and collaboration (Fuller & Haugabrook, 2001; Grace, 2000; O'Halloran, 2007). But what is meant by collaboration in the university college? What types of collaborations exist, and how are they organized to best impact student learning? Kuh (1996) describes cross-campus collaboration, particularly between academic affairs and student affairs, and identifies six principles that guide integration of the curriculum and the cocurriculum. These include generating enthusiasm for institutional renewal, creating a common vision of learning, developing a common language, fostering collaboration and cross-functional dialogue, examining the influence of student cultures on learning, and a focus on systematic change. Similar characteristics of successful collaborations emerge from the descriptions of university colleges included throughout this monograph.

For example, effective collaborations move beyond "superficial affiliations" toward "substantive partnerships" as is the case with the university college at Buffalo State University (see case in this chapter). Buffalo State's residential learning communities illustrate the characteristics of substantive partnerships: interdependence, authentic participation from a wide range of constituent groups, and a focus on institutional mission and student learning.

Another hallmark of substantive partnerships is resource sharing—whether physical, personnel, or financial. Shared resources across units necessitate shared dialogue. At Indiana University

– Purdue University Indianapolis (IUPUI, see the case study in this chapter), joint faculty positions were created. The university college leadership brought together groups of faculty from all schools at IUPUI to provide oversight for the entire array of academic programs in the university college. In addition, to facilitate development of cocurricular engagement in the first-year experience, the university college offered to create and jointly fund a position with student affairs. This shared administrative position (assistant vice chancellor for student life and learning) supports the integration of cocurricular learning, both on and off campus, into the first-year experience at IUPUI. Financial support is provided for joint positions and cooperative programming across campus.

Being able to speak a common language is also critical for successful collaborations. At Montana State University (see case in this chapter), Student development theory has provided a way for both faculty and student affairs administrators to talk about and plan for students learning and success. Bringing student development theory and practice to the faculty and their teaching practices for first-year students provides a clear pedagogical partnership between academic affairs and student affairs and creates the platform from which to grow an understanding of each other's expertise.

Effective leadership is also critical for the development and enhancement of collaborations in university colleges. Successful collaboration depends upon finding and empowering an effective leader. This person must be trusted by faculty and staff across campus, be known as a student-centered advocate and as someone who listens well and invites participation from a range of constituent groups. Case studies from both University of Texas at El Paso (this chapter) and Appalachian State University (chapter 3) illustrate the work of leaders who were effective in bringing together campus partners, valuing all voices, and taking multiple perspectives into account in the collaborative process of program development.

Benefits of Collaboration

Collaboration requires significant and intentional strategizing. In some ways, it appears to be harder than the work we expect to do or want to do. It challenges us to put our own ideas and ourselves on the table for discussion, dissection, and modification. In other words, ideas move from being the product of one individual to the product of a team of individuals. Collaborations are energizing and benefit the faculty and staff involved in the process. The result is better programs and a shared pool of workers who are invested in those programs and the success of the students they serve.

Often collaborative efforts in higher education lead to successes at the program, department, and institution level. These benefits include solid, functioning bridges between institutional silos; diminishing internal competitions among units; reduction of cross-institutional barriers and boundaries; reduction of waste and redundancy; ability to maximize talent on campus; increased ability for fiscal responsibility through cost sharing; enhanced relationships with other educational institutions (i.e., both P–12 and community colleges); and increased student satisfaction.

Kellogg (1999) notes that collaborative work in higher education benefits student learning, including improved cognitive, interpersonal, and organization skills; self-discipline; self-understanding; responsibility for self and community; increased leadership and citizenship; academic success; and retention. These benefits are most successfully realized when an institutional structure like a university college is present to ensure all campus partners are engaged in the work of improving student learning and success.

Conclusion

Genuine collaboration in higher education truly gives meaning to the notion that the whole is greater than the sum of its parts. As educators—faculty and administrators alike—work together in shared ownership, the most efficient and effective strategies to develop the whole student can be employed. The case studies in this chapter provide excellent models for how university colleges can collaborate to enhance student learning and success. More specifically, they detail partnerships between university colleges and campus partners such as student affairs, academic affairs, enrollment services, honors programs, and residence life. Collaborations with community partners such as P–12 systems and two-year institutions will also be discussed.

Yet, readers will quickly notice that the theme of collaboration repeats itself in every chapter and in nearly every case study in this monograph. While the overriding focus of chapter three is the importance of the undergraduate curriculum to student success, an effective undergraduate curriculum is made possible by interdisciplinary teams working together in a variety of ways. In chapter four on holistic support for learning, the same is true. While cases describe programs that provide learning support, each of those initiatives is collaborative in some way. Finally, chapter five thematically addresses assessment, and the work exemplified by each case is highly collaborative in nature.

References

American College Personnel Association (ACPA). (1994). *The student learning imperative: Implications for student affairs.* Washington, DC: Author.

Coll, J. E., Oh, H., Joyce, C., & Coll, L. C. (2009, April). Veterans in higher education: What every adviser may want to know. *The Mentor: An Academic Advising Journal, 11*(2). Retrieved from http://www.psu.edu/dus/mentor

Fuller, T. M. A., & Haugabrook, A. K. (2001). Facilitative strategies in action. *New Directions for Higher Education, 116,* 75–87.

Grace, T. (2000). The integrator: Linking curricular and cocurricular experiences. In J. L. Bess (Ed.), *Teaching alone, teaching together: Transforming the structure of teams for teaching* (pp. 151–172). San Francisco, CA: Jossey-Bass.

Keeling, R. P. (Ed.). (2004). *Learning reconsidered: A campus-wide focus on the student experience.* Washington, DC: National Association of Student Personnel Administrators and American College Personal Association.

Kellogg, K. (1999). *Collaboration: Student affairs and academic affairs working together to promote student learning.* Washington, DC: Institute for Education Policy Studies, Graduation School of Education and Human Development, The George Washington University.

Kolins, C. A. (1999). An appraisal of collaboration: Assessing perceptions of chief academic and student affairs officers at public two-year colleges. *Dissertation Abstracts International, 60*(11).

Kuh, G. D. (1996). Guiding principles for creating seamless learning environments for undergraduates. *Journal of College Student Development, 37*(2), 135–148.

Martin, J., & Murphy, S. (2000). *Building a better bridge: Creating effective partnerships between academic affairs and student affairs.* Washington, DC: National Association of Student Personnel Administrators.

O'Halloran, K. C. (2005). A classification of academic and student affairs collaboration in higher education from a student affairs perspective. *Dissertation Abstracts International, 65*(11).

O'Halloran, K. C. (2007). The state of student and academic affairs partnerships. In J. H. Cook & C. A. Lewis (Eds.), *Student and academic affairs collaboration: The divine comity* (pp. 33–52). Washington, DC: National Association of Student Personnel Administrators.

Schuh, J. H. (1999). Guiding principles for evaluating student and academic affairs partnerships. In J. H. Schuh & E. J. Whitt (Eds.), *Creating successful partnerships between academic and student affairs* (pp. 85–92). San Francisco, CA: Jossey-Bass.

Strommer, D. W. (1993). *Portals of entry: University colleges and undergraduate divisions* (Monograph No. 12). Columbia, SC: University of South Carolina, National Resource Center for The Freshman Year Experience.

U.S. Department of Veterans Affairs. (2009, May 15). *Over 25,000 post-9/11 GI Bill applications received in first two weeks*. Retrieved May 15, 2009, from http://www1.va.gov/opa/pressrel/pressrelease.cfm?id=1675

Chapter 2 Case Studies

Buffalo State

A Case Study in Student Affairs/Academic Affairs Partnership

Scott L. Johnson

The Institutional Context

Located in Buffalo, New York, Buffalo State is the largest of the comprehensive liberal arts colleges in the State University of New York system. Buffalo State is a master's comprehensive institution, offering 140 different academic programs. The undergraduate enrollment in the fall of 2008 was 9,371 with a total enrollment of 11,234. The first-year class at Buffalo State averages 1,500 students per academic year. The majority (80%) of Buffalo State students commute; however, almost 60% of the first-year class lives on campus. More than half (59%) of the undergraduate students are women, and historically underrepresented groups comprise 18.2% of the undergraduate population. Buffalo State takes tremendous pride in its history of academic excellence, its service to the community, and its commitment to diversity.

University College

Established in 2004, the University College at Buffalo State is the administrative home for Buffalo State's undeclared students and oversees the design and administration of the First-Year Programs and the Intellectual Foundations (general education) program. Students find a diverse array of academic support programs to help them maximize their potential as learners and members of our community. Lastly, University College broadens the intellectual lives of Buffalo State students through its transdisciplinary enrichment programs. The Honors, International and Exchange, and Undergraduate Research programs enhance student experiences beyond the curriculum. By striving to ensure that all students experience intellectual discovery and community at appropriate levels of educational challenge while receiving academic and social support, the programs of the University College augment student learning and satisfaction.

Academic Affairs/Student Affairs Collaboration

Although Buffalo State did not create a university college until 2004, the College implemented learning communities in 2001 as a way to improve its first-year experience. Since many successful academic learning communities are residential and the majority of Buffalo State's first-year students live on campus, this initiative required a working partnership between academic affairs and student affairs. The lead participants in the design and implementation of learning communities became the director of the Center for Interdisciplinary Studies from academic affairs and the associate vice president for Residence Life and Auxiliary Services from student affairs. While Buffalo State successfully implemented learning communities, it was clear to many of the participants that the program could be improved. Student affairs had made a substantial investment in rehabbing a residence hall floor and allocating funding for cocurricular programming. However, the academic affairs contribution was not as strong initially. The Center was relatively new, had low visibility among campus constituencies, and did not have direct authority over faculty. As such, the learning communities program did not maximize its potential in certain areas, such as engaging faculty participants, funding extracurricular programming, and recruiting students. The creation of University College strengthened the academic affairs contributions to this partnership. University College had high campus visibility and was headed by a dean with explicit authority over the first-year experience. Further, because University College had more resources at its disposal than residence life, it was able to compensate faculty and supplement extracurricular programming. These changes overcame significant logistical hurdles, which allowed the partnership to grow and made substantive contributions to the nature and content of the program.

For example, faculty introduced a linked-course, themed structure with a one-credit class devoted to integration of thematic concepts. Student affairs greatly enhanced that structure by asserting student success strategies should be taught as a part of the integrated hour because it was a graded course as opposed to an optional workshop. Residence life also reconfigured residence hall space to provide lounge, study, and teaching space for learning communities. These spaces better connected commuter students to the other students and the campus by allowing them a place for out-of-class learning and community building with other learning community students. All learning community students participated in theme-related residence programming. Student affairs colleagues supported the cocurricular program through funding and logistical planning that supplemented students' classroom experiences.

Lastly, many faculty integrated student development theory into their pedagogy because of the relationships developed with their student affairs colleagues during the program as well as the outcomes witnessed over time. Learning communities rest on the premise that once students bonded with each other, they would work collaboratively and spend more time on task, resulting in greater learning. Faculty saw that as student affairs professionals addressed these issues and intentionally developed out-of-class programming that enhanced the lessons in the classroom, student engagement increased dramatically. Students became more confident in themselves, and their writing and their attendance improved. The quality and interest in cocurricular activities also improved. This was a significant development in that the more accurate understanding of students' cognitive and social development caused many professors to modify their teaching in ways that allowed students to achieve more rigorous standards, directly challenging some colleagues' misperception that programs such as these compromised academic standards of the institution.

Perhaps the most significant manifestation of the partnership between academic and student affairs in this program has been the creation of the student affairs liaison—a recognized position on each learning community team. These professionals assist faculty in developing cocurricular events, present on college transition issues to students and faculty, and intervene proactively with students determined to be at risk. The development of this position has increased faculty awareness and appreciation of out-of-class issues and their effect on students' academic performance. Liaisons have in turn developed a new appreciation for demands on faculty and challenges in teaching and learning.

Results and Lessons Learned

Buffalo State considers its learning communities program a success. Retention data show that one-year retention in learning communities has been higher than in the general first-year student population throughout the program's existence. Available data show that GPAs have been higher as well, although these differences are not significantly different. Student evaluation data have been consistently positive. As pertains to the collaboration between academic and student affairs, student evaluation data reveal that students highly value the quality of the cocurricular experiences. In addition, creating a resident space accessible to commuter students has been successful. Students are especially appreciative of the opportunities to deepen relationships with faculty and each other. Faculty also noted in their evaluations satisfaction with the relationships they have built as members of a team. These connections remain the most important factor in motivating faculty participation in the program. While some faculty were hesitant to formalize the partnership with student affairs by including them as members of the instructional team, evaluations show that these fears were overcome quickly and the professors valued the contributions.

Key Elements

How was the learning communities program at Buffalo State able to develop this meaningful partnership between student affairs and academic affairs? Certainly the commitment of all participants to the success of the program was critical to the success of the endeavor. The participants' openness to the perspectives and expertise of those from the other division was essential as well. However, two distinct elements of the experience at Buffalo State stand out as critical to the creation of strong, successful partnerships between academic and student affairs.

First, both student affairs and academic affairs made substantial contributions to the project. Residential learning communities struggled initially because the contribution of academic affairs was limited. When this is the case, the perception that a project can succeed without full participation of all parties can lead to the devaluation of some contributors by other team members. Exchanges become superficial or nonexistent, leading to mere presence instead of partnership. Substantial contributions necessitate interdependence among team members. The substantive, collaborative exchanges rooted in this interdependence would more accurately represent the common perception of true partnership.

In the case of Buffalo State, academic affairs contributed courses that counted toward general education credit and limited class sizes to mirror best practices in learning communities. Student affairs offered residence hall space, special amenities in that space, unfettered access for commuter and faculty participants, and an intentionally designed cocurricular program. All parties knew that the program could not succeed as planned without these elements. The resultant sense that the work was valued created stakeholders and motivated participants to perform at high levels. Moreover, since all parties recognized the larger programmatic value in each contribution, they adapted their contributions when appropriate so that the program capitalized on the potential of each idea, demonstrating the importance of a sense of interdependence on such interdivisional project teams.

Secondly, to generate successful collaborations, team members must have authentic voice, which is the ability of participants to offer their expertise, experience, and opinions in a welcoming environment. There must be a climate of trust in which all parties are free to express themselves. Failure to capitalize on the skill sets of those involved diminishes the quality of the project. Understandably, faculty are very protective of their classrooms. Concerns that someone without a similar level of disciplinary expertise or teaching experience would attempt to control a professor's course content or pedagogy are justified. Similarly, it is inappropriate to believe that expertise in an academic discipline qualifies someone to dictate the management of a residence hall. In a cooperative venture between academic and student affairs, voices are often silenced or conditioned by the perception of political hierarchy and contextual relevance. Both speakers and listeners silence voices. All must be willing to share and listen. The issue becomes one of appropriate exchange and input. Listening to research and experience about student learning, transition, and success does not impinge on one's rights or responsibilities as the deliverer of the content of a course. Assertions that a cocurricular event may not reinforce learning as originally intended indicate that faculty do not recognize the contributions of out-of-class learning activities. The context must allow for these deeper dialogues if the participants are going to have substantive partnerships as opposed to superficial affiliations.

The Buffalo State experience demonstrates successful collaboration in that faculty presented the model of learning community they wanted to pursue, and student affairs presented research on student development that would maximize the likelihood of that success. Disagreements occurred and compromises were made, but all stakeholders felt sufficiently safe and empowered to inform one another based on expertise and experience. When it became clear that these ideas were bearing fruit in the classroom and the program, everyone shared and listened more intentionally. This moved the relationship beyond professional courtesy to trusted partnership.

Conclusion

Undoubtedly, learning communities at Buffalo State could not be successful without the intentional collaboration between academic affairs and student affairs. Although the teaching faculty were fully committed to the success of this program, they did not fully understand the complexity of certain dimensions of the student experience or their importance in generating classroom success. Partnering with student affairs equipped them to become better teachers through integration of student development theory into their pedagogy, appreciation of intentional cocurricular design, and recognition of students in distress. Student affairs professionals were able to design a cocurricular program intentionally linked to students' course experiences rather than general issues of student success and transition. The student-centered, learning-driven, transdisciplinary missions of university colleges present a unique opportunity to merge the strengths of student affairs and academic affairs. The example of the learning communities program in the University College at Buffalo State represents what is possible when consequential contribution and authentic voice are present in these interdivisional collaborations.

Indiana University–Purdue University Indianapolis

Academic and Student Affairs Partnerships Supporting First-Year Students

Frank E. Ross & David J. Sabol

The Institutional Context

Indiana University–Purdue University Indianapolis (IUPUI) is a public, four-year commuter institution located in downtown Indianapolis, Indiana. With more than 28,000 students representing 49 states and 139 countries, IUPUI is the second-largest campus in the Indiana University statewide multiple-campus system. IUPUI is an urban research and academic health sciences campus, with 22 schools and academic units that grant degrees in more than 200 programs from both Indiana University and Purdue University.

In fall 2008, IUPUI enrolled 28,722 students, 19,970 of whom were at the undergraduate level, with 3,040 new beginning students. The University has an enrollment of 17,932 full-time students and 10,840 part-time students. IUPUI has a significant adult (age 25 and over) student population represented by 13,261 learners. Approximately 1,100 students live on campus. Of those, 64% are first-year students.

More than half (57%) of IUPUI students are female. Total minority enrollment represents almost 16% of the total student population: African American (9.1%), Asian/Pacific Islander (4%), and Hispanic (2.5%). Finally, 44% of undergraduate students are first-generation, defined as neither mother nor father having completed a college degree.

University College

As part of institutional efforts to provide one portal of entry to the multiple degree units and support student success, the IUPUI Faculty Council approved the formation of University College in spring 1997. The founding faculty (representing all degree-granting schools at IUPUI) and the dean were appointed soon thereafter, with the first students entering the college in summer 1998. The founding faculty approved the following mission statement:

> University College is the academic unit at IUPUI, which provides a common gateway to the academic programs available to entering students. University College coordinates existing university resources and develops new initiatives to promote academic excellence and enhance student persistence. It provides a setting where faculty, staff, and students share in the responsibility for making IUPUI a supportive and challenging environment for learning.

All students entering IUPUI are granted admission to University College (either full or dual admission with a degree-granting school). Students remain in University College until they have declared a major and meet the necessary conditions for transfer to a degree-granting school. Approximately 6,500 are enrolled in University College each year.

Programs and services offered by University College focus on assisting students with the development of the knowledge and skills needed for success in the collegiate environment, including academic advising, academic support, first-year seminars, themed learning communities, academic mentoring, new student orientation, and the campus honors program. University College also offers several college readiness programs, which focus on helping area students become college bound.

Collaborations With Academic Units

University College at IUPUI has built a reputation with all the schools on campus as being a truly collaborative unit. From its inception, University College was designed to function under the auspices of a collaborative group of faculty from all the schools in the University. Because this collaborative group has the oversight responsibility for all the academic programs within University College, these faculty also serve to strengthen ties between University College and their academic units in the role of liaison. A high level of commitment to student success in the first year is necessary to be a faculty member in University College. Faculty chosen to serve in the College demonstrate this commitment through successful teaching (as evidenced in positive student evaluations, peer observations, and annual reports) or by providing support services in their academic units.

University College maintains a number of joint faculty lectureships with various academic units across the IUPUI campus. Lecturers are required to teach and provide service equally between their academic unit and University College. At IUPUI, lecturers teach 12 hours per semester, which equals four three-credit-hour courses. Generally, University College lecturers teach two courses for their academic unit and two or more courses for the College, which can vary from semester to semester. Lecturers divide their service commitments between University College and their academic departments according to individual agreements. Because first-year seminar courses have typically been one-credit hour courses, these additional administrative responsibilities with the joint lecturer position have allowed the faculty member to teach only two first-year seminar courses (or their equivalency) per semester and still meet the six-hour semester requirement for a lectureship. The other four hours are spent scheduling and staffing courses and staying current with trends in first-year seminars and learning communities in order to provide quality training and faculty development support.

One of the first joint lectureships between University College and an academic unit involved a composition faculty member. This position also included administrative coordination with the first-year seminar courses and the English Department. There grew a need to expand seminar course offerings to meet the demands of an increasing entering student population. With the expansion came additional administrative coordination by the joint lecturer, including the recruitment of faculty, providing faculty training and development, scheduling the linked first-year seminar courses with academic courses, staffing the linked courses each semester, and general ongoing curriculum and faculty development for the linked courses. The University College has expanded its joint lecturer positions to include other academic units: Communication Studies, Biology, Anthropology, Math, Career Services, and Education. These joint lecturer positions allow for a more consistent delivery of first-year seminars linked with various discipline courses to provide students with support in their chosen field. The collaborations between University College and each of these schools also strengthens first-year programs across IUPUI's campus.

The joint lectureship and linked course models have been quite successful at IUPUI. Because the University is a commuter campus, students entering in their first year need the support of caring instructors to help them navigate the system and to make meaningful connections to the institution. The linked courses provide opportunities for students to get to know each other and to bond more closely with their instructors, which in turn provides a sense of safety and belonging. While retention rates still can be improved, documentation has shown that joint lectureships and linked courses are helping entering students remain at the University.

Collaborations With Student Affairs

In the fall of 2002, the IUPUI student affairs division was restructured to create a key staff position (associate director of campus and community life) to work strategically with University College in the support of first-year student learning. Because University College does not have a distinct student affairs office, this staff position performed a variety of functions to encourage and support the integration of cocurricular engagement into the first-year experience at IUPUI. Cocurricular engagement is described as student involvement both on campus and in the community. The position was administratively housed within the student activities area (Campus and Community Life) and worked with all areas of University College, initially new student orientation and learning communities.

Within new student orientation, this administrator worked with University College staff to develop programming to enhance entering students' awareness of involvement opportunities, both on and off campus. For example, the newly developed program, First Year in a FLASH, provided students with a fun, fast-paced experiential overview of their first year at IUPUI.

In working with learning communities, the position also assisted first-year seminar instructional teams, particularly in advancing the goal of students making use of campus resources and services that support learning and campus connections. This staff member implemented specific initiatives related to first-year seminars, including cocurricular program development, instructional team development and support, and a weekly newsletter of campus and community happenings.

An expanded calendar of cocurricular activities designed specifically to meet the developmental needs of first-year students was also introduced. This calendar provided many opportunities for both on-campus and off-campus involvement. Additionally, a robust agenda of cultural programming designed to help first-year students explore issues of diversity was offered.

Intentional professional development for first-year seminar instructional team members was implemented to educate faculty regarding the important role cocurricular learning plays in first-year student success. Instructional team members were taught how to integrate this learning into their courses and appropriate ways to engage students in reflection about the learning. Faculty also took advantage of individual consultations. Additionally, regular classroom presentations in first-year seminar courses encouraged involvement in student life through student organizations, leadership workshops, community service, and other student activities.

The introduction of an electronic newsletter for all first-year students was a significant development in our enhancement of cocurricular learning in the first-year seminars. This newsletter detailed opportunity for campus involvement as well as engagement in the city. Additionally, weekly study tips, provided by the academic advising center on campus, were included.

While the collaboration between student affairs and University College proved very successful, it soon became apparent there was more good work to do and too much to be accomplished by one individual. The associate director for campus and community life advocated for additional staffing within student affairs to support this. Eventually, a full-time coordinator for first-year programs (paid for by student affairs) and a first-year programs graduate assistant (paid for by University College) were added to the student affairs staff roster.

The additional collaborative staffing allowed the student activities unit to have greater outreach in new student orientation and learning communities. Additional programming, including a new student convocation and Weeks of Welcome, followed. Also, the new coordinator assumed leadership as the advisor of the University College Student Council, working with representatives of each first-year seminar class to enhance the student experience for first-year students at IUPUI.

In 2007, the collaboration between student affairs and University College expanded with the development of a new position: the assistant vice chancellor for student life and learning. This joint-funded position supervises five administrative units within student affairs, strengthening their adherence to the academic mission of the University and also provides leadership within University College for the integration of cocurricular learning and student engagement at all levels.

Results and Lessons Learned

Collaborations With Academic Units

From its inception, University College has maintained sustainable budgets for joint lecturer positions with various academic units who share the costs. The benefits of better retention rates and higher student GPAs tend to offset the expenditure for these positions. Reporting structures are in place to allow for joint lecturers to be reviewed and promoted based on performance in both their academic unit and University College. Official faculty appointments for University College joint lecturer positions reside within the various academic units rather than with University College since the academic units maintain degree-granting status. This also allows the lecturers to retain academic rank.

Because the joint lecturer positions are full-time rather than part-time/adjunct faculty, entering students benefit from faculty whose main priority is their success. The IUPUI first-year seminars taught primarily by joint lecturers produce positive retention rates and are recognized nationally as being among the best models for student success. Joint lecturers in University College help students navigate both the details of particular disciplines and the vastness of the university system. This effort attracts faculty members who are willing not only to share their expertise in a discipline but also to provide the larger context of what it means to be a member within the University culture.

Collaborations With Student Affairs

University College has created a strong environment of collaboration with student affairs. This has been realized through financial support for joint administrative positions and cooperative programming. The administration of University College has been intentionally inclusive in inviting student affairs staff members to have presence at key meetings and to join standing committees. This successful partnership is due in large part to the University College administration and faculty realizing the critical importance of cocurricular engagement in first-year students' learning and success. New student orientation exit survey data provide evidence that entering students are learning about involvement opportunities on campus and in the community at rates higher than before collaborative efforts began.

Additionally, the effectiveness of this collaboration is evident from National Survey of Student Engagement (NSSE) data, which suggest that these initiatives were successful in enhancing cocurricular student engagement for first-year students at IUPUI. The data support first-year seminar participation having a statistically significant positive impact on specific measures of cocurricular engagement, including participation in a community-based project as part of a class; attendance at an art exhibit, gallery, play, or theatre performance; participation in community service or volunteer work; and hours per week spent participating in cocurricular activities.

Montana State University

University College: A Collaboration

Gregory Young & Allen Yarnell

The Institutional Context

Founded in 1893 in the scenic Gallatin Valley just north of Yellowstone National Park, Montana State University (MSU) is a residential campus located in Bozeman, Montana. It has an enrollment of more than 13,000 students and a faculty of 802. MSU is a Carnegie classification Very High Research Activity university. Montana State offers baccalaureate degrees in 51 fields, master's degrees in 42 fields, and doctoral degrees in 18 fields. Accredited by the Northwest Commission on Colleges and Universities, its students are 47% female, 65% Montana residents, 32% out-of-state residents, 3% international (from 70 countries), and 18% first-generation college (neither parent has a bachelor's degree). The largest ethnic minority groups on campus are Native Americans at 3%, with all other minority groups combined comprising another 3%.

University College

In 2003, MSU created and filled the position of vice provost for undergraduate education to enhance undergraduate education at an institution that was rapidly moving forward in faculty research productivity. The creation of University College in 2004, to bring together several university-wide programs under the authority of the new vice provost, was a natural next step. It also facilitated raising the profile of the general studies program, which serves as an entry point for more than 700 incoming undeclared majors annually.

Changing the name of General Studies to University Studies was intended to give legitimacy to exploratory study as a lower-division major. Some of our best students enter University Studies because they are interested in several fields and wish to make a well-informed choice of major.

University College offers several important academic programs to students, regardless of major. Undergraduate research and creative activity, interdisciplinary study, thematic research seminars, major/career exploration, and National Student Exchange are just a few of the many opportunities available. Specific programs, with enrollments, include the University Honors Program (750); the Undergraduate Scholars Program (200); University Studies (1,300); Leadership Fellows Certificate (12); and two new interdisciplinary degree programs, Liberal Studies (225) and American Studies (25, first offered fall 2007).

Collaboration With Student Affairs

University College at Montana State University serves as a portal of entry for one third of the incoming first-year class who have yet to declare a major and plays an important role in providing several other campus-wide academic opportunities. Upon the formation of University College, it became apparent that to best serve the undergraduates, collaboration with student affairs would be crucial. University College staff have since developed excellent channels of communication with student affairs on issues such as financial aid, advising, retention, recruitment, and the first-year seminar program. Student success is enhanced when the knowledge and perspectives of people who work in student affairs are integrated into course design, especially in courses like the first-year seminar. The vice president for student affairs and the vice provost for undergraduate education, who serves as dean of University College, cochair a group called the Student Progress Oversight Committee (SPOC), which provides student success and retention recommendations to the University budget and strategic planning committees. This SPOC collaboration resulted in University funding for 2007–2009 initiatives, which included (a) offering Supplemental Instruction (SI) in the residence halls, (b) reducing the size of first-year English composition sections, (c) expanding the location of the Math Help Center to the residence halls, (d) funding an out-of-class experience for faculty/student connection in first-year seminar, and (e) designing and printing an advisor toolkit.

SI is an academic assistance program that uses peer-assisted study sessions for historically difficult, large lecture courses (e.g., Math 181:Calculus). SI sessions are regularly scheduled informal review sessions in which students compare notes, discuss readings, develop organizational tools, and predict test items. Students learn how to integrate course content and study skills while working together. SI leaders are students who have successfully completed the class. They attend all classes, conduct two SI sessions per week, plan interactive learning activities, prepare handouts for SI sessions, conduct exam review sessions, and model outstanding student behavior and successful academic practices.

Empirical evidence suggests that a number of negative outcomes are associated with increasingly large class size (Cuseo, 2007). Reducing the size of first-year composition classes (English 121) from 33 to 25 was a University goal that never reached a high enough priority level for funding until it was recommended by SPOC as a retention initiative with a possible return on investment in terms of tuition dollars and student success. An argument was made that getting closer to the national average on section size for this course was important for student success in future courses and that having at least two required small-class settings for first-year students, composition and first-year seminar, would improve retention.

Expanding the Math Help Center to provide additional tutoring in the evenings in the residence halls met a demand that was evident by specific student requests as well as by grades. This followed the model of the Writing Center, which expanded their services in 2005 to the main library and the residence halls.

Approximately 130 sections of first-year seminar are taught each year. In fall 2007, we began providing a budget of $10 per student to seminar instructors to have an out-of-class event, such as making dinner together, attending a special lecture followed by discussion and coffee, or doing an outdoor activity. Several instructors have done this successfully in the past, and research shows that making a faculty/student connection in the first six weeks of the semester is an important factor in retention (Levitz & Noel, 1989). A survey of faculty who participated revealed that they were overwhelmingly positive about this activity. Thus, it continues to be an option for all first-year seminars.

A concise, graphically interesting advisor toolkit is printed and distributed to advisors before the preregistration period each semester. Although departments handle advising in different ways, all advisors need access to vital information to aid students with academic course selection and extra-academic issues. A clear, concise, and comprehensive set of resources to help answer questions and refer students was needed. Professional advisors in the Advising Center in University College designed this toolkit, and faculty have found it very helpful.

Collaboration also enabled student affairs to fund a new position in University College called the students-in-transition advisor, based upon the premise that a student probably will not get the best advice from an advisor whose expertise lies in the very department the student wishes to leave. Such students need someone who has a comprehensive knowledge of all the available academic programs and can skillfully help them navigate the transition process. The Board of Regents of the Montana University System requested student success proposals for base funding adjustments, and University College staff submitted a request for the students-in-transition advisor as part of a larger proposal by student affairs.

Student recruitment is another area where University College has collaborated with student affairs, especially with regard to academic content in promotional materials. For example, our new core curriculum—with its inquiry courses in arts, humanities, natural sciences, and social sciences—is regularly featured in publications from student affairs, such as the view book. Because University College welcomes such a large portion of the incoming class, collaboration on recruitment is important. It is also critical to relay the message to prospective and first-year students that they are not expected to immediately declare a major and that their decision should be well informed.

The First-Year Initiative is a student affairs program that helps students manage the transition to college through individual counseling and workshops on study skills and time management. Two of the main tools used to identify potential at-risk students are the College Student Inventory (CSI), given at orientation, and mid-semester grades of D or F, solicited from the faculty as an early-alert system. In an effort to reach out to more at-risk students and to encourage student/faculty interaction, the CSI is being added to the first-year seminar curriculum. First-Year Initiative advisors will provide a group interpretation on the CSI within the classroom followed by individual student meetings with the instructor or an academic advisor.

Raising the level of awareness of the importance of academic advising is another area of campus-wide collaboration that has been achieved through (a) a new MSU Academic Advising Council; (b) expansion of the Academic Advising Center in University College to reach out to departmental and faculty advisors; (c) advising workshops for faculty to explore best practices; and (d) electronic advising software to facilitate the course selection and curriculum requirement process, enabling instructors to spend more time on advising related to careers in the discipline.

The Academic Advising Council is chaired by the vice provost for undergraduate education and is made up of professional advisors from University College and other campus departments, faculty, and Student Affairs staff. This group works with the Academic Advising Center to find out where departments need help with advising, since advising is handled in a variety of ways across campus, some with more success than others. With that information, the Council plans advising workshops for faculty in which different models are presented, often customized by a particular department, followed by question and answer sessions.

A first-year convocation was initiated in the fall of 2007 and was inspired by findings from the National Survey of Student Engagement (NSSE, 2004), which suggested that bonding through common experience was an important retention tool. A new summer reading project, coupled with the first convocation was a direct collaboration between University College administrators and student affairs. New York Times bestseller *Three Cups of Tea* was the first MSU summer reading, and book author, Greg Mortenson, was the convocation speaker. Two thousand students attended the program, which received favorable reviews. MSU Parent/Family Association also provided a web cast of the event and made it available to the parents of first-year students.

In the summer of 2007, MSU created a Living and Learning Advisory Board, comprised of administrators from University College and student affairs. This was intended to integrate academics with residence life and minimize the silo effect of academia, which often limits meaningful dialogue across divisional boundaries. Residence hall floors with specialized living/learning environments, such as outdoor pursuits or discipline-specific themes, continue to be piloted and reviewed to meet the goals of the students and the staff.

Ideas for future collaboration include analyzing NSSE data to better inform decisions on student success programs, collaborating on funding for our Student Advocacy for Financial Education, and conducting student focus groups to learn more about campus-specific retention issues.

Results and Lessons Learned

Collaboration between University College and student affairs was a natural alliance for MSU because the units have similar goals, most of which focus on student success. It also positioned University College to be a player in working on certain aspects of the University's five-year vision, such as retention. University College and student affairs membership representation on SPOC contributed to the retention committee's success along with a willingness on the part of its members to quickly move forward with researching effective strategies. Within two weeks of the group's formation, SPOC had a refined proposal to present to the budget committee, and allocations were made quickly in an environment that often favors caution over risk when it comes to funding. During the budget committee deliberations, it was evident that considerable thought from a representative group of MSU personnel had gone into the retention proposals, which helped secure the necessary program funding.

One retention challenge is determining why students are choosing to leave MSU, as many students often cite personal or financial reasons, even though it might be only partially true. By using NSSE, we hope to better assess the problem areas and more effectively implement solutions. The students-in-transition advisor has been especially important in counseling students who do not make it through the sophomore-level academic gates in high-demand programs, such as architecture, film, and nursing.

Recommendations for other institutions include (a) collaborating with student affairs units to achieve common goals, (b) establishing a campus-wide Academic Advising Council with a variety of advising entities represented to assess the state of advising on campus and address any problems, (c) initiating a summer reading program and a new student convocation, (d) making the case to the central administration that University College can and should play a critical role in recruitment and retention, and (e) raising the profile of University College by taking on key roles in fulfilling the university's strategic goals.

References

Levitz, R., & Noel, L. (1989). Connecting students to institutions: Keys to retention and success. In M. L. Upcraft & J. N. Gardner (Eds.), *The freshman year experience: Helping students survive and succeed in college* (pp. 65–81). San Francisco, CA: Jossey-Bass.

Cuseo, J. (2007). The empirical case against large class size: Adverse effects on the teaching, learning, and retention of first-year students. *The Journal of Faculty Development, 21*(1), 5-21.

National Survey of Student Engagement (NSSE). (2004). *Student engagement: Pathways to collegiate success.* Bloomington, IN: Indiana University Center for Postsecondary Research and Planning.

University of Akron

University College Evolves to Meet Campus Needs

Karla T. Mugler

The Institutional Context

The University of Akron (UA) is a Carnegie classification Doctoral/Research Intensive university, which focuses on the success, retention, and graduation of its undergraduate students. UA is part of the University System of Ohio and receives state support. As of fall 2008, the University served 26,000 students and offered approximately 300 associate's, bachelor's, master's, doctoral, and law degree programs and 100 certificate programs at sites in Summit, Wayne, Medina, and Holmes counties in northeast Ohio. A metropolitan university with a sizeable nontraditional student population (23.3%), UA welcomes more than 4,000 first-year students each fall. Minority students comprise 16.2% of the undergraduates, 50% of whom are first-generation.

University College

UA has the necessary support structure to help students succeed—University College. Founded originally in 1935 as General College, University College has continued to evolve to meet the needs of the institution and the students it serves. At one time University College had responsibility for the instruction of all general education courses, ROTC, Women's Studies, the Honors Program, and the Center for Conflict Resolution. Since 1989, general education courses have resided in their respective colleges, the Honors College was established, and reporting lines for other units have changed. In 1994, the University College dean reported to both the provost and the vice president of student affairs, but since 1996 University College has reported to the provost. Students in University College reflect the diversity of the UA student population: 50% of the students are male; 16.6% are adult learners; and 18.1% are African American, Hispanic, Asian/Pacific Islander, or Native American.

Some of the ongoing initiatives supported by University College that illustrate our commitment to students' success include (a) required new student orientation for traditional-aged, adult, and transfer students; (b) an opening convocation for new students in the fall; (c) a common reading program with a first-year lecture; (d) professional advisors who work with University College students until they transfer to UA's degree-granting colleges; (e) an extensive learning communities program; (f) a number of courses (e.g., Student Success Seminar, Career Planning, Information Tools for Success) to help students transition to the University or to a degree program; (g) the Majors Mosaic program in October, which highlights programs where students can earn majors, minors, and certificates; and (h) student academic support, including peer tutoring and learning assistants.

University College is one of 11 undergraduate colleges at The University of Akron; although not a degree-granting college, professionals within University College work with faculty and administrators across campus to promote student academic success. While opportunities for collaboration with the Division of Student Affairs remain strong, University College administrators are also working on a Learning Commons with the Library, Instructional Technology, and the Institute for Teaching and Learning. University College's leadership in service-learning, the Post Secondary Enrollment Option Program (a dual high school/college credit program), and the

Transfer Student Services Center have demonstrated University College's unique collaborations throughout northeast Ohio, which benefit our students and the greater Akron community.

Campus-Wide Collaborations

University College collaborates with various units across campus and in the community to help students succeed at The University of Akron. University College professionals are active in the greater Akron community creating access opportunities for potential students who might not have considered higher education upon high school graduation. For example, administrators work with faculty, counselors, and administrators in the Akron public school system and Summit Education Initiative on the Destination College program and other programs that encourage students to continue their education. They also participate in campus recruitment events, interview perspective students for competitive scholarships, work with administrators in Enrollment Management and the Office of Undergraduate Admissions, and share information about the various programs offered to ensure success at the college level.

University College provides new student orientation for all incoming undergraduate students, including international, adult, honors, developmental, and minority students. These one-day orientation programs include sessions focusing on the basics of a college experience, placement testing if not already completed, academic advisement, the resident or commuter student experience, technology tools including the course management system, and the University's web enrollment and student information system. In addition, the learning community program includes all of these student groups as well as commuter students. Faculty and administrators from across campus teach learning community courses and work together to provide student/faculty interaction outside of class for their students. As many UA students are the first in their families to attend college, University College collaborates with the UA Adult Focus office, which reports to the provost, and Commuter Central in Student Affairs to secure mentors for these first-generation students, 23% of whom are 25 or older.

University College's Office of Student Academic Success (OSAS) collaborates with faculty in each of the degree-granting colleges. OSAS provides tutoring for all general education and first- and second-year classes at the University. In 2000, the University community was concerned about the number of students who withdrew from, or earned substandard grades in, courses required for entry into specific majors. Too many students were not making satisfactory progress toward their degree objective. Faculty members were asked to recommend students whom they felt might be successful as tutors. In preparation for their assignment, these students completed a series of one-credit hour courses highlighting learning theory and issues they might face as learning assistants (LAs). Initially undertaken as a collaborative effort between University College and Buchtel College of Arts and Sciences, seven peer tutors, who were certified at the most advanced level by the College Reading and Learning Association, were placed as LAs in these key classes.

Learning assistants help students select and manage appropriate learning strategies, think about the learning process, and plan and orchestrate sound practice with regards to mastery of course material. The University's LAs are not, however, used for Supplemental Instruction, grading, or formal teaching. The value of LAs in the classroom includes their ability to

◇ Assess learning styles and present material in a variety of ways, thereby making that material accessible

◇ Strengthen the relationship within the classroom between students and faculty, as well as among students

◇ Provide a comfortable way for students to ask questions that they deem too insignificant to ask the faculty
◇ Offer the faculty insights into which parts of the course content are the most problematic to the students
◇ Suggest possible solutions, directions, and strategies that help students develop greater independence

The LAs are introduced by the faculty member to the students in the target class; they attend the class regularly so that they know exactly how the professor explained concepts to the class; and they provide tutoring for students as well as review sessions before exams. UA students appreciate working with and learning from another student who models successful student behavior. The program has also improved academic performance. The number of students earning *A*s, *B*s, and *C*s increased significantly (i.e., between 19% and 73%) in classes where an LA was assigned.

Faculty have been pleased with the success of their first- and second-year students who work regularly with LAs and have championed the program in major University meetings. Faculty from degree-granting colleges that have not traditionally had LAs are now requesting them for their classes. LAs are now assigned to more than 60 first- and second-year courses in Buchtel College of Arts and Sciences; Summit College (the only college on the main campus offering associate's and bachelor's degrees); and the Colleges of Business, Creative and Professional Arts, Engineering, Health Sciences and Human Services, and Nursing.

Another successful collaboration is University College's work with the public school systems within our service area—a five-county region—to provide the opportunity for their students with strong academic records to take college courses at the University. Akron's Post Secondary Enrollment Option Program (PSEOP), which is the largest among the state-assisted universities within Ohio, is administered by University College. High school students participate in a new student orientation program where they meet with an academic advisor who assists them in selecting courses that will fulfill high school graduation requirements while also being applicable toward a college degree. Students may elect to take their courses via distance learning or by attending classes on campus. In both cases, they participate with Akron undergraduates in the target course. During the past few years, about 33% of the students who have participated in PSEOP have matriculated at The University of Akron, and many were selected for the Honors College and/or have received other scholarships for their studies.

Administrators in University College have worked with professionals in the Division of Student Affairs to support an AmeriCorps-VISTA volunteer who helped staff the Office of Service Learning and Civic Engagement. University College professionals partnered with those in Student Affairs to write successful grant proposals to secure and fund the VISTA as well as the Midwest Campus Compact Citizen-Scholar program. Both programs are supported by Ohio Campus Compact. University College professionals join with community leaders from the University Park Alliance (a 40-block area surrounding the campus) to develop service-learning opportunities for students; more than 120 students in the Pre-Education and Exploratory learning communities work with first through fourth graders to improve their reading skills in two Akron elementary schools located within walking distance of the campus. This collaborative effort also involves the College of Education, which provides a graduate assistant to serve as a site coordinator for this initiative and to critique the journals in which students write reflective statements about their service-learning experiences. University College also provides the funding for the background checks and tuberculosis tests required by the school district. Thanks in part to these first-year students' efforts, the reading scores on the children's standardized tests rose so significantly that one of the elementary schools moved from *on watch* to *satisfactory* status. University College administrators and students also participate with volunteers from local churches and businesses to clean up the neighborhoods in which they work and live on Make a Difference Day as part of the national day of service.

University College also has responsibility for transfer services at the University. The College works with faculty at UA and administrators at community colleges and other institutions to develop articulation agreements as well as course equivalencies to ensure a smooth transition for students transferring to The University of Akron. Since the Ohio Board of Regents' Articulation and Transfer Council developed Transfer Assurance Guides (TAGs) for 42 disciplines, the University College dean has sought faculty from each of the undergraduate degree-granting colleges to serve on statewide panels to review TAG learning objectives as well as course submissions from colleges and universities across the state. The Transfer Student Services Center staff work with admissions officers at college fairs and visits community college campuses to let students know about UA. In addition, faculty members in each of the colleges review course descriptions from other institutions to determine bilateral course equivalencies; faculty have developed course equivalencies for more than 140,000 courses that have been entered into the online system, U.Select. Evaluations of students' course work from previous institutions are sent to the students once they have registered for the Transfer Transitions orientation program. This daylong program provides transfer students with the services they need to begin their course work at the University. UA typically enrolls about 1,470 new transfer students each year who have remarked that the University is transfer friendly due to the array of services provided to help them in their transition.

The University of Akron's University College has more responsibilities today than when it was first established. As University administrations, faculty, and students have changed, the services that University College provides in collaboration with our partners within and outside of the academy have been modified to ensure student academic success.

Results and Lessons Learned

Over the past 15 years, University College leaders have focused on students' success. Programs that have been implemented—including a required new student orientation program for all undergraduates, a common reading program, a first-year lecture, learning communities, learning assistants, and the student success seminar—have been evaluated to determine whether they impacted students' (a) knowledge about what it takes to succeed at the college level, (b) cumulative grade point averages, (c) retention to the second year and beyond, (d) promotion to the degree-granting college, and (e) persistence to graduation.

The University of Akron participated in the Foundations of Excellence self-study in 2005–2006. Responses from the Educational Benchmarking, Incorporated, Foundations of Excellence Student Assessments indicated that first-year students understood UA academic expectations, out-of-class opportunities, academic majors, college costs, and financial aid better than students at peer/benchmark institutions who responded to the same instrument. Collaborative relationships built over time between University College professionals and faculty and administrators in other units have benefited the programs and services that UA provides to students. The strength of this collaboration has withstood the negotiation of a faculty union contract with the administration. Even in the months when tensions were high, no one involved waivered in their concern for students' success.

The development of UA's learning assistant program evolved over the past seven years. Each year the number of students withdrawing or earning failing grades was reviewed and compared to figures of students remaining in the class with an LA, while controlling for the faculty member teaching the course section. Participating faculty members and LAs get together several times each term to share strategies for engaging students in the targeted classes. Topics related to learning styles, diversity of learners, and communication skills are addressed. As the program grows—currently 63 class sections have LAs—faculty representing different disciplines and all undergraduate colleges discuss effective pedagogy. Faculty who have experienced a greater engagement in their classes recommend the program to colleagues so requests for LAs continue to grow.

Students who work with the LA at least five times during the term have seen a significant improvement in the grades earned in the target course. There was an increase in the number of C grades from students who would have ordinarily withdrawn or earned a D or F. The LAs indicated that having a peer in the class to whom students can pose questions helps all of the students—even average to above-average students who seek out the LA can improve their grades.

Regular assessment of programs helps refine or improve them. Students' success data have also helped to determine University funding. University College, along with the other colleges and administrative units, must present priorities for the year at annual budget hearings. Armed with information regarding students' completion of courses, progress toward degree, and attendance in succeeding terms, key administrators understand the value of University College programs and services.

Many provosts and presidents have not previously served at institutions with a University College structure, so upon arrival on campus, they may not realize its value. It is incumbent on the dean or director to illustrate how effective a University College can be in building collaborative relationships that benefit the entire university. An investment in a University College—and the collaborative programs it provides—can pay huge dividends for the institution, faculty, students, and the greater community.

University of Texas at El Paso

Partnering for Student Success: The College Readiness Initiative

Dorothy Ward & Joyce Ritchey

The Institutional Context

The University of Texas at El Paso

The University of Texas at El Paso (UTEP) is a doctoral, research-intensive, four-year public institution located on the U.S.-Mexico border. A commuter campus, UTEP's fall 2006 enrollment was 19,842 students, including 11,237 full-time undergraduates and 2,544 first-time, first-year students. Undergraduates were 76.1% Hispanic. International students included 8.3% from Mexico and 1.3% from a country other than Mexico. Additional undergraduate populations included 9.1% White, 2.8% African American, 1.1% Asian American, and 0.2% Native American. Females were 55.1% of the undergraduate population. The average age was 23 with 27.6% being older than 25. More than half (54%) were first-generation college students (neither parent has a college degree).

El Paso Community College

El Paso Community College (EPCC) is a two-year, multicampus institution. A commuter campus, EPCC's fall 2006 enrollment was 25,306, including 18,424 full-time and 4,037 first-year students. At 85.5% of the student body, Hispanics were the largest population. International students were 2.9%. Additional populations included 8.4% White, 2.15% African American, 0.8% Asian/Pacific Islander, and 0.3% Native American. Females were 60.5% of the student population. The average age was 25 with 32% being older than 25. First-generation students were 48.5% of the student body.

University College

UTEP's Entering Student Program (ESP), established in 1999, was a partnership between academic and student affairs, linking key programs that served first-year students. As its mission statement indicated, ESP was designed to promote "the academic, social, and personal success of all entering students at UTEP" and was led by a director who was also the associate vice president for academic affairs. Using a matrix-management approach, a model in which employees maintain their vertical reporting lines while also reporting across unit lines to a project manager, ESP departments operated across academic and student affairs functional reporting and budget lines to provide innovative programs to support the success of entering students.

The University College was created in 2001 as a result of the Entering Student Program's success and the recognition that a matrix management model relies on the willingness of key people to collaborate. Thus, a change in personnel might have negatively impacted the spirit of cooperation. The University College created a single reporting line that allowed for program sustainability. College status also elevated the visibility and prestige of the programs, facilitating collaborations on and off campus and improving opportunities for grants.

UTEP's University College grew to include the Academic Advising Center, Admissions and Recruitment, Developmental Education, Enrollment Services Center, Entering Student Program (i.e., first-year seminar and learning communities), Financial Aid, New Student Orientation, Registrar, Student Assessment and Testing, and Student Success Programs (i.e., Honors, Junior Scholars, Student Leadership Institute). It also offered a Bachelor of Multidisciplinary Studies. Though its focus remained on assisting entering students, University College served essentially the entire UTEP student population.

College Readiness Initiative

The College Readiness Initiative (CRI) was established in 2005 to increase students' college readiness and decrease the large number of entering students at EPCC and UTEP who require one or more developmental courses. Both institutions draw the majority of their students from El Paso County: in fall 2006, 93.8% at EPCC and 82.1% at UTEP. Knowing that students who place directly into college-level courses persist and graduate at a higher percentage than students who have precollege course requirements, the CRI engages UTEP, EPCC, and the 12 Region 19 Independent School Districts (ISDs) in a collaborative effort to increase high school students' college readiness prior to their enrolling in courses at institutions of higher education, and once, they are admitted to EPCC or UTEP, to accelerate their enrollment into college-level courses. The CRI's ultimate desired outcomes are to increase the number of college-going students, placement into college-level courses, and the number of college graduates as well as to decrease students' time to college graduation.

In fall 2005, this partnership was formalized as The College Readiness Consortium, cochaired by EPCC's vice president of instruction and UTEP's provost. In addition to the EPCC and UTEP members, the Consortium's membership includes representatives from the 12 Region 19 superintendents' offices, the Region 19 Central Office, and the El Paso Collaborative for Academic Excellence. The Consortium's written charge is, in part, to "design strategies that will ensure that college bound high school graduates' initial enrollment is in entry-level college courses." A major strategy of the Consortium is to administer the ACCUPLACER, the exam used for math, reading, and writing placement at EPCC and UTEP, to students while they are still in high school and to provide interventions followed by a retest for those students who place at the developmental level.

The CRI is truly a collaborative effort. In 2005–2006, the cost of the ACCUPLACER exams was shared equally by UTEP, EPCC, ISDs, and the El Paso Collaborative for Academic Excellence. In 2006–2007, the ISDs paid for the ACCUPLACER exams, many using allotted state funds. UTEP and EPCC Student Testing Offices adopted ISDs to help them with the testing and to train their personnel in preparation for the ISDs becoming their own ACCUPLACER test sites. In addition, in fall 2005, the College Readiness Implementation Committee was established. The CRI Committee is made up of representatives from UTEP, EPCC, and Region 19 ISDs and is cochaired by EPCC's dean of Arts, Communications, and Social Sciences and UTEP's associate dean of University College and director of the Entering Student Program. This Committee developed an ACCUPLACER orientation PowerPoint presentation and script for use by the high schools. The Committee also created an ACCUPLACER Score Interpretation PowerPoint presentation and handouts. In addition, the Committee identified a procedure to share the joint applications for admission to UTEP and EPCC that students complete prior to taking their initial

ACCUPLACER exam and developed the procedure for high schools to upload ACCUPLACER scores to UTEP and EPCC databases. In the high schools, CRI components include

- ◇ An ACCUPLACER orientation at least two weeks prior to the administration of the exam to explain its purpose and design and to provide a list of resources for pretest review
- ◇ Completion of a joint admissions application to EPCC and UTEP
- ◇ ACCUPLACER testing during students' junior or senior year
- ◇ Interventions for students whose ACCUPLACER scores indicate developmental placement
- ◇ ACCUPLACER retesting of students after interventions

Even with the short turn around between the planning and the implementation phase, in 2005–2006, six ISDs tested 3,550 students with an initial ACCUPLACER exam. One ISD and one high school in another ISD also made interventions and retests available to their students, and 75 students participated in the retests.

In 2006–2007, the number of ISDs participating in high school ACCUPLACER testing increased to nine, and 7,262 students took the initial ACCUPLACER exam. In addition, eight of the districts extended ACCUPLACER testing to include juniors. This move toward testing juniors will allow ISDs to provide interventions during the students' senior year before retesting. Nine ISDs provided interventions, and all nine made retests available though not all made the retests a requirement. In the nine ISDs, 1,584 students retested.

For the students who retested, the interventions provided varied between and within ISDs. Interventions include integration of content and strategies into English, math, and reading curriculum; after school, Saturday, intersession workshops and tutoring; and use of commercial products, such as the *Princeton Review*.

At EPCC, the CRI components include a Developmental Summer Bridge Program designed to help entering students earn three hours of college-level credit, improve ACCUPLACER scores, and ease transition to the college environment. The Summer Bridge Program is a five-week program consisting of a first-year seminar and a daily two-hour workshop in math, reading, and writing. Table 2.1 suggests the value of this program for improving test scores. In addition to the Summer Bridge Programs, EPCC offers several developmental courses in a mini-mester (eight weeks) format to accelerate students' time through developmental into college-level courses.

At UTEP, the CRI components include Enhanced New Student Orientation (ENSO) math workshops that are embedded in the five-day orientations for first-year students who place into a developmental math class. Upon completion of the three-day, six-hour workshop, students retake the math portion of the ACCUPLACER. In 2006, of the 1,603 developmental math students who retested, 777 (48%) retested one or more math courses higher, and 514 (31%) tested from developmental to college-level math.

A second component of CRI at UTEP is course redesign, which includes changes in instructional format, academic support, and options to help accelerate students' progress through developmental courses, enrolling them as quickly as possible into college-level classes. Rather than requiring a sequence of traditional semester-length courses that serve as prerequisites and extend the time a student is in developmental coursework, UTEP shifted to placing students into target core classes and providing them with as much concurrent and supplemental support as they need to accelerate their progress.

In 2006, UTEP offered new course formats for math. One option is a hybrid version of the developmental course MATH 0311 Intermediate Algebra that uses an Internet-based algebra tutorial and assessment application (i.e., Math-Zone). A second new format consists of compressed courses, which provide two math classes offered in consecutive eight-week minimesters.

Table 2.1

Impact of Summer Bridge Participation at El Paso Community College

	2006 (*n* = 62)	2007 (*n* = 83)
Writing		
Number of students retested	10	---
Number (percentage) of students retested college-level	7 (70%)	---
Reading		
Number of students retested	43	61
Number (percentage) of students retested one or more courses higher	21 (49%)	39 (64%)
Number (percentage) of students retested college-level	14 (33%)	30 (49%)
Math		
Number of students retested in math	52	73
Number (percentage) of students retested one or more courses higher	24 (46%)	34 (47%)

Recognizing that different majors have different math needs, UTEP also developed a new college-level math course in 2006. MATH 1319, Mathematics in the Modern World, is a college-level core curriculum course for students in majors that do not require statistics or other math classes. Students in these majors (e.g., education and most liberal arts majors), who formerly would have placed in MATH 0311 (developmental), now enroll in MATH 1319 (college-level) to satisfy their math requirement. In fall 2006, of the 72 students who placed into the developmental class but who qualified for the college-level course, 51 (72%) successfully completed (i.e., *A, B,* or *C*) MATH 1319, passing at a higher percentage rate (70%) than the 201 students who placed directly into this class.

Also effective fall 2006, students who are business or analytical social sciences majors who score in the upper third of MATH 0311 placement are admitted to the college-level MATH 1320, Mathematics for Social Sciences, with a supplemental MATH 0120 lab support. Of the 171 students who placed into MATH 0311 but who qualified for the college-level class and lab, 103 (60%) successfully completed MATH 1320, which is comparable to the success rate (63%) of those students who placed directly into this course.

The MATH 1320 with lab support is built on a previously developed model. Beginning in 2001, students whose scores were in the upper portion of the developmental course ENGL 0311 placement were admitted to the college-level ENGL 1311, Basic English Composition, with a supplemental workshop: ENGL 0111, Expository Composition Workshop. From 2001–2005, of approximately 271 students per fall semester who placed into developmental English but who qualified for the college-level course and workshop, an average of 80% successfully completed ENGL 1311. As a result of this success, in 2006, the placement score for ENGL 1311 was changed to mirror the state identified college-level score, and the placement into this class and workshop was adjusted accordingly. This change in placement meant that an even greater number of students tested out of the developmental course. In fall 2006, of the 128 students enrolled in the combination college-level classes, 82 (64%) passed.

At UTEP, oversight for the CRI logically resides in University College, which houses key programs and departments for entering students. Moreover, the goals of CRI correspond to the goals of University College that include preparing students for college-level work and supporting their "achievement through innovative educational programs" and engaging University College in "collaboration with our partners in education."

Lessons Learned

The El Paso CRI partnership is a unique collaboration between two institutions of higher education along with 12 ISDs working cooperatively toward the same goal. This is due, in part, to the vision and work of EPCC's vice president of instruction and UTEP's vice provost who initially gave presentations to ISD academic leadership teams showing them how their high school graduates performed on the ACCUPLACER. It is also due to ISD superintendents who responded to the information with a desire to immediately develop a collaborative effort that would help improve their graduates' college readiness. Instead of placing blame or pointing fingers, the emphasis was placed on what could be done together to help "our" students. A team of EPCC and UTEP administrators made follow-up visits to all 12 area superintendents to solidify the commitment to CRI. Numerous successes have resulted from the ISD, EPCC, and UTEP collaboration.

◇ There was a 100% increase in the number of ISDs participating from 2005–2006 to 2006–2007, and a 50% increase in the number of districts testing. This resulted in a 105% increase in the number of students who took the initial ACCUPLACER test in the high schools. Of those students who retested in 2006–2007, 30% improved in math, 22% in reading, and 49% in writing.

◇ By 2006–2007, more than 75% of the 12 ISDs had become their own test site. The remaining ISDs have indicated a clear desire to become one. The creation of high school test sites provides schools with the opportunity to test and retest at their own convenience and schedule.

◇ Interventions in the ISDs, EPCC, and UTEP are helping students achieve college readiness before or during their first semester of college.

Conclusion

The CRI is a large, collaborative effort. The breadth of the project requires effective communication among all participating parties. In the large ISDs, communication from the administrative offices to the personnel in each high school who will orchestrate the CRI on their campus can become complicated. In addition, data exchange between the ISDs and EPCC and UTEP is often delayed, pre-empted by state reporting requirements faced by the ISDs. In the small ISDs, the complications arise less from communication than from having limited staff with multiple job responsibilities placing demands on their professional time.

Ongoing meetings and training sessions that bring together a variety of work groups representing the ISDs, EPCC, and UTEP are necessary to ensure effective communication and appropriate procedures and to address any areas of concern.

In a relatively short period of time, the College Readiness Initiative has made a difference in the academic lives of students in the El Paso region. This collaborative effort is one that can be replicated in other regions of the United States. It simply requires institutions in a region to assume a shared sense of responsibility for their students' academic success.

CHAPTER 3

Dynamic Engagement With the Undergraduate Curriculum

Barbara Jackson

National research literature, as well as the experience of practitioners, underscores the importance of connecting first-year student support initiatives to the undergraduate curriculum and its faculty (Erickson & Strommer, 2005; Koch, 2001). Ensuring effectiveness and excellence in the undergraduate curriculum can be achieved only when student motivations and perspectives on their learning are synchronized with the values, resources, and politics of universities. The university college model thus advocates curricula and pedagogies that honor the worldview of contemporary students while exciting and enabling them to become active, lifelong learners. Of crucial importance is attention to faculty development, which provides support and reward for doing this work. Equally critical are changes in the university culture leading to greater value being placed on work with entering students and to an adequate investment of resources to support that work.

The primary focus of this chapter is an examination of how university colleges establish a solid connection to the undergraduate curriculum for entering students. The overarching strategy is for the university college to coordinate and support student engagement with important touchstones (i.e., guides, benchmarks, barometers, or indicators of a student's ability to navigate the academic environment) of that curriculum. First-year seminars, learning communities, general education, and developmental education are all vital structures for helping students access touchstones of academic success.

Engaging faculty and securing their support is essential for the success and institutionalization of the aforementioned programs. While there are many strategies, including various types of faculty appointments to the university college unit, a widespread practice is to create programs for faculty development and communities of practice among those engaged in first-year initiatives. Survey and case study data will be presented below to demonstrate ways in which strong faculty connections to first-year initiatives have been developed and sustained, resulting in a positive impact on their institutions.

Before proceeding with an examination of how university colleges offer support or articulate with these programs, however, we should address the question of why such efforts should be strongly connected to the university college. It is not unusual for successful learning communities, first-year seminars, developmental education, and most certainly general education to be situated elsewhere within the institution. Speaking from the collective experience of the monograph authors and other university college colleagues, there are multiple reasons for university college involvement with these structures supporting academic success. Some of these reasons relate to efficient use of resources and minimizing duplication of effort as when the university college provides the umbrella for coordinating learning communities and first-year seminar scheduling, enrollment and staffing or a one-stop information and service shop for entering students. In addition to such practical considerations are the less obvious, but ultimately more significant, advantages of a single first-year structure. These include the synergy and quality enhancement created by colocation of programs, the opportunity for students to achieve a more holistic and less fragmented understanding of their curriculum's components, and the chance for faculty to understand and engage with students.

We are not affirming that all such programs must reside completely within the university college structure. Among the more recently formed university colleges (e.g., Appalachian State University and Kennesaw State University), there is an attempt to have more comprehensive and finite structural and budgetary assignments. However, in many institutions, particularly those with longer histories of a university college structure (e.g., Pennsylvania State University), a collaborative and coordinating role for university colleges of the structures that facilitate access to the touchstones of academic success remains an effective model.

Structures Providing Access to Touchstones of Academic Success in the Undergraduate Curriculum

Several types of initiatives have been used by many university colleges to structure the undergraduate curriculum in such a way as to facilitate student access to the touchstones of academic success. By design, these initiatives—first-year seminars, learning communities, developmental education, and general education—also create new and solid bridges to faculty. Each is described in greater detail below.

First-Year Seminars

An extensive body of research consistently documents how and why first-year seminars have been embraced by colleges and universities as a key strategy to enhance student persistence, satisfaction, and academic success. Comprehensive overviews and guides to the literature, including the rationale, assessment, and characteristics of successful first-year seminars, are presented by both Hunter and Linder (2005) and Tobolowsky (2008). While offered in a variety of formats, universal goals of the seminars are to help the student establish a positive personal connection to the institution and to articulate clearly the institution's values, expectations, and resources (Barefoot & Fidler, 1996). Nationally, first-year seminars tend to be graded courses that are offered for credit and have solid academic focus directly supporting the general education curriculum (Tobolowsky).

Data from our survey demonstrate that involvement with an institution's first-year seminar is one of the most frequent ways university colleges connect to the undergraduate curriculum. While 74% have primary responsibility for the first-year seminar, an additional 17% share responsibility with other units on campus for offering such courses.

Kennesaw State University's (KSU) first-year seminar KSU1101 provides an outstanding model of how such a course provides a solid link between the university college and the first-year curriculum. The seminar's curriculum is centered on 11 learning outcomes, several of which focus explicitly on academic success, including enhanced study, cognitive, and critical thinking skills and increased connectivity to faculty and peers. Many seminar sections are linked to other courses (i.e., a learning community structure), providing students with the opportunity for meaningful application of content from the first-year seminar to general education courses and introductory courses in the major.

One of Pennsylvania State's iterations of the first-year seminar is Library Logistics, an innovative course introducing students to doing scholarship using state-of-the-art information technology. This seminar was developed primarily for entering exploratory students who are members of Discovery House, sponsored by PSU's university college equivalent, the Division of Undergraduate Studies. By engaging in hands-on learning experiences, the students develop skills and insights that support their academic success across the curriculum.

Learning Communities

The practice of enrolling a common cohort of students in two or more courses, often linked around an interdisciplinary theme, has widely come to be termed a learning community (MacGregor, Smith, Matthews, & Gabelnick, 2002). Learning communities are recognized as a powerful pedagogy and are increasingly used by universities to connect first-year students to the general education curriculum and encourage active and critical learning (Lardner & Malnarich, 2008). The significant contribution of learning communities to learning and academic success for first-year students has been proven by assessment data from numerous and diverse institutions (Hansen & Williams, 2005; Stassen, 2003; Zhao & Kuh, 2004). Data cited in the KSU case study in this volume related to retention and grade point average are representative of national findings.

Learning communities embody the major components of a holistic approach to student learning in microcosm: They build student-to-student social connections around an academic activity; create opportunities for faculty to know students as whole persons; encourage students to make connections between general education course work and their individual, academic, and professional goals; and provide a model for multi- (often inter-) disciplinary learning. Institutions responding to our survey affirm this with 72% of respondents having significant responsibility (i.e., primary or shared) for offering learning communities on their campus.

Most of the pioneering efforts with learning communities were developed on residential campuses with small class sizes and the possibility of faculty working in an organic fashion to develop unique sets of courses with curricula integrated around a theme of common interest to participating faculty. Such a model is the Cadillac of learning communities, but it may not be possible on all campuses. In these cases, institutions may opt for models that allow them to offer some benefits of learning community participation to most entering students rather than limiting a potentially wider range of benefits to just a few students. At institutions like the University of Akron and other large publics, both faculty development resources (e.g., significant release time to develop new thematic, integrated learning communities), as well as scheduling (e.g., large class sizes, space) and budgetary constraints, have resulted in the development of other models, such as small learning community cohorts within larger classes and paired or clustered courses. This has allowed the extension of learning community benefits to the large number of entering students such institutions serve. The case studies from The University of Akron and Penn State similarly illustrate the incredible flexibility and adaptability of learning communities to meet the needs of different students and to their responsiveness to campus resources and environments. For example, Penn State's Division of Undergraduate Studies has used learning communities to address the special needs of exploratory students on that campus, focusing on their exploration and choice of academic majors.

The establishment of a successful first-year learning community program depends on an intentional program of faculty and staff development (Shapiro & Levine, 1999), particularly one that promotes collaborations (Gammill & Hansen, 1992; Scharff & Brown, 2004). The Kennesaw State and University of Akron case studies highlight some of the strategies required to engage faculty in learning community initiatives. In their description of learning communities at KSU,

Hoerrner and Goldfine affirm that faculty need "direction, encouragement, and time" and that faculty development activities for learning community participation must be responsive to varied and changing faculty needs. Williams, describing The University of Akron, summarizes the key components as preparation of faculty for a new experience, participation by full-time senior faculty, provision of appropriate administrative leadership, and collaboration with other academic units and student affairs.

Developmental Education

Developmental education is currently defined as a field of practice and research within higher education that seeks to promote cognitive and affective growth by developing the skills and attitudes necessary for the attainment of students' academic, career, and life goals (National Association for Developmental Education, 2009a, 2009b). Higbee (2005) articulates the rationale for significant recent changes from remedial education, offered to only those students who are at obvious and extreme risk, to a model promoted by Astin (1985) and others, which focuses on making support, especially in the first year, available to all postsecondary learners. Further, Higbee identifies many emerging models of assessment, placement, and instruction, including Supplemental Instruction and developmental learning communities.

For many of the units represented in our sample, the need to provide academic support to underprepared entering students has historically been a defining part of their mission for the first college year. A third of the units in our sample have primary responsibility for developmental math (33%), reading (31%), or writing (31%). An additional 15% (i.e., math 16%, reading 14%, and writing 16%) share responsibility for these courses and programs.

Even as some of the traditional models of remedial education, especially in reading, are being abandoned by four-year institutions, the need to provide support for collegiate-level academic readiness has produced some innovative and effective programs developed in collaboration with academic departments. Institutions that fully embrace the university college model have taken national leadership in revitalizing developmental education as exemplified by Miller's case study of IUPUI's critical inquiry. Based on a model developed by Bell and the Brooklyn College SEEK Program, University College U112 (Critical Inquiry) is a one- to two-credit-hour course linked to IUPUI general education courses, particularly those that have been problematic to both students and faculty. The course uses a variety of strategies tailored to disciplines and individual instructors focused on developing college-level, text-based skills of analysis.

Some recommendations for best practice in developmental education courses, which fit with the comprehensive model of academic support advocated here, include the following:

- ◇ *Courses should not be identified as remedial.* This label sends defeatist, negative messages to students, such as "we need to fix you in order for you to become a real college student."
- ◇ *Courses should be offered by or in close collaboration with academic departments.* Faculty in core curriculum classes are best able to identify deficits in specific academic skills and provide substantive materials for addressing them. Additionally, students are more highly motivated to engage in development work when it is applied to "real" coursework.
- ◇ *Course content must be clearly meaningful academic work.* Students should be able to see some of the immediate benefits, in terms of increased engagement and learning in their coursework.
- ◇ *Courses should develop transferable academic skills.* Effective curriculum is organized to provide students the opportunity to acquire strategies of active learning, critical reading, and analysis that transcend the requirements of a particular course.

◇ *Courses need to harness the power of the learning community model.* The infusion of collaborative, active, and interdisciplinary learning both extends the platform of pedagogies available to instructors and enhances student motivation to engage with developmental coursework.

General Education

That university colleges have a role in general education seems obvious. These courses are the foundation of all undergraduate degree programs and the building blocks for the major. Furthermore, they are courses in which entering students are primarily enrolled. So, connecting general education curricula to the structures that support first-year students is a goal that many institutions have intentionally embraced. However, establishing and implementing these connections is complicated. General education curricula almost always extend beyond the needs of entering students who have been the primary focus of these units. Moreover, offering general education courses frequently has political and economic dimensions beyond student learning. In most institutions, academic departments jealously guard their traditional prerogatives for offering general education courses and the credit hours they generate. For example, Douglas Koritz (personal communication, July 8, 2008), assistant dean for Intellectual Foundations at Buffalo State University, asserts that, in the beginning, faculty reaction was that the university college was "taking away resources" and that there continues to be some faculty opposition to the first-year seminar. In that context, we are not surprised by survey results showing that only 7% of the sampled units claim to have primary responsibility for general education. However, more than one third of the units (36%) report shared responsibility for general education on their campus. As the following discussion illustrates, the how of university college involvement with general education reflects a great range of diversity related to unique institutional features.

A significant trend among newly created or reorganized university colleges is to structure very direct involvement with general education course requirements, including offering courses, hiring faculty, and faculty development. This seems to be most often achieved when institutions are re-imagining and restructuring their general education curriculum and university college unit simultaneously. Buffalo State University and Appalachian State University are instructive examples of how institutions are coming to embrace the model of connecting faculty work and student learning needs around general education.

Administrative appointments and assignments structured to work collaboratively with faculty governance represents a powerful strategy for connecting a university college with campus general education. At Buffalo State, Intellectual Foundations is overseen by an all-campus faculty Senate committee. Their University College's assistant dean for Intellectual Foundations—a new position—serves as the ex officio chair of the body that reviews and approves proposals for new courses based on their ability to meet particular learning outcomes. It also monitors quality and pedagogy of Intellectual Foundations courses. At Appalachian State, University College promotes shared responsibility among units that provide and support the general education initiative. It houses three programs offering interdisciplinary general education and works collaboratively with the campus-wide General Education Council charged with oversight of course approvals, assessment, and review of academic policies related to general education. The collaboration between faculty governance, academic units, and University College is strengthened by the vice provost for undergraduate education also serving as the dean of University College.

Kennesaw State is a good illustration of a university college in a campus environment where general education offerings reflect more traditional school or department silos, but whose university college has managed to become significantly involved in the general education curriculum in a variety of ways. However, for many institutions, history, politics, budgets, and limited resources constrain such a direct involvement with curriculum and pedagogy in general education and mandate a less direct, but nonetheless significant impact. The Division of Undergraduate Studies at Penn State, primarily an academic advising unit, has taken on the responsibility of establishing a meaningful connection to the general education curriculum for exploratory students by linking these basic academic courses to their individual academic exploration, experience, enthusiasm, and excitement about learning in general. Similarly, Illinois State's university college has a less direct connection to faculty and general education course offerings but is a key player in collaborating with academic departments to ensure that sufficient seats in appropriate courses are available to entering students.

In recent years, an emerging trend has been the increasing number of university colleges, especially those with fully configured structures, that play an active leadership role in the process of change and innovation. The cases from Appalachian State University (this chapter) and Buffalo State University (chapter 2) demonstrate how the university college serves as a locus for enhancing and reforming general education. In both cases, the role of the university college is not simply to offer courses; rather, it is to support interdisciplinary perspectives and ensure consistency of institution-wide outcomes.

Faculty Engagement and Development

Engagement and identification of the undergraduate faculty with the university college's mission is the most critical element of successful implementation of this model. It is, however, one of the most difficult to achieve. Faculty appointments are traditionally made to departments representing specific academic disciplines, and it is these departments (not the university college) that determine professional advancement and rewards. At four-year institutions, faculty engagement with undergraduates tends to be focused on recruiting and training majors. General education courses are too frequently treated as service courses with little attention paid to the learning needs of the entering students who populate them and even less attention paid to the opportunities they present for developing the collegiate-level learning strategies faculty desire in their advanced undergraduates.

All of our case study institutions recognize the importance of putting faculty at the center of their efforts to connect new students with the undergraduate curriculum. At Appalachian State, the reconfigured University College represents a deliberate strategy on the part of the provost "to increase faculty involvement in all aspects of students' education," and the innovative new general education program "succeeded only because faculty were involved at every step of the way." The Critical Inquiry Program at IUPUI succeeded where a traditional program of developmental reading did not because it was designed and has evolved through a collaborative effort of critical inquiry and general education faculty. At Pennsylvania State, it was only through involvement of faculty librarians that the learning community could deliver on the goal of providing "a culture of classroom instruction" for first-year students.

Yet, involving faculty in interdisciplinary collaboration is not without challenges. At Appalachian State, some faculty "retreat[ed] to hyper-disciplinarity and a simplistic approach to the principle that faculty (i.e., tenure-track faculty untainted by administrative duties) should control all curriculum decisions" in the face of organizational changes.

In our model, the definition of *faculty development* then is to engage faculty with the university college's mission of enhancing academic success for entering students. This is a slow, often frustrating, and certainly incremental process, but one that is crucial to the viability of the initiatives discussed above. Identification, by appointment or teaching assignment, with entering, exploratory students is too generally regarded as a form of second-class faculty citizenship. Most of the institutions that have embraced the university college model have taken steps to encourage faculty recognition. Three significant strategies that our surveyed institutions have used or recommended for enhancing faculty engagement and identification with entering student success are discussed below.

Faculty Appointments

The most potent way to ensure and institutionalize faculty support for first-year initiatives is through faculty appointments to the university college. Nothing affirms status as an authentic academic unit more solidly than the appointment of tenure-track faculty to the unit. Such faculty appointments convey campus credibility for first-year seminars, learning communities, general education reform, and other first-year academic initiatives. This was recognized by former Kennesaw State University President Betty Siegel. In founding that institution's University College, she designated a significant number of faculty lines to the new unit. According to University College dean Ralph Rascati (personal communication, May 7, 2008), KSU's University College employed 29 faculty in 2007, most of whom teach courses in their disciplines as part of their workload. Recently, they have moved to hire faculty with joint appointments in University College and a disciplinary department, with a formalized distribution of teaching responsibilities between both units.

At this point in time, however, primary appointment of tenured or tenure-track faculty to university colleges is rare. Even the appointment of full-time instructors is far from normative. Of the 58 institutions responding to our survey, only 10 reported the assignment of tenure-track faculty to the university college. These institutions reported a range of faculty appointments from 0 to 30, with an average number of four tenure-track faculty members per university college. Yet as Hammett-McGarry and Haney note in their description of Appalachian State's university college, the appointment of tenure-track faculty is a complex issue, which must balance the need for a stable University College faculty against the dangers of "second-class status for such faculty."

Some institutions have engaged senior faculty on their campuses through honorary, adjunct, or joint appointments to the university college unit. When IUPUI founded its University College, having a senior faculty who would take ownership of developing first-year programs and academic policy was deemed crucial. With no budgetary resources available for tenure or tenure-track lines, a model analogous to graduate school appointment was adopted. Forty senior faculty, noted for commitment and accomplishment in undergraduate student teaching and learning, are appointed for three-year (renewable) terms. These faculty, representing all academic units on campus, but especially those heavily involved in general education, act as leaders and advocates for the unit and its programs (Evenbeck & Jackson, 2005).

Formal Faculty Development Initiatives

While only 16 of the institutions in the sample reported either primary or shared campus responsibility for faculty development, many of the case study institutions describe significant efforts of their university college to provide continuing education for faculty engaged in programs for entering students. Institutions with successful learning communities programs generally have regular annual events, such as KSU's Maymester, IUPUI's Learning Communities Symposium, and Akron's Learning Communities Institute (see case studies for further description). Systematic support for faculty engaged in innovative developmental education and general education, such as IUPUI's Critical Inquiry Retreat and Buffalo State's Summer Institute for Intellectual Foundations, is also a crucial component.

Evenbeck and Jackson (2005) offer a number of suggestions for the content and structure of faculty development initiatives, such as

◇ Including content and discussion on the characteristics of contemporary incoming students by using local data as well as national research (e.g., on attitudes and motivations of millennial students)
◇ Providing access to national literature on the scholarship of teaching and learning
◇ Using presentations by both national and local experts to provide cross-institutional context and validate campus initiatives
◇ Tailoring learning opportunities to diverse needs (e.g., novices/veterans, science/humanities, hi-tech/low-tech)
◇ Including others (e.g., peer mentors, academic advisors, student life personnel) who are involved in instructional efforts
◇ Ensuring that faculty have a central role in planning and assessing events
◇ Providing ample time for small-group collaborations and informal discussion
◇ Creating mechanisms (i.e., live and/or electronic) for continuing the conversation throughout the academic year

Institutional Rewards

Limited availability of institutional rewards and resources constitute a major barrier to full implementation of university college models. This is especially true with regard to faculty involvement. While subsequent chapters will address the need for comprehensive campus commitment of resources, here we will identify issues related to traditional university faculty reward structures.

Resources for developing learning communities and first-year seminars or for revitalizing general and developmental education are almost never available to fully compensate for faculty time and effort. It is a real testimony to a growing undercurrent of faculty concern for student learning that so many of the programs of formal faculty development described above operate on truly minimal allocations. Support for faculty participation is generally modest and of more symbolic than actual value. For example, Buffalo State provides a mere $200 stipend for Summer Institute participation (D. Koritz, personal communication, July 8, 2008).

Other incentives that university colleges have been able to use to engage faculty include modest amounts of speaker funding for collaborating faculty, support for cocurricular events, faculty fellowships for conducting and disseminating scholarship of teaching, and small grants for course development. Compensation for teaching first-year seminars, themed learning communities, and special sections of general education courses are most often only available to resident faculty as overload at part-timer rates, rather than full course buyout. Despite these severe resource limitations, significant numbers of faculty at many institutions appear to accept the benefits as being those they see in student learning and improved pedagogy. Full faculty buy-in, however, will only come when institutions place significant value on working with entering students in the reward structure (i.e., tenure, promotion, and raises).

Summary and Conclusion

As both the survey data and the institutional case studies demonstrate, there is no single structural or strategic path to achieving a dynamic engagement with the faculty and curriculum. The specific programs developed for entering students, the way that they are connected to general education and the way faculty are engaged, are very different and reflect unique institutional history, resources, and students. Some have had the opportunity to embrace rapid structural and curricular changes. Others are in the slow but deliberate process of "teaching old dogs new tricks." Some use learning communities as the centerpiece for curriculum integration and faculty engagement. Others lean heavily on interdisciplinary studies and honors. Some have tenure-track faculty appointments, others part-time and term faculty appointments. What all these institutions have in common is a firm and sustainable connection to the undergraduate curriculum and its faculty.

References

Astin, A. W. (1985). *Achieving educational excellence*. San Francisco, CA: Jossey-Bass.

Barefoot, B. O., & Fidler, P. P. (1996). *The 1994 National Survey of Freshman Seminar Programs: Continuing innovations in the collegiate curriculum* (Monograph No. 20). Columbia, SC: University of South Carolina, National Resource Center for The Freshman Year Experience and Students in Transition.

Erickson, B. L., & Strommer, D. W. (2005). Inside the first-year classroom: Challenges and constraints. In M. L. Upcraft, J. N. Gardner, & B. O. Barefoot (Eds.), *Challenging and supporting the first-year student: A handbook for improving the first year of college* (pp. 241–256). San Francisco, CA: Jossey-Bass.

Evenbeck, S. E., & Jackson, B. (2005). Faculty development and the first year. In M. L. Upcraft, J. N. Gardner, & B. O. Barefoot (Eds.), *Challenging and supporting the first-year student: A handbook for improving the first year of college* (pp. 257–274). San Francisco, CA: Jossey-Bass.

Gammill, L., & Hansen, C. (1992). Linked courses: A method to reinforce basic skills. *Journal of Education for Business, 67*(6), 358–360.

Hansen, M. J., & Williams, G. A. (2005). Assessing learning communities at Indiana University–Purdue University in Indianapolis: Comprehensive approaches, leveraging results, lessons learned, and remaining challenges. *Metropolitan Universities Journal, 16,* 69–90.

Higbee, J. L. (2005). Developmental education. In M. L. Upcraft, J. N. Gardner, & B. O. Barefoot (Eds.), *Challenging and supporting the first-year student: A handbook for improving the first year of college* (pp. 292–307). San Francisco, CA: Jossey-Bass.

Hunter, M. S., & Linder, C. W. (2005). First-year seminars. In M. L. Upcraft, J. N. Gardner, & B. O. Barefoot (Eds.), *Challenging and supporting the first-year student: A handbook for improving the first year of college* (pp. 275–291). San Francisco, CA: Jossey-Bass.

Koch, A. K. (2001). *The first-year experience in American higher education: An annotated bibliography* (Monograph No. 3, 3rd ed.). Columbia, SC: University of South Carolina, National Resource Center for The First-Year Experience and Students in Transition.

Lardner, E., & Malnarich, G. (2008, July-August). A new era in learning community work: Why the pedagogy of intentional integration matters. *Change, 40*(4), 30–37.

MacGregor, J., Smith, B. L., Matthews, R., & Gabelnick, F. (2002). *Learning community models.* Retrieved May 19, 2009, from http://www.evergreen.edu/washcenter/lcfaq.htm

National Association for Developmental Education. (2009a). *Definition of developmental education.* Retrieved December 1, 2009, from http://www.nade.net/aboutDevEd/definition.html

National Association for Developmental Education. (2009b). *Goals of developmental education.* Retrieved December 1, 2009, from http://www.nade.net/aboutDevEd/goals.html

Scharff, C., & Brown, H. (2004). Thinking through computing: The power of learning communities. *Computer Science Education, 14*(4), 297–320.

Shapiro, N. S, & Levine, J. H. (1999). Creating learning communities: A practical guide to winning support, organizing for change, and implementing programs. San Francisco, CA: Jossey-Bass.

Stassen, M. L. A. (2003). Student outcomes: The impact of varying living-learning community models. *Research in Higher Education, 44,* 581–613.

Tobolowsky, B. F. (2008). *2006 national survey of first-year seminars: Continuing innovations in the collegiate curriculum* (Monograph No. 51). Columbia, SC: University of South Carolina, National Resource Center for The First-Year Experience and Students in Transition.

Zhao, C., & Kuh, G. D. (2004). Adding value: Learning communities and student engagement. *Research in Higher Education, 45,* 115–138.

Chapter 3 Case Studies

Appalachian State University

Integrating the First-Year Educational Experience Through the University College

Carter Hammett-McGarry & Dave Haney

The Institutional Context

Appalachian State University, located in Boone, North Carolina, is a coeducational, residential, master's comprehensive public university within the University of North Carolina system. For the academic year 2007–2008, Appalachian enrolled students from 46 states and 61 foreign countries. The undergraduate enrollment for 2007–2008 was 13,997 students, of whom 6,907 were men and 7,090 were women. First-year students who enrolled totaled 2,737; 11.5% were first-generation college students. The University has an undergraduate minority enrollment of 7% and a 7.2% enrollment of students over age 25.

University College

Appalachian's University College, founded in 2007 and reporting to the vice provost for undergraduate education, includes both university-wide curricular and cocurricular units and academic student support services: general education, the honors program, cross-college interdisciplinary degree programs (i.e., Women's Studies, Sustainable Development, Appalachian Studies, Global Studies, and Interdisciplinary Studies), Watauga Global Community (i.e., an alternative interdisciplinary residential learning community of about 100 students), service-learning, student research, the learning assistance program, advising for undeclared and preprofessional students, orientation, the writing center, a university-wide lecture committee, the summer reading program, and the testing center. The University College did not, in the first three years, hire its own tenure-track faculty. Faculty members will have disciplinary homes and be reassigned as needed (with incentives to departments) to University College programs.

General Education Reform

The establishment of University College was both an intentional effort to enhance undergraduate education at Appalachian and an organizational solution to a series of challenges and opportunities that presented themselves somewhat independently. Since 2004, Appalachian has seen a near-total change in upper administration, following a period of unusual stability, with a chancellor who had been in office for 10 years and a provost who had led academic affairs for 24 years. Thus, significant internal change would have been inevitable even without the increasingly louder external calls for accountability and responsiveness to a rapidly changing world. In his first year of office (2004–2005), the new provost set up two task forces—general education and honors—that directly influenced the development of a university college.

The General Education Task Force consisted of faculty, administrators, and students who met weekly for two and one-half years, producing an integrated, interdisciplinary, and vertical general education model, implemented in fall 2009, which drew on the national best practices articulated and promoted by organizations such as the Association of American Colleges and Universities. The task force developed a set of learning outcomes with four main goals. Ideally, students would leave Appalachian (a) thinking critically and creatively, (b) communicating effectively, (c) making local to global connections (e.g., understanding local cultures and systems in their necessarily global contexts), and (d) understanding responsibilities of community membership. All students take an interdisciplinary first-year seminar and a first-year writing course, followed by a writing course in the second year, a third-year writing course in the major, and a senior capstone in the major.

The heart of the curriculum is a series of four perspectives—aesthetic, historical and social, science inquiry, and local to global—within which students take thematically integrated courses that come up for periodic review. Additional requirements include wellness literacy, quantitative literacy, and information/communication/technology literacy. Throughout the process, the campus and other constituencies (i.e., high schools, community colleges, employers, and alumni) were involved through a series of open forums, surveys, and focus groups. The high level of administrative infrastructure this general education requires led to the realization that a university college, reporting directly to academic affairs, would provide a natural home. The administrative costs of this program are offset by the elimination of two stand-alone offices (i.e., Freshman Seminar and Freshman Learning Communities) that were subsumed into the university college structure. The new program is administered by a director of general education and a faculty coordinator reporting directly to the vice provost for undergraduate education, as well as a full-time assistant director, a half-time faculty coordinator of the first-year seminar, and committees involving 41 faculty members in curriculum oversight and decision making. Despite some opposition from departments who felt their autonomy threatened by the elimination of a menu of disciplinary courses in favor of an interdisciplinary program, the new curriculum was approved in fall 2007, for implementation in fall 2009.

Honors, Interdisciplinarity, and Student Support: Further Justification for University College

Enhancing the honors program has become a priority for the chancellor and provost, as Appalachian has become more selective and has begun an effort to recruit high-achieving students. A task force recommended a variety of curricular changes and that an honors college be established under an honors dean. The latter was strongly opposed by the existing college deans, which led to the decision to place the honors program in the University College, where the vice provost for undergraduate education could help the program achieve its goals.

Concurrent with the work of the honors and general education task forces was a conversation about interdisciplinarity that led to the decision to disband the Department of Interdisciplinary Studies (IDS) effective in fall 2008 and to house cross-college interdisciplinary degree programs in University College. While the decision to disband IDS has had some difficult consequences, especially for interdisciplinary faculty who are now credentialed in disciplinary departments, the IDS faculty are cautiously optimistic about a university-wide context and the opportunity to collaborate with other programs. The University College now offers interdisciplinary degree programs in sustainable development, women's studies, Appalachian studies, global studies, and interdisciplinary studies.

Following the dissolution of IDS, Watauga Global Community, a lower-division alternative residential community, moved to University College in fall 2008. Watauga Global Community has developed a plan to internationalize the Living-Learning Center, which houses Watauga students, teaching fellows, and international students. Watauga's director explains that while in the past Watauga College and IDS saw it as important to be isolated from the mainstream of Appalachian State in order to pursue an alternative vision, they now want to help guide the new interdisciplinary vision that is developing at the university level.

As these conversations occurred on the faculty and curricular side of the house, a parallel conversation was taking place in the areas of academic student support and cocurricular programs in the divisions of academic affairs and student development, both of which sought closer partnerships. A broadly conceived model of student success, crossing divisional boundaries and encouraged by the University of North Carolina system's demand for higher retention and graduation rates, evolved in contexts such as the Student Achievement Team, a group that includes representatives from all areas that directly touch students' lives. Locating advising, orientation, and some other student support units in Enrollment Services enabled close links with Admissions and the Registrar; however, there was a growing disconnect between these programs and the faculty, especially full-time, tenure-track faculty members, as well as a separation between units that had developed into successful but autonomous programs. Some reporting lines that had evolved historically no longer made sense: Freshman Learning Communities and the learning assistance program reported through the Office of General Studies to the associate vice-chancellor for enrollment services while Freshman Seminar and the University Writing Center reported to the senior associate vice chancellor for academic affairs. Testing Services, which had long ago cut ties with the Counseling Center, and service-learning—a very successful academic program—were housed in the Division of Student Development.

Without exception, the directors and coordinators of all these units saw University College as a good opportunity to implement a more unified program of curricular and cocurricular student success than we had had in the past. The vice-chancellors and associate vice-chancellors to whom these units reported saw the wisdom of moving these units into University College to promote opportunities for greater institution-wide collaboration.

Results and Lessons Learned

Critical Elements for Success

- ◇ *Personal and financial commitment from the upper administration.* The provost not only provided the necessary resources but also gave his personal support for the development of University College programs to those involved and through public statements.
- ◇ *A strong student-centered perspective in academic affairs and student development.* Those units were able to put aside turf battles in order to support students; for example, student development fully supported the new general education curriculum, and academic affairs embraced the importance of cocurricular programs for student success.
- ◇ *A commitment to success in undergraduate education as a strategic priority for the University.* Even before the actual curriculum was approved, the four goals of the new general education program had become part of institutional discourse as shorthand for the University's overall educational priorities, and the implementation of the general education program is one of the key indicators in our new strategic plan's commitment to "intellectually engage students with active, interdisciplinary learning environments."
- ◇ *Personal relationships between responsible individuals in a variety of arenas.* Our chancellor and provost, partly under the influence of Collins' (2001) *Good to Great*, firmly believe that the most important first step in creating a great institution is to get the right people

in place. Without key individuals in the faculty and administration who build trust and complement each other's skills, this kind of reorganization would be impossible.

◇ *A recognition that structures dependent on individuals are unsustainable in the long term.* In the past, certain programs have succeeded or failed only because particular people were in charge. Our recent turnover has shown us how important it is to create a sustainable administrative structure that is not dependent on particular individuals but that will provide structural opportunities for the right people to work with each other.

◇ *Acceptance of external and internal pressures that nurture creative solutions and collaborations for shared resources.* In the past, individual programs have competed for resources without clear accountability. In the face of calls for greater accountability by our campus administration, the University of North Carolina General Administration, and the public, the University has embraced outcomes-based educational decisions while actively seeking collaborations that will make more efficient use of resources. These more efficient collaborations in turn can be better for students.

◇ *The continuous involvement of the faculty.* The three-year process of general education revision succeeded only because faculty members were involved every step of the way. Now faculty members are taking initiative in developing and linking courses in the context of the new general education curriculum, and more faculty members are interested in interdisciplinarity and liberal education. University College, along with related groups such as the Student Achievement Team and the Learning Communities Council, are helping faculty members, student support administrators, student affairs professionals, and other University personnel understand how these various roles fit together for student success.

Challenges to Implementation

The general education administrative team and the faculty committees have a crucial role to play in shifting faculty culture from a comfort in disciplinary silos and a loyalty to departments to a culture that values metadisciplinary efforts and cross-college collaboration. While University College programs have brought faculty members together with other groups on campus, these changes, especially the new general education curriculum, have made some faculty members retreat to hyper-disciplinarity and a simplistic approach to the principle that faculty (i.e., tenure-track faculty untainted by administrative duties) should control all curriculum decisions. Though it is agreed that curriculum *approval* is a function of elected faculty bodies, it is essential to maintain the view that curriculum *development* and *implementation* be a shared responsibility of administrators and faculty members. As Gaff (2007) has pointed out, "While the faculty are generally responsible for academic decisions, they are seldom held accountable either for student learning or for the fiscal results of their decisions" (p. 6). Greater involvement by the faculty requires a more sophisticated notion of shared governance than we currently have.

Faculty term-limited appointments to University College academic efforts (i.e., honors, general education, interdisciplinary programs) must also be put in place in return for temporary lines to cover departmental curricula. In the long term, careful decisions need to be made about whether and how to appoint and tenure faculty directly through University College programs, weighing the necessity for a stable University College faculty against the danger of second-class status for such faculty.

In addition, appropriate evaluation procedures for promotion and tenure that recognize University College teaching must be designed and implemented through Faculty Senate. In part, this means moving beyond the traditional mode of valuing only what Boyer (1997) terms the "scholarship of discovery" (p. 16) and including the scholarship of teaching and learning and the scholarship of engagement as valued contributions to scholarly work. As Schneider (1998) has noted, stewardship (e.g., faculty work in the development of programs) is not easily captured by the triumvirate of teaching, scholarship, and service, but needs to be incorporated into the faculty rewards system.

Lastly, complex reporting lines must be designed to enhance the professional growth of the people in affected positions rather than penalize or frustrate them with too many bosses and conflicting agendas.

Conclusion

The provost saw a comprehensive University College as an appropriate organizational structure to accommodate curricular changes, to increase faculty involvement in all aspects of students' education, to promote synergy among programs, and to enable a more efficient distribution of resources. This change is also part of his attempt to provide the Office of Academic Affairs with a more rational organizational structure, including the appointment of a vice provost who is explicitly responsible for undergraduate education. The establishment of the University College addresses Appalachian's position as a growing institution with a need for a variety of programs—both curricular and cocurricular—to unite in a shared vision of student success. It is hoped that University College will provide both support and accountability for a complex mission that includes introducing students to a rigorous liberal education, fostering innovative interdisciplinary teaching and research, promoting engagement with diverse communities both inside and outside the classroom, and providing the students with the support that will enable their highest achievement.

References

Boyer, E. L. (1997). *Scholarship reconsidered: Priorities of the professoriate.* San Francisco, CA: Jossey-Bass.

Collins, J. (2001). *Good to great: Why some companies make the leap and others don't.* New York, NY: Harper Business.

Gaff, J. G. (2007). What if the faculty really do assume responsibility for the educational program? *Liberal Education, 93*(4), 6–13.

Schneider, C. G. (1998). President's message. *Liberal Education, 84*(4), 1–2.

Indiana University–Purdue University Indianapolis

Critical Inquiry Courses: Promoting First-Year Student Success in the Second Semester

Leslie Miller

Institutional Context

Indiana University–Purdue University Indianapolis (IUPUI) is a public, four-year commuter institution located in downtown Indianapolis, Indiana. With more than 28,000 students representing 49 states and 139 countries, IUPUI is the second-largest campus in the Indiana University statewide multiple-campus system. IUPUI is an urban research and academic health sciences campus with 22 schools and academic units that grant degrees in more than 200 programs from both Indiana University and Purdue University.

In fall 2008, IUPUI enrolled 28,722 students, 19,970 of whom were at the undergraduate level, with 3,040 new beginning students. The University has an enrollment of 17,932 full-time students and 10,840 part-time students. IUPUI has a significant adult (age 25 and over) student population represented by 13,261 learners. Approximately 1,100 students live on campus. Of those, 64% are first-year students.

More than half (57%) of IUPUI students are female. Total minority enrollment represents almost 16% of the total student population: African American (9.1%), Asian/Pacific Islander (4%), and Hispanic (2.5%). Finally, 44% of undergraduate students are first-generation, defined as neither mother nor father having completed a college degree.

University College

As part of institutional efforts to provide one portal of entry to the multiple degree units and support student success, the IUPUI Faculty Council approved the formation of University College in spring 1997. The founding faculty (representing all degree-granting schools at IUPUI) and the dean were appointed soon thereafter, with the first students entering the college in summer 1998. The founding faculty approved the following mission statement:

> University College is the academic unit at IUPUI, which provides a common gateway to the academic programs available to entering students. University College coordinates existing university resources and develops new initiatives to promote academic excellence and enhance student persistence. It provides a setting where faculty, staff, and students share in the responsibility for making IUPUI a supportive and challenging environment for learning.

All students entering IUPUI are granted admission to University College (either full or dual admission with a degree-granting school). Students remain in University College until they have declared a major and meet the necessary conditions for transfer to a degree-granting school. Approximately 6,500 are enrolled in University College each year.

Programs and services offered by University College focus on assisting students with the development of the knowledge and skills needed for success in the collegiate environment, including academic advising, academic support, first-year seminars, themed learning communities, academic mentoring, new student orientation, and the campus honors program. University College also offers several college readiness programs, which focus on helping area students become college bound.

Critical Inquiry in University College

The IUPUI Critical Inquiry (CI) Program, titled UCOL U112: Critical Inquiry, is a one- to two-credit-hour course linked to certain introductory, general education classes that have considerable reading requirements. Students choose to take the CI class at the suggestion of their academic advisors with whom all University College students meet regularly in the first year. Through advising sessions and student records, advisors determine which students need assistance with dense reading, are conditional admits, and/or are on academic probation. These students are encouraged to take U112 Critical Inquiry to assist them with their course work or to fulfill the requirements of their admission.

Beginning as a request from the IUPUI campus that University College develop an academic success intervention to replace its traditional, remedial program of reading and study skills, the dean of University College appointed a Transitional Education Task Force to examine national best practices and recommend a new program appropriate to IUPUI's particular institutional context. This task force reviewed the literature, employed consultants, and made site visits to selected peer institutions, particularly Brooklyn College, which had pioneered this kind of support class and on whose model the task force made its proposal (G. Williams, personal communication, October 24, 2007). The task force recommendations were affirmed by the University College faculty. The orientation, enrollment, staffing, and advising branches were set in place to direct students into the CI classes, and U112: Critical Inquiry was first implemented in 2000, taking its place alongside other first-year experience student support initiatives located in University College, such as learning communities, themed learning communities, structured learning assistance, and the Summer Academy Bridge Program (G. Williams, personal communication, October 24, 2007).

Currently, the IUPUI first-year experience courses take effect for all new enrollees in the fall semester. These students are placed into U110: Learning Community sections, nearly all of which are linked to one or a series of general education course. In the second semester, however, not all of these students are required to take a support course, and so the numbers of students who take U112: Critical Inquiry is smaller.

Nevertheless, U112: Critical Inquiry was designed to follow the first-semester U110: Learning Community course, both chronologically and conceptually. In practice, learning communities are supported by an instructional team of four members (i.e., faculty member, academic advisor, student mentor, and librarian). In the second-semester Critical Inquiry course, however, the instructional team is comprised of only the CI faculty member, the general education course faculty member, and a librarian. Thus, a U112: Critical Inquiry class can be linked, for example, with a Psychology B104: Introduction to Psychology, and the CI instructor will collaborate with the psychology instructor on how the CI class can increase student learning using the psychology course and textbook as a foundation for critical inquiry. Also, U110 focuses on orientation to the IUPUI campus, whereas U112 focuses on academic orientation to learning (i.e., how students need to think about their courses' subject matter).

Vitally important to the understanding of the CI Program is its separation from remediation; that is, students in CI are engaged in reading praxis and strategies that lead them to deeper understanding of classroom texts that presupposes existing fundamental reading skills. Thus, the CI course is not remedial, but rather designed for those students with narrowly defined risk factors in writing and/or reading (G. Williams, personal communication, October 24, 2007).

In order to develop the conditions for such demanding work with students, Critical Inquiry classes meet twice weekly for a total of 2 ½ hours of instructional time, either immediately before or after the general education courses to which they are linked. The classes are typically limited to 27 students and represent only a part of the total enrollment of the general education course to which it is linked. An American history class, for example, may enroll 60-90 students; some of these students, however, will volunteer to take a CI class to help them with the class's considerable reading. Those students will be grouped under a separate course number within the history class, and only they will attend the CI class.

As a result, a built-in control group exists within the general education course section to compare the effects of the additional instruction. Consequently, the success of CI students has been assessed against the control groups with regard to their course grade, GPA, and student satisfaction with learning. Furthermore, students have had the choice of many CI classes linked to more than 14 first-year, introductory classes in biology, American history, sociology, anthropology, and psychology, among others. The class work in CI occurs in the context of these linked general education courses, implemented, however, through distinctive active-learning strategies and course requirements.

The Critical Inquiry emphasis reveals the programmatic understanding of the students' increased need to approach course work more critically as they proceed through the University. In keeping with the mission of supporting academic excellence and improving student persistence, CI classes are dynamic places of learning where both the CI and general education faculty are closely involved in curriculum design and implementation. CI also emphasizes transferable academic skills wherein students come to understand the distinctive expectations and requirement for successful college learning and gain strategies of active learning, critical reading, and appropriate communication. Finally, CI classes also help students practice learning activities resulting in the acquisition of text-based strategies of critical analysis. As a result, the CI classes form a learning community similar to what students experience in their first semester built around using the powerful elements of peer connections, active and collaborative learning strategies, multidisciplinary perspectives, and positive interactions with faculty (Hansen, Jackson, & Williams, 2004). In this way, CI classes bear the institutional responsibility to all admitted students to promote their success, especially to those who can benefit from its transitional, academic support (G. Williams, personal communication, October 24, 2007).

Results and Lessons Learned

To measure the courses' impact, the CI program has been assessed since its inception using both qualitative and quantitative methods, summative and formative approaches, and multiple measures from different sources. Course evaluations have been administered at the end of each semester in order to understand students' perceptions of course benefits and self-reported learning gains by means of both closed- and open-ended questions. In-class focus groups and questionnaires with open-ended questions have also been used, as well as comparisons made between participants and nonparticipants with regard to academic performance and retention while controlling for background differences. In addition, the feedback from both CI and general education course faculty has been used to gauge the progress and effectiveness of the program and to make planning decisions.

End-of-semester evaluations for the spring 2006 period demonstrate the success of the CI model. CI students were more likely to be retained to the next year than the control group (CI = 69%; control group = 64%) and had GPAs 0.07 points higher (Hansen, 2007) than control group students. Students themselves noted how much they valued the discussion and the assistance with the reading. One student wrote, "Great discussion! Lead [*sic*] me to develop better understanding of subjects." In the same vein, another student wrote, "The class helped clear up anything I did not understand" (Hansen & Pederson, 2006). Many similar comments have been recorded, and taken together, these positive evaluations highlight the benefits of the Critical Inquiry program to influence student success and retention.

Although CI is a success story, outside threats reveal the need to prepare for the future. A public perception that the course is for remediation persists even though such a view is not held within University College. Conceivably, some public relations effort will be needed to convey the understanding that CI is a challenging academic course. In addition, the ability to increase the number of CI classes to meet the demand competes with other organizational needs—financial and programmatic.

Further, the need for professional development of CI faculty has become increasingly evident. In the years since its inception, CI faculty have met as a group only one time during the year—the CI retreat in the fall. While faculty have respond positively to the retreat, their busy schedules seldom allow them time to have periodic interaction with each other or to keep up with current learning theory. Although a CI listserv is available, few exchanges have been recorded. In some ways, the CI faculty have become isolated even though they tend to be a lively and innovative when together. Consequently, morale is low.

The student responses from evaluations and other assessment tools have also included suggestions for revision. When students expressed dissatisfaction, it was because they thought the class would be something like a study hall, a familiar classroom model from high school. The seminar-like, active-learning environment of the CI class is so foreign that some students struggle to adjust to the added responsibility they must take for their own learning. As a result, they sometimes report they would like CI to have a more traditional learning path similar to general education courses. It appears that CI instructors need to do a better job of translating the learning theory that underpins CI into language students understand and help them see how the class can translate into their own academic success. Also, further study is needed to consider student dissatisfaction with a one-credit-hour course that meets for 2½ hours per week (a decided majority of the CI classes).

More difficult to express is the need for the CI program to adapt to the changing needs of the University, the faculty, and the students. IUPUI is in a time of opportunity as leadership changes, finances fluctuate, and enrollment grows. Therefore, research and study is required to plan for the future and to answer these questions:

◇ In what ways does the CI program need to adapt to changes in the University?
◇ How can CI adapt to the needs of incoming students?
◇ How can CI establish reasonable and useful professional development?

References

Hansen, M. J. (2007). *IUPUI critical inquiry spring 2006 evaluation report.* Unpublished report, Indiana University–Purdue University Indianapolis.

Hansen, M. J., Jackson, B. D., & Williams, G. A. (2004, May). *Assessment of critical inquiry: A new model for transitional education.* Presentation at the annual forum of the Association of Institutional Research, Boston, MA.

Hansen, M. J., & Pedersen, J. (2006). *IUPUI University College critical inquiry courses: Understanding student perceptions of critical inquiry courses, spring 2005 and 2006.* Unpublished report, Indiana University–Purdue University Indianapolis.

Kennesaw State University

Faculty Development Within a Large Learning Community Program

Keisha L. Hoerrner & Ruth A. Goldfine

The Institutional Context

Kennesaw State University (KSU), 30 miles northwest of Atlanta in Kennesaw, Georgia, is a four-year, comprehensive university with expanding undergraduate and graduate programs. Founded by the University System of Georgia's Board of Regents in 1963 as a two-year institution, KSU has grown rapidly and is now the third-largest university in the state. Residential communities opened in 2002, and more than 13% of KSU's undergraduates now live on campus.

KSU's fall 2009 student population included 20,304 undergraduates. Of those students, 76% were enrolled full time, and 14% were first-year students. The majority (59%) were female. While the students had an average age of 24, the median age was 22. The minority population constituted 25% of the total undergraduate population, and 6% of undergraduates were from foreign nations. KSU students can choose from more than 60 undergraduate, master's, and doctoral degree programs and have access to more than 150 student groups and organizations.

University College

KSU's University College was established in 2004 to provide greater visibility to the numerous interdisciplinary programs for first-year students and students in transition who have been integral to KSU for more than a decade. University College houses the Department of First-Year Programs (FYP), which directs the nationally recognized first-year seminar course and the learning communities program as well as the Department of University Studies that is home to numerous interdisciplinary programs for students in transition (e.g., learning support, Honors, the Interdisciplinary Studies degree program). University College is also home to the director of First-Year Retention Initiatives and the American Democracy Project/Political Engagement Project and provides oversight for the Advising Council. The Center for Student Leadership is housed jointly in the college and the Division for Student Success and Enrollment Services.

The FYP Department offers more than 140 sections of the first-year seminar each academic year, serving more than 3,000 students. Some of those sections are part of learning communities. Approximately 40 theme-based communities are offered each academic year. The department includes 16 faculty, numerous part-time instructors, and three professional staff members.

Faculty Development and Learning Communities

KSU's learning communities (LCs) initiative has grown exponentially since it began in fall 2000, when eight sections of the first-year seminar course were paired with one general education course. While initial results showed that first-year students in these LCs had higher GPAs than a random sample of students enrolled only in the seminar or students not enrolled in either the seminar or a LC (i.e., 2.52 compared to 2.32 and 2.24, respectively), Casey & Hoerrner (2005) referred to the first LCs as learning coincidences. The LCs were not themed, and faculty participants did little to explicitly integrate the paired courses.

Eight LCs were again offered in 2001 with little change in pairings or integration; in 2002, the number increased to 16. Fall of 2003 brought a significant increase in the offerings (25) of LCs and integration within the courses. All LCs were thematically based and faculty worked to integrate these themes into their coursework. The first residential students moved into KSU's new living/learning communities in 2003 and were required to join an LC during their first semester. Commuter students were also encouraged to participate. Assessment data illustrate the success of these learning communities (Table 3.1).

Table 3.1

Assessment Data From Fall 2003

Student group	n	First-semester GPA	Fall 2004 retention
LC students	388	3.01	81% ($n = 314$)
KSU 1101 only	421	2.86	80% ($n = 339$)
Neither LC or 1101	1,174	2.61	74% ($n = 869$)

Note. Adapted from Building the Case for CLASS: Best Practices in Learning Communities, by R. Casey and K. Hoerrner, 2005, paper presented at the Southern Regional Learning Communities Conference, Atlanta, GA.

Informal feedback from LC faculty demonstrated a need for faculty development. While faculty were eager to collaborate on curriculum intersections, they needed direction, encouragement, and time. Thus, a faculty development program for LC faculty was initiated.

The literature on faculty development among LC instructors is clear on two points: (a) faculty development is greatly needed, particularly for those new to the LC experience, and (b) insufficient resources are available to support such programs (Hill, 1985; Smith, 2001). Formal methods and strategies for enacting such training have been suggested by some authors (e.g., Shapiro & Levine, 1999).

Despite the need for faculty development, LC faculty report that much of their training comes from collaborations with colleagues and through trial and error (Gammill & Hansen, 1992; Scharff & Brown, 2004). That was true for KSU faculty who participated in the early years. The inaugural Maymester program, designed to formalize the collaborative process and provide guidance and support, was a two-day training session in 2004 that combined information-sharing with opportunities for social connections. LC faculty learned about national research on the effectiveness of learning communities, heard from a student panel of former LC students, and had dedicated time to brainstorm course intersections. Participation was voluntary, and funding allowed for a small stipend ($500) for attendees. The program occurred during the first two days of a two-week period between the end of spring semester and the beginning of summer semester, which KSU calls Maymester.

In fall 2004, faculty taught in 34 communities. That number increased 60% by fall 2005 thanks to the development of University College and a first-year curriculum requirement that took effect that semester.

KSU's administration launched University College in fall 2004 and created the University College Advisory Council (UCAC) to ensure campus-wide input for its initiatives. UCAC proposed a curriculum requirement that every first-time, full-time student with 0 to 15 semester transfer hours enroll in either a seminar or an LC. The goal was to provide first-time, full-time students with a consistent first-semester experience without designing a one-size-fits-all requirement. The proposal passed the multiple levels of curriculum review, including the final Undergraduate Policies and Curriculum Committee. Beginning fall 2005, students were required to enroll in one of four curriculum options: (a) an independent section of KSU 1101; (b) a learning community that included KSU 1101 and/or BIOL 2101 (i.e., a discipline-specific first-year seminar for biology majors); (c) a learning community that did not include KSU 1101 and/or BIOL 2101; or (d) an independent section of BIOL 2101. All options introduced students to the same 11 learning outcomes[1]:

- ◇ Enhance study skills
- ◇ Promote cognitive/academic skills
- ◇ Improve critical-thinking skills
- ◇ Provide greater connection to faculty
- ◇ Provide greater connection to student peers
- ◇ Increase out-of-class engagement opportunities
- ◇ Increase student knowledge of campus policies
- ◇ Increase student knowledge of academic services
- ◇ Promote skill in managing time and priorities
- ◇ Improve knowledge of wellness
- ◇ Enhance understanding of global perspectives

To accommodate the increasing number of students and promote greater faculty participation, KSU initiated a proposal process for LC themes that invites faculty across campus to develop either discipline-based or general-interest communities.

The growth in the overall number of communities and faculty participants prompted expansion of the Maymester faculty development program and the creation of other development opportunities for LC faculty. The Maymester 2005 program spanned four days and included a keynote speaker, who focused on helping faculty understand incoming students and strategies for challenging and supporting them. Other featured speakers addressed the demographics of the incoming first-year class and the scholarship of teaching and learning within LCs. Both faculty and student panels were also included.

Each day of the program allowed time for LC colleagues to collaborate on thematic integrations. Each faculty cohort completed a description of their plan to achieve each of 11 learning outcomes. (In December, cohorts were asked to provide an assessment of how effectively they met each outcome.) During Maymester, faculty were also able to choose dates for out-of-class engagement opportunities, which they then included on their syllabi.

Funding restrictions limited Maymester 2006 to three days with only internal speakers and guests. Faculty engaged in planning more than 50 communities, and the agenda focused yet again on the incoming students, active pedagogy, and the scholarship of teaching and learning. Participants received books on student development theory and a notebook of relevant articles, important dates, and other ancillary information. Feedback from the previous Maymester indicated LC veterans were bored with the repetition of program basics, yet those new to the program were unclear on the concept of LCs and confused by the jargon. Therefore, participants were initially split into two groups: those new to LCs and veterans. Separate programs facilitated by LC veterans brought the new LC faculty up to speed while the veterans explored how to better integrate technology and enhance collaboration.

The 2007 Maymester program was limited to two days and featured an external speaker who discussed benefits and limitations of research on the millennials and its implications. Participants received copies of either *Generation Me* (Twenge, 2006) or *My Freshman Year* (Nathan, 2005) to enhance their understanding of the millennial generation. Faculty were again separated into groups of novices and veterans for part of the program; while novices learned the essential details of LCs, experienced LC faculty explored student motivation issues. Peer leaders were part of Maymester for the first time, allowing faculty to meet their leaders and discuss their responsibilities in the community.

In addition to Maymester, LC faculty were invited to biannual community-planning luncheons in April and December. These luncheons provided an opportunity for faculty cohorts to meet while having access to the LC leadership for questions related to the learning outcomes, out-of-class engagement events, and other LC issues.

Finally, an e-mail group was created each semester to encourage communication between University College and LC faculty across campus. Small groups of LC faculty have also initiated their own faculty development/scholarship initiatives. For example, faculty who taught the spring 2007 gender studies community met with those who would be teaching the two fall sessions to explore assignments, lessons learned, implications for research projects, and student reactions. Also, a group of seven LC faculty, representing four of KSU's seven colleges, spent more than a year examining interdisciplinary learning in LCs. This was both a faculty development opportunity and a research initiative that resulted in presentations and a publication.

Results and Lessons Learned

Maymester programs were assessed through a quantitative moment-in-time survey of participants. Beginning in 2005, data were compiled and used to plan the following year's program. Responses were overwhelmingly positive, with faculty reporting greater (a) understanding of the LC initiative, (b) appreciation for their role in achieving LC goals, and (c) ability to see intersections between their course and the other courses in their communities.

The survey consists of seven Likert-scale statements and several open-ended questions. The open-ended questions asked faculty to list the most and least valuable aspects of the program and to make suggestions for improvement. Response rates were strong. In 2005, 27 of the 46 participants (59%) returned evaluation surveys; for 2006 and 2007, there were 34 (44%) and 33 (67%) respondents, respectively.

Respondents from 2005, 2006, and 2007 (Table 3.2) reported similar experiences, expressing that they gained knowledge and understanding of leaning community structures and resources to help them feel more confident in the classroom. They also enjoyed hearing from previous LC faculty and from former LC students (those agreeing ranged from 24 to 27 across the three years). More valuable to the event planners, the open-ended responses noted the importance of both practical and theoretical information. Participants were as pleased with the dedicated time set aside to learn about each other's course content and brainstorm points of connection as they were with the guest speakers. KSU faculty have consistently remarked on the importance of social and planning time together, which costs little money and takes little time to plan but pays large dividends in interdisciplinary integration. The same can be said for materials provided to LC faculty. Although new

LC faculty members possess disciplinary expertise, it would be presumptuous—and foolhardy—to assume each is well-versed in the research regarding student development, first-year programs, and/or interdisciplinary collaboration. Thus, it is imperative that they be provided with materials that address these three primary components of first-year student success.

Table 3.2

Faculty Responses to Maymester

	2005 (*n* = 27)	2006 (*n* = 34)	2007 (*n* = 33)
Maymester aided in my understanding of LCs.	21	28	20
I now feel comfortable fulfilling the LC objectives.	27	30	29
Looking forward to collaborating with LC colleagues	27	32	30
Learned about resources to make LC successful	22	27	24
Understand the curriculum requirement	25	28	30

Note. Data reflect the number of faculty agreeing that participating in Maymester helped them *much* or *very much* in achieving these outcomes.

Maymester was a successful program for a period of time; however, it faced a significant budgetary challenge. The program was never a line item within either the department or college budget. The food for the event could not be supplied with state funds, so KSU 1101 textbook royalties helped defray this cost. Stipends, honoraria for guest speakers, and materials were generally funded through end-of-year requests, which meant that planning for Maymester could not begin until February or March. For these budgetary reasons—as well as the recognition that a majority of the faculty who now teach in LCs are veterans of LCs and Maymester—the new coordinator for learning communities chose to discontinue Maymester in 2008.

Clearly, faculty development is vital for the continued growth and enhancement of learning communities. Recognizing this, and in the face of budgetary limitations, the LC administrators have become more creative in devising LC faculty development initiatives. Future plans include a resource web site for LC faculty and more social opportunities for collaboration. Finally, special half-day training programs for new LC faculty will continue to ensure they have a basic understanding of their role within this important first-year initiative.

KSU's experience shows that successful faculty development programs can be low-budget lunches that provide LC faculty time to collaborate, or they can be multiday, expensive programs requiring months of preparation. Clearly, the cost of the program seems to have little impact on its success. Rather, the success of LC faculty development programs can be attributed to the inclusion of three key components: (a) dedicated time for planning and discussion, (b) materials that will allow faculty to expand their teaching capabilities and understanding of their first-year students, and (c) an assessment plan. Therefore, given the importance of LC faculty development, even LC administrators on a shoestring budget should—and should be able to—offer their faculty some development opportunities.

Notes

[1] In 2009 the 11 outcomes were reduced to four. Seminar courses promote life skills, strategies for academic success, connections to campus and community, and provide a foundation for global learning. Learning communities promote skills in interacting with others, demonstrate cross-disciplinary connections, reflect upon the value of global learning for engaged citizenship, and enhance critical-thinking and problem-solving skills.

References

Casey, R., & Hoerrner, K. (2005, October). *Building the case for CLASS: Best practices in learning communities.* Paper presented at the second Southern Regional Learning Communities Conference, Atlanta, GA.

Gammill, L., & Hansen, C. (1992). Linked courses: A method to reinforce basic skills. *Journal of Education for Business, 67*(6), 358–360.

Hill, P. (1985, October). *The rationale for learning communities.* Paper presented at the Inaugural Conference on Learning Communities of The Washington Center for Undergraduate Education, Olympia, WA.

Nathan, R. (2005). *My freshman year: What a professor learned by becoming a student.* Ithaca, NY: Cornell University Press.

Scharff, C., & Brown, H. (2004). Thinking through computing: The power of learning communities. *Computer Science Education, 14*(4), 297–320.

Shapiro, N., & Levine, J. (1999). *Creating learning communities: A practical guide to winning support, organizing for change, and implementing programs.* San Francisco, CA: Jossey-Bass.

Smith, B. (2001, March). *The challenge of learning communities as a growing national movement.* Paper presented at the Association of American Colleges and Universities Conference on Learning, Providence, RI.

Twenge, J. M. (2006). *Generation me: Why today's young Americans are more confident, assertive, entitled—and more miserable than ever before.* New York, NY: Free Press.

The Pennsylvania State University

Discover House: A Living-Learning Community for First-Year Students

Eric R. White

The Institutional Context

The Pennsylvania State University is a multicampus, public, land-grant institution with administrative headquarters in State College, Pennsylvania. Undergraduate degree opportunities are available at the University Park campus in State College and 20 other campus locations throughout the Commonwealth. The University was chartered by the Pennsylvania legislature as the Farmers' High School in 1855. Today, the total student enrollment is more than 90,000. Control of the University is vested in a 32-member Board of Trustees; general operations of the institution are supported by appropriations of the state legislature and from tuitions, fees, and the other income sources. Penn State is accredited by the Middle States Commission on Higher Education and is a member of the Association of American Universities.

For fall 2009, the undergraduate enrollment at the University Park campus totaled 38,630 of whom 37,754 were baccalaureate degree candidates. Most undergraduates (71.3%) were from the state of Pennsylvania, and 54.8% were male. The ethnicity of the undergraduate population was: African American (1,399), Asian American (1,915), Hispanic American (1,635), Native American (30), International (1,663), and White (31,599). The 2003 cohort six-year graduation rate was 84.6%, and the 2004 cohort five-year graduation rate was 83.2%.

Division of Undergraduate Studies

The Division of Undergraduate Studies (DUS) provides four major programs:

◇ Enrollment Program for students who want to explore the University's academic opportunities before deciding on a field of study and for students in transition from one college/major to another

◇ First-Year Testing, Consulting, and Advising Program (FTCAP) for all entering first-year students and their families

◇ Academic Advising Practices and Information Program including a network of programs coordinators

◇ Academic Advising and Educational Planning Program for anyone who requests assistance

DUS is one of the oldest and most comprehensive programs of its kind in American higher education. The earliest predecessor of DUS, the Division of Intermediate Registration, was created in 1948 to help meet the academic needs of returning World War II veterans. In 1956, DIR was replaced by the Division of Counseling, which, as part of its work, helped students better understand their personal characteristics and how these characteristics related to their new educational environment.

In 1973, after a three-year study, the University Faculty Senate recommended the creation of DUS to improve enrollment and advising programs for students as they developed their academic plans and to create a university-wide academic information and advising system. On October 1, 1973, Penn State's Board of Trustees established the Division of Undergraduate Studies.

When founded, DUS enrolled nearly 400 students. With more than 7,000 students at 20 Penn State campuses (approximately 3,000 at the University Park campus and 4,000 at the other campuses), DUS is now Penn State's largest unit of enrollment for entering baccalaureate students. DUS also provides academic advising to 730 provisionally admitted students,

Discover House: A Living-Learning Opportunity for Exploratory Students

The Division of Undergraduate Studies sponsors Discover House. It is a unique initiative for a unit charged to advise undecided students and enhance academic advising university wide. Discover House has enabled DUS to enhance its academic mission, collaborate with others units of Penn State, and interact with students outside the traditional advisor's office. Discover House began in 2000 with a grant from the William and Flora B. Hewlett Foundation. An original goal was to introduce the content of general education into the curriculum via specific courses. For example, the introductory English composition course (English 15, Rhetoric and Composition) used texts such as the *Declaration of Independence* and the *Harvard Redbook* as readings.

Another goal of Discover House is to provide a living-learning opportunity for students who wish to explore more than one academic option before declaring a major. Currently located on the fifth floor of Beaver Hall on Penn State's University Park campus, Discover House is a community of 70 first-year students. In addition to the usual social and informational services, this residential life experience includes academic advising and special programming to help students choose academic majors and appreciate the value of general education in a university curriculum.

Discover House is based upon the premise that exploratory students (i.e., also referred to as undeclared or undecided students), despite their growing numbers, feel isolated among students who have declared majors or claim to know their educational goals. This sense of isolation can be addressed within a residential community so students learn they are not alone and will value the exploratory process.

Discover House offers residents special sections of general education classes. To enhance students' appreciation for general education, they are encouraged (at significantly reduced rates) to attend special events, lectures, and performances on campus. Out-of-classroom activities are offered to assist students with their academic exploration. A special first-year seminar designed for Discover House students introduces them to the role of libraries in the 21st century.

Students also have opportunities for leadership and academic growth through community service, public scholarship, and participation in Discover House activities. In consultation with their academic advisor, Discover House students select cocurricular activities that support their areas of exploration. For example, a student interested in advertising or marketing may be encouraged to join the Marketing Club. Students with interests in writing are often referred to the student newspaper. Special programming in the House features an introduction to University opportunities, including the full array of majors and minors, learning support programs, student organizations, internships, career services, and international study.

A unique aspect of the Discover House experience is that participation in any course or activity is voluntary. There are no deliberately clustered courses; rather, students select their own unique combinations in consultation with their academic advisor. A student's schedule is drawn from a general education distributional list, from the requirements of any major or minor under consideration, and appropriate elective courses.

Discover House is staffed with an undergraduate program assistant, usually a previous Discover House student, and a resident assistant. An academic advisor from the Division is assigned to oversee the activities of the House on a half-time basis and serves as the primary academic advisor to the majority of Discover House students. The program assistant lives in Discover House and supports the academic and social programming but does not have the disciplinary responsibility of the resident assistant.

The Discover House Curriculum

Over the years, the Discover House curriculum has been expanded beyond introductory English composition to courses and recitation sections exclusively for Discover House students. Unlike other living-learning environments, there was no need to hold classes in the residence halls. In fact, given the intense nature of the residential experience, having the students leave their residence to take classes appeared to be a more desirable approach. Feedback from other programs where courses were offered in residence halls was not always positive. Faculty reported that students approached their academic work too casually (e.g., the come-to-class-with-your-bedroom-slippers-on syndrome). Offering too many classes in the residence hall also fostered greater insularity. When students had no reason to venture outside their residence, they did not.

Living and learning together and working collaboratively, sometimes competitively, appears to have a positive impact on learning. Sections of courses set aside for Discover House students have included Introduction to Sociology, Fundamentals of Acting, Environmental Science, Geography of International Affairs, Race and Ethnic Relations, American Civilization Since 1977, History of Landscape Architecture, and Effective Speech. Faculty report Discover House students are active in class, unlikely to be absent, and generally turn in quality work.

The first-year seminar, Library Logistics, offered by the faculty of the University Libraries and described below is especially significant.

> This course will examine the library behind the scenes. The entire library will serve as a lab to engage the student and provide hands-on experience in how libraries acquire, organize, and make available information in all formats. Students will learn valuable skills that will empower them as university scholars in all disciplines and as lifelong learners through student-centered, active-learning situations directed by a team of service-oriented library professionals.

Librarians had not considered offering a first-year seminar, although they are authorized to teach them, until they were approached with the idea. They, however, do teach courses using the Library Studies rubric, such as Library Studies 490, Archival Management. They eagerly accepted the challenge of developing a course that would respond to the needs of exploratory students, bring them into the library (an ongoing challenge), and innovatively present the 21st century library. Not only would students begin to understand the purpose of libraries from historical and contemporary perspectives, they would also learn how libraries function, how books and other manuscripts are preserved, and how information is organized and retrieved. Unlike other introductory library classes, this course extends beyond the guided tour approach to examine how students might use a library to benefit their own academic exploration. Unique aspects of the seminar dealt with electronic plagiarism, how to cite electronic documents, and online safety and security.

Results and Lessons Learned

The assessment of Discover House includes examining changes in attitude toward general education, responses to programming and suggestions for enhanced activities, and feedback from faculty and staff who have worked with Discover House students. Specifically, we have learned that such living-learning opportunities create significant bonding among the students lasting well past graduation and can challenge students academically to understand the value of general education.

What Worked and Why

One obvious outcome, while unexpected, was the overwhelming sense of identity, allegiance, and spirit of community that developed. This sense of community was manifested in Discover House residents who continued to room together after leaving Discover House and maintained friendships well after graduation. This spirit fostered a sense of commitment to the physical entity known as Discover House, leading one Discover House cohort to sponsor a painting party to brighten their common hallways and create a wall design that enhanced the look of the House.

From an academic perspective, assessments indicated students used general education courses in their own academic exploration process and realized a university education should go beyond the vocational.

The use of former Discover House residents as coaches for current residents reinforced the notion that students learn from other students, specifically addressing the disadvantage of making premature decisions about what major to choose. Pre- and post-Discover House assessments have indicated increased appreciation for general education and associated cocurricular activities. For example, students who previously indicated they saw no purpose in taking science courses, acknowledged later the relevance of such study even though they were contemplating majors outside the science realm.

The first-year seminar in Library Studies worked because of its hands-on focus and relevance to the students. Students learned how to use general library resources as research tools, and guests from disciplinary-based libraries focused on the specifics of their fields. As a result, students developed the skills to find material regardless of the majors they were contemplating.

Discover House participants indicated they developed new habits of intellectual inquiry. Residents learned that one can be stretched intellectually at college. Understanding higher education and associating with faculty and staff empowered Discover House students to create networks throughout the University, and participants have graduated from all 12 academic colleges of Penn State.

Challenges and Barriers

The tight-knit Discover House community presented a disadvantage in one classroom setting. When an instructor innocuously made comments that singled out a House member, the entire class rallied around the targeted student, becoming highly protective, going so far as to disrupt instruction. Discover House staff now include a discussion with future instructors about this phenomenon.

Attending plays, concerts, and other artistic events has been built into the Discover House cocurriculum. Originally, the entire cost of attending an event was covered by grant support. Ironically, free admission did not lead to greater participation. Students now cover a minimal amount of the cost, thus assuring some commitment to use the ticket.

Since it should not be assumed that all students are technologically savvy, instructors in the first-year seminar decided that pretesting students at the beginning the semester would help them understand the range of knowledge students have about library technology. In addition, these instructors needed to adjust their pedagogy to accommodate the types of students in their class. Not all students thrive in a seminar approach and may find a lecture approach, at least initially, less threatening. A class with particularly loquacious students, however, may respond more readily to seminar pedagogy.

Critical Elements

A project of this scope needs a high level of personal commitment. Success occurs because the individual in charge understands the students' academic advising needs and also comes from a residence hall background. Coordination with other units is important, as is the ability to negotiate with faculty and departments, the residential life staff, and the academic advising community. Likewise, the first-year seminar succeeded because the chosen instructors were ready for and comfortable with the traditional classroom experience where behavior management techniques may have to be used and grading is a factor.

Critical to the success of this course is having a wired classroom and the technological infrastructure to support such instruction. Having the course taught under the Library Studies rubric allows for it to be credit bearing, thus giving librarians, who have academic rank and are in the tenure track, the opportunity to teach formally designated courses. The Discover House experience reinforced the role of librarians as faculty, not only in their own library setting but in the classroom as well. In fact, such an approach helps to combat the stereotypic notions that students have about librarians, a goal all librarians applaud.

Conclusion

The concept of Discover House can transfer to any college or university with residence halls. The costs to start such a program are not excessive, although realigning some professional responsibilities is necessary. At University Park, the Office of Residence Life eagerly collaborated, underwriting some of the room and board costs of the program assistant. A second Discover House was initiated using the University Park model at Penn State Berks in fall 2006.

The first-year seminar represents a proactive model in which the librarians collaborated with an academic unit of enrollment. Such a seminar can easily be implemented at any college. The course is designed to be team taught because of its modular construction and can be adapted to an online instructional modality.

Ultimately, what Discover House can achieve is a host of outcomes that virtually all colleges and universities value: appreciation for general education, collaborative study, lifelong learning habits, student understanding that curriculum can be used to explore educational options, lasting friendships, and institutional loyalty.

University of Akron

The University of Akron's Learning Communities Program
Bonnie Williams

The Institutional Context

The University of Akron (UA) is a Carnegie classification Doctoral/Research Intensive university, which focuses on the success, retention, and graduation of its undergraduate students. UA is part of the University System of Ohio and receives state support. As of fall 2008, the University served 26,000 students, and offered approximately 300 associate's, bachelor's, master's, doctoral, and law degree programs and 100 certificate programs at sites in Summit, Wayne, Medina, and Holmes counties in northeast Ohio. A metropolitan university with a sizeable nontraditional student population (23.3%), UA welcomes more than 4,000 first-year students each fall. Minority students comprise 16.2% of the undergraduates, 50% of whom are first-generation.

University College

UA has the necessary support structure to help students succeed—University College. Founded originally in 1935 as General College, University College has continued to evolve to meet the needs of the institution and the students it serves. At one time University College had responsibility for the instruction of all general education courses, ROTC, Women's Studies, the Honors Program, and the Center for Conflict Resolution. Since 1989, general education courses have resided in their respective colleges, the Honors College was established, and reporting lines for other units have changed. In 1994, the University College dean reported to both the provost and the vice president of student affairs, but since 1996 University College has reported to the provost. Students in University College reflect the diversity of the UA student population: 50% of the students are male; 16.6% are adult learners; and 18.1% are African American, Hispanic, Asian/Pacific Islander, or Native American.

Some of the ongoing initiatives supported by University College that illustrate our commitment to students' success include (a) required new student orientation for traditional-aged, adult, and transfer students; (b) an opening convocation for new students in the fall; (c) a common reading program with a first-year lecture; (d) professional advisors who work with University College students until they transfer to UA's degree-granting colleges; (e) an extensive learning community program; (f) a number of courses (e.g., Student Success Seminar, Career Planning, Information Tools for Success) to help students transition to the University or to a degree program; (g) the Majors Mosaic program in October, which highlights programs where students can earn majors, minors, and certificates; and (h) student academic support including peer tutoring and learning assistants.

University College is one of 11 undergraduate colleges at The University of Akron; although not a degree-granting college, professionals within University College work with faculty and administrators across campus to promote student academic success. While opportunities for collaboration with the Division of Student Affairs remain strong, University College administrators are also working on a Learning Commons with the Library, Instructional Technology, and the Institute for Teaching and Learning. University College's leadership in service-learning, the Post Secondary Enrollment Option Program (a dual high school/college credit program), and the

Transfer Student Services Center have demonstrated University College's unique collaborations throughout northeast Ohio, which benefit our students and the greater Akron community.

Learning Communities Program

One of UA's major First-Year Experience Program initiatives, the Learning Communities Program, was originally created in 1995 with the design of developmental LCs for the most academically at-risk first-year students. From their inception through the academic year 2000–2001, developmental LCs focused on basic math, basic writing, and study skills. Because of the retention success of these LCs, the program was expanded to include more of the first-year class in various majors, special interest groups, and in living-learning communities. The first-year seminar (i.e., the Student Success Seminar) serves as the anchor for the majority of learning communities. LC teams consist of full- and part-time faculty, administrators, academic advisors, and graduate teaching assistants. UA learning communities use variations of three basic models (i.e., student cohorts in larger classes; paired courses; and team-taught, fully thematic, integrated LCs) all designed to promote and accomplish active learning and civic engagement. The LCs now encourage diversity by design since they meet entering students' needs across the educational spectrum, as evidenced by provision of the following academic and special interest learning communities:

◇ *Major-specific LCs* include, but are not limited to, nursing, education, engineering, business, communications, liberal arts, criminal justice, allied health, political science, statistics, developmental, and honors. During fall 2009 semester, UA piloted a new STEM Exploratory Learning Community for first-year, nondeclared majors, adopting Science Education for New Civic Engagements and Responsibilities (SENCER) pedagogy and integrating a STEM-driven civic issue into multiple disciplines across the University. The thematic course sequence is purposefully designed and heavily focused on scientific inquiry, applied data analysis, discovery, service-learning, and information literacy within a project-based, situated learning environment. Biology, chemistry, mathematics, public health, and engineering concepts are integrated into well-developed student writing, speaking, and teamwork assignments.

◇ *Nontraditional LCs* involving adult students—25 years of age or older and now equaling 23% of UA's undergraduates—have been created to help foster community for adult learners who are beginning or returning to college. The UA Adult Focus Program, an academic support service created and administered specifically to help nontraditional, adult students, provides two learning communities offering five-week courses revisiting effective study strategies (e.g., memorization techniques, study tips, test-taking strategies, and critical thinking). The Student Success Seminar and the Career Planning Course are also included in the learning communities.

◇ *International LCs* have been created to aid foreign-born students in acclimating to the urban Akron, Ohio area, American customs and traditions, college life in general, and specifically to the traditions and culture of UA. The International Learning Community also provides ESL sections of English Composition and Speech.

◇ *Students of Color LCs* were designed to promote social and academic integration of this population and to develop strong UA affiliations through personalized advising and peer mentoring. They include the Preparing Akron Students for Success and Great Expectations (PASSAGE) LC and the Four Phase Advising System (4PAS) LC. Another new pilot learning community is the African American Male Learning Community, intended to address high dropout rates during the first year. Addressing self-image and retention through leadership, civic engagement, and participation in the Student African American Brotherhood (SAAB), the LC confronts challenges faced by African American male students within the academy.

◇ Residential and Commuter LCs extend the program's academic basis, enabling students to experience the atmosphere of a small college within the facilities and programs of a large university. Campus life is a great way to experience the unique UA culture and diversity.

◇ Special Interest Living-Learning Communities support and enrich the academic major LCs (e.g., Business Leadership Connection; Dance and Theatre: The Artists' Community; Future Education Professional; Honors Emerging Leaders Community; Ritchie Emerging Leaders Community; Nursing: Living, Learning, and Leading; Women in Engineering; and Exploratory Learning Communities). Each is designed to extend and solidify the academic LCs through increased faculty support, formation of study groups, exploration of creative and intellectual potential, scheduled guest speakers, social activities, and provision of unique mentoring and support opportunities.

Alliances have been built with all the undergraduate colleges, evolving into a team of dedicated professionals who clearly strive to change the learning culture on UA's campus. Learning communities have increased by 93% since fall 2003.

Another unique feature of UA's learning communities is their origin. While many LC programs nationwide are residential programs, UA's began with an academic foundation and then branched into the living-learning component. Living-learning communities were established in 2001 to provide an educational setting where academic success would be supported through the residential experience. In each of these communities, the students live on a common floor in the residence halls to create a network for leadership, communication, and reinforcement of major-specific skills.

Because UA is a large research university, it was necessary to use three nationally accepted curricular models (i.e., student cohorts within larger classes; paired or clustered courses; and fully integrated, team-taught programs) with the ultimate goal that all would evolve into team-taught programs. The following LC examples demonstrate the three models:

◇ *Small LC cohort in larger classes.* The four Nursing Learning Communities, cohorts of 20–25 students, are part of large lecture sections (i.e., more than 250 students) in Introduction to General, Organic and Biochemistry and in Introduction to Sociology. The student cohorts are then self-contained in English Composition, the large lecture's lab sections, and the Student Success Seminar, taught by the University College academic advisor specifically assigned as liaison to the College of Nursing. The academic advisor/LC instructor creates an intentional, collaborative, and ongoing partnership with the students, sharing accurate and timely information that enables students to navigate the educational system and reach educational, personal, and career goals.

◇ *Paired or clustered courses.* The three Statistics Learning Communities each pair the Statistics for Everyday Life lecture and the Student Success Seminar. The faculty in these classes work together to coordinate their syllabi and assignments to help beginning statisticians grasp statistics concepts and apply and integrate them into daily life.

◇ *Team-taught programs.* The four Exploratory (i.e., undecided majors) and two Pre-Education LCs exemplify truly integrated, thematic LCs. A service-learning project partners these LCs, comprised of 120 UA students, and two of the Akron Public School district's elementary schools. UA students work with elementary children by tutoring them in reading. All LC curricula (i.e., English Composition, Intro to Public Speaking, the Student Success Seminar, and Career Planning) focus on active learning, varied teaching pedagogy, civic engagement, and integration of assignments and curriculum. The capstone portfolio project represents the cumulative result of classroom teaching and curriculum integration, service-learning, and mentoring relationships between the UA students and the elementary school children developed through the service-learning project.

Results and Lessons Learned

Time necessary to coordinate the program creates a significant administrative challenge. Tasks such as cultivating relationships with departments, scheduling courses, working to streamline logistics, faculty recruitment and professional development, student recruitment, and program evaluation take considerable time. Learning communities have an administrative home in University College; nonetheless, many courses are taught in other colleges. Campus leadership team participation has helped to spread feelings of ownership and responsibility for the LC effort. Since more people on campus have shared the vision of what LCs can accomplish, more support and assistance has become available.

Nevertheless, obtaining faculty buy-in and enlisting their participation in the LC program has been an ongoing challenge. Instructors teaching first-year learning community students include full-time and part-time faculty, administrators, contract professionals, and graduate teaching assistants. Due to individual teaching loads, research and professional development activities, and the time required to integrate LC curricula, it is difficult to attract senior faculty to the program. While part-time faculty have participated in the LC Professional Institute and are interested in the LC concept, some are reluctant to spend the extra time out of class needed for coordination and planning.

The creation of the annual Learning Communities Professional Institute, however, has helped to overcome unfamiliarity LC goals and pedagogy innovations and has increased faculty buy-in. During the Institute, faculty spend dedicated planning time shaping the goals and assessment efforts of each community. This kind of early focus on learning outcomes has provided direction and integration of classroom assignments and grading.

To demonstrate the effectiveness of the Learning Communities program to faculty, staff, administrators, and the university community at large and to improve the program on a continual basis, a plethora of qualitative and quantitative assessment tools have been used, including descriptive and inferential statistics, student and faculty surveys, student and faculty focus groups, faculty professional development training, and an on-site visit by representatives of the National Learning Communities Project at the Washington Center for Improving the Quality of Undergraduate Education. The LC Program concluded a longitudinal, outcome-based assessment examining student satisfaction, progression toward degree, academic standing, cumulative GPA, and overall retention. Results of the three-year assessment include the following:

⋄ LC students tend to earn more credits per semester than non-LC students.
⋄ LC students have higher retention rates than non-LC students.
⋄ According to UA's Office of Institutional Research, retention from fall 2007 to fall 2008 semesters for UA's first-time, full-time first-year cohort was 68%; retention of Learning Communities Program participants overall, from fall 2007 to fall 2008, totaled 73%.
⋄ The 73% LC retention rate is the highest retention figure for any UA undergraduate program, four-year or two-year at UA within the last 20 years.

Conclusion

The University College Learning Communities Program could not be successful without the cooperation of the other undergraduate degree-granting colleges at The University of Akron and their respective faculties. Another key component in the program's success is the synergistic collaboration with UA's Student Affairs Division, specifically the Registrar's Office and the Residence Life Program, and other unique campus outreach programs (i.e., the Learning Assistants Program and the University Park Alliance Business Association) as well as the UA's Institutional Research and Center for Organizational Research.

From its inception, the mission of UA's Learning Communities Program has been to enhance the quality of undergraduate education; foster a climate of innovation; increase the sense of community and collaboration between students and faculty; improve first-year students' retention, overall GPA, and credit hour production; and promote a climate of assessment of student learning. Assessment results provide evidence that the program has achieved these goals and that learning communities have become a vital component of UA's First-Year Experience initiative.

CHAPTER 4

Holistic Support for Learning

Dorothy Ward

While involvement in undergraduate curriculum is an essential element of the university college model (as addressed in chapter 3), university colleges' support of student success is not limited to the classroom. Recognizing that teaching and learning occur in a variety of venues, through a variety of instructional approaches, at a variety of learning points or opportunities, university colleges administer a wealth of effective instructional programs that provide holistic support for student learning. This chapter examines how university colleges increase student learning through the connection of curricular and cocurricular support, enhanced instructional services, and development of students as teachers and learners.

Since the last half of the 20th century, institutions of higher education have broadened their view of who should have an opportunity to earn a college degree. With access to college no longer restricted to the select few, colleges and universities recognize the need, as well as their obligation, to provide effective programming to support student development and learning and to increase students' opportunities for academic and personal success. As stressed in a recent National Leadership Council for Liberal Education and America's Promise (LEAP) report (2007), institutions of higher education must also recognize that it is not sufficient to offer a collection of courses that add up to a degree; educational programming must help students learn to "integrate and apply their learning" and build "real-world capabilities" (p. 4). Drawing on data from the National Survey of Student Engagement (NSSE) Annual Report, Kuh (2007) describes effective educational practices as ones that

◇ Require students to invest significant "time and effort to purposeful tasks"
◇ Require students to "interact with faculty and peers about substantive matters"
◇ Increase students' interaction with individuals "who are different than themselves," helping them "develop new ways of thinking"
◇ Allow students to receive "frequent feedback about their performance"
◇ Encourage students to apply their learning "in different settings"
◇ Engage students in activities that help them "better understand themselves in relation to others and the larger world" (pp. 7–8)

University colleges provide a structure that allows for a more comprehensive approach by offering programs that provide holistic support for student learning. These programs help students with the integration and application of their learning both inside and outside the classroom, both on and off campus, making their learning more relevant to their lives. As such, university colleges work to support effective educational experiences in a variety of contexts.

The case studies and data provided by colleges and universities in response to the recent survey conducted by the authors of this monograph (see chapter 1) demonstrate the breadth of programming university colleges provide to support student development and success. Holistic learning support includes innovative approaches to instruction through the classroom venue, but learning support also wraps around the classroom. Acknowledging that learning occurs both inside and outside the classroom, university colleges offer programs to educate the whole student, contributing to the student's academic and personal development. Table 4.1 demonstrates the breadth of learning support for which university colleges have responsibility as evidenced by our survey. These programs are, of course, in addition to the first-year seminar and learning communities already addressed in chapter 3.

Table 4.1

University College Responsibility for Learning Support Services

Service	Primary responsibility	Shared responsibility
Learning centers	60%	26%
New student orientation	41%	47%
Study skill instruction	41%	40%
Tutoring/mentoring	41%	38%
Supplemental Instruction	41%	24%
Academic advising	34%	60%
Peer advising	31%	24%
Career planning	12%	40%
Service-learning	7%	22%
Student leadership development	3%	33%
Instructional technology	2%	9%

Such programs are also likely to introduce students to the kinds of educational experiences advocated by Kuh (2007). These programs deepen students' learning, enhance their academic lives, and support their personal development, providing them with learning opportunities that are relevant to their growth as individuals as well as their success as students.

Connection of Curricular and Cocurricular Support

The traditional separation of the curricular and cocurricular experiences of students is no longer viable if colleges and universities are to meet the challenge laid out in the LEAP (National Leadership Council, 2007) report calling for institutions to "become far more intentional themselves—both about the kinds of learning students need, and about effective educational practices that help students learn to integrate and apply their learning" (p. 4). In order to support the development of the whole student versus focusing only on the academic side of the student, university colleges provide intentional learning opportunities that extend beyond the classroom walls. In fact, many of their programs integrate the students' curricular and cocurricular experiences, blurring the traditional boundary between academic and psychosocial support.

Generally housed in academic affairs, university colleges often form collaborative bonds with student affairs to integrate students' curricular and cocurricular experiences. Those collaborative connections may be as formal as jointly funded positions or shared responsibilities for the administrative oversight of programs, or as informal as first-year seminar instructors requiring students to participate in campus activities and organizations. As described in a chapter 2 case study, at Indiana University Purdue University at Indianapolis (IUPUI), university college and student affairs jointly fund the position of assistant vice chancellor for student life and learning to assist with the integration of curricular and cocurricular experiences. This shared position works to effectively promote activities that help engage students with their campus and their community. This type of formal connection helps to reduce what Boyer (1990) describes as "bureaucratic fiefdoms" that divide academic and "student life concerns" (p. 4).

Another common university college supported connection that helps to integrate curricular and cocurricular experiences for students is the living-learning community. While living-learning models vary, all residence-based learning communities seek to connect students' academic and social lives by organizing around disciplines or themes. The residence facility generally provides space for instruction, tutoring, and advising, and special programming that is both academic and social. In living-learning communities, the faculty presence varies from simply attending special programming or teaching in the residence hall to keeping an office in the students' residential facility or actually living in the residence hall.

An additional key educational practice that extends student learning beyond the classroom and into the community is service-learning. Jacoby (1996) defines service-learning as "a form of experiential education in which students engage in activities that address human and community needs together with structured opportunities intentionally designed to promote student learning and development" (p. 5). As indicated by the definition, service-learning places students in environments that allow them to interact with a variety of individuals outside the classroom where they can apply what they are learning in the class to meaningful activities. While 29% of respondents to the survey for this monograph indicated either primary or shared responsibility for administering service-learning on their campus, the percentage of university college programs, such as first-year seminars, learning communities, and student leadership programs, engaged in service-learning may be higher. In fact, of the institutions that responded to the 2006 National Survey on First-Year Seminars, 40.2% indicated that they include service-learning in their first-year seminars (National Resource Center for The First-Year Experience & Students in Transition, 2006).

Service-learning is an effective extension of student learning beyond the classroom. A summary of service-learning research in higher education from 1993–2000 shows that service-learning has a positive effect on students' personal, social, and learning outcomes and improves students' satisfaction with college (Eyler, Giles, Stenson, & Gray, 2001).

University colleges also provide student leadership programs. While only 3% of university colleges that responded to the survey for this monograph reported primary responsibility for student leadership development, 33% indicated shared responsibility. It is not surprising that student leadership development is a responsibility for one third of university colleges. First, university colleges focus on supporting the development of the whole student; leadership development addresses the individual's academic and psychosocial abilities. Second, university colleges offer programs that help students connect with their campus community; student leadership is an approach that extends the development of the institutional connection initiated through first-year programming. Additionally, university college units such as learning centers, new student orientation, first-year seminars, and mentoring programs all potentially use student leaders. Leadership development programs help prepare students to assume important peer educator roles in university college programs.

These are just a few of the ways that university colleges seek to provide holistic support for student learning, but they exemplify the manner in which university colleges seek to respond to Boyer's (1990) challenge for institutions of higher education to connect students' curricular and cocurricular lives: "How can life outside the classroom support the educational mission of the college?" (p. 5).

As is apparent, university colleges develop programs that foster the connection, and sometimes the integration, of curricular and cocurricular support for student success. Collaboration among university college units and between university college and the broader campus allows for a network that supports students' academic and personal development. This holistic support helps prepare the students for success in the classroom and beyond.

Enhanced Instructional Support

University colleges are generally creative in their varied approaches to supporting student success. This creativity may result in part from the university college's commonly held mission to assist with students' successful transition into institutions of higher education, which requires a network of support for students. It also stems from the understanding that the whole student must be addressed for the successful transition to occur. This creativity extends to the manner in which university colleges provide instructional support.

University college units commonly create teams to assist with instruction of students. This team approach allows students to benefit from the expertise of each member and broadens the network of support for the students. The team approach is commonly used in first-year seminars. In fact, 43.7% of the institutions that responded to the 2006 National Survey on First-Year Seminars indicated that they use the team approach for their first-year seminars (National Resource Center for The First-Year Experience & Students in Transition, 2006). Learning communities also use the team approach, but this varies depending on the design of the community and level of integration among the courses. With learning communities, the team approach can be as simple as course instructors working together to monitor the progress of students in their linked courses or may be as sophisticated as coordinated studies programs where instructors team-teach an interdisciplinary theme.

Whether for a first-year seminar or a learning community, the instructional team members are intentionally selected to provide a network of learning support for students. Depending on the type and design of the first-year seminar or learning community, the instructional team may consist of faculty who are dedicated to university college programs, in joint appointments, or selected from across campus; staff or administrators from academic or student affairs, undergraduate or graduate students, academic advisors, librarians, and counselors, including career counselors. As is evident by the list of potential members, the team often includes representatives from offices commonly viewed as external to the traditional classroom.

The team approach is used at IUPUI and addressed in one of this chapter's case studies. At IUPUI, all first-year seminar courses and themed learning communities are taught by an instructional team consisting of a faculty member, academic advisor, librarian, and peer educator. Though all members provide support for student success, they play different roles on the instructional team.

Using a team approach to instruction also increases students' interaction with key university staff members, such as academic advisors. This integration of academic advisors into the classroom or learning environment provides opportunities for students to interact with advisors throughout the semester rather than the students' more traditional once-a-semester visit to an advisor's office. As a result, students receive real-time responses to their advising-related questions and concerns, develop a stronger relationship with an advisor, and gain an appreciation of the importance of academic advising and planning to their academic success and career goals. Students' interaction with academic advisors has a significant impact on their students' development. The 2007 annual report of the National Survey of Student Engagement (NSSE) indicated that "frequent contact with the advisor was related to greater self-reported gains in personal and social development, practical competence, and general education, and more frequent use of deep approaches to learning" (p. 23). Students with greater advisor contact also indicated that they were "generally more satisfied with their institution" (NSSE, p. 23).

The importance of advisors and effective advising to student development and success is further emphasized by Light (2001) when he stated, "Good advising may be the single most underestimated characteristic of a successful college experience" (p. 81). The survey results for this monograph indicate the important connection between university colleges and academic advising, with 34% of university colleges reporting primary responsibility and 60% reporting shared responsibility for academic advising. University colleges recognize that advisors can work in a range of venues through a variety of collaborations to support students' educational development and personal growth.

Learning centers, which are responsible for providing tutoring and other academic support programs for students, are university college units with which academic advisors often collaborate. At many universities, academic advisors have responsibility for administering special programs for at-risk students. These at-risk students may be individuals who entered the institution with a probationary status or students whose academic performance has identified them as at-risk students. Often, mandatory tutoring or attendance at workshops conducted by the learning center is monitored by academic advisors. Such is the case at Ball State where participation in such a program allows disqualified first-year students the opportunity to re-enroll. This relationship between advising and the learning center makes evident to students the institution's intentional network of support for student success that extends beyond the classroom.

Instructional support for students can also be enhanced through technology. Students entering colleges and universities today have grown up using computers, Internet, and state-of-the-art technology for entertainment, information, and instruction. Technology can enhance learning for the Net Generation student, especially when it is used to provide instruction that is interactive and engaging. Web-based course management tools, such as Blackboard, can help facilitate student-to-student discussions; student-to-faculty communications; and delivery of course materials, such as the course syllabus, calendars, articles, and assignments. These course management tools can also administer quizzes and exams, allow students to submit assignments online, and access the course material at their convenience 24 hours a day. Technology can engage students in course instruction both inside and outside of the classroom.

Online programs and modules can support classroom instruction in highly interactive ways. Commercial programs such as DISCOVER allow students to examine their values, abilities, and interests in relation to career options. Other programs, such as Alcohol 101 Plus, engage students in thinking critically about alcohol use. Though only 9% of respondents to the survey for this monograph indicated shared responsibility for instructional technology, university colleges at some institutions (e.g., The University of Texas at El Paso) have developed online modules to support instruction of academic skills, such as time management, lecture note-taking, and annotation in the first-year seminar. Instructors can integrate these modules into the course curriculum, but the interactive design of the modules also allows students to revisit them as frequently as they deem necessary. Whether commercially produced or university produced, the interactive nature of online programs are likely to engage students and enhance instruction.

Effective use of technology is not limited to formal courses. Academic advising, learning centers, and writing centers can also use technology to provide instructional support to students. Web sites, videos, and podcasts all allow students to access instructional support when they need it.

Whether through a team approach or effective integration of technology, creative techniques for supporting instruction of students allow university colleges to provide learning support in the classroom and beyond. These instructional enhancements help prepare the student for success in college.

Students as Teachers and Learners

University colleges recognize the positive effect of employing students in peer educator roles. Such employment allows university colleges to intentionally harness the powerful impact peers have on students' academic and personal development (Astin, 1993; Pascarella & Terenzini, 2005). Serving as peer educators also has a positive impact on students who assume such roles (McDaniels, Carter, Heinzen, Candrl, & Wieberg, 1994; Hart, 1995). Recognizing that the role of peer educator allows a student to serve as both teacher and learner, university colleges employ peer educators in many of their units and in a variety of positions. Students assume roles including, but not limited to, peer educators in first-year seminars and learning communities, student orientation leaders, peer advisors in advising centers, Supplemental Instruction leaders, mentors for transitioning students, and tutors in learning centers.

In addition to working directly with students, peer educators can also be employed to help create and administer programs that support student development and academic success. The challenging role of peer educator requires students to apply their learning to real-world situations. These experiences also demonstrate characteristics Kuh (2007) described for effective educational practices because they "challenge students to develop new ways of thinking about and responding . . . to novel circumstances as they work side-by-side with peers on intellectual and practical tasks, inside and outside the classroom, on and off campus" (p. 8). Regardless of the specific type of peer educator role, the position provides numerous benefits for all involved. Peer educators benefit the students they serve, the institution for which they work, and they, themselves, gain personally from the experience.

Students have a significant influence on other students. Since peer educators are students who have successfully transitioned to the college or university, they can serve as effective role models for entering students. They represent the values of the institution, and they can help students translate the university experience. Lynch (2001) explains that peer educators serve an important role for transitioning students because they can "model cultural codes while acting as translators of the new language so that new students do not become marginalized and frustrated" (p. 23).

Astin (1993) concludes that "the student's peer group is the single most potent source of influence on growth and development during the undergraduate years" (p. 398). The peer educators' closeness in age and experience to the students they assist gives them credence that students might not grant to a faculty or professional staff member who does not resemble the student population in age or professional status. This credibility makes peer educators especially effective in addressing appropriate behavioral or skill set development for success in the collegiate environment. Peer educators can talk about academic success skills, such as time management or test preparation, and they can address issues related to responsible behavior in academic and social settings with an authority not awarded by students to most faculty or staff members who, as professionals, are removed from the experience the students are living. Through interaction with peer educators, students gain important instruction they need to support their academic and personal development.

The closeness in age and experience may also make the peer educator seem to students more approachable than perhaps the faculty or professional staff member. This identification with peer educators provides students a sense of comfort that allows them to ask peer educators questions or voice concerns that might otherwise remain unasked or not addressed.

There are numerous ways that peer educators benefit institutions of higher education. A major responsibility of colleges and universities is to promote student learning and development. Through the employment of peer educators, institutions can intentionally determine and direct the student's leadership development. For example, as reported in the Kennesaw State case study in this chapter, the former president, Betty Siegel, advocated for the institution's responsibility to lead students "to a deeper understanding of the values of service, moral imagination, civic responsibility, and diversity." With this charge in mind, Kennesaw State created the Center for Student Leadership in an effort to develop "a culture where leadership was fundamentally connected to engaged activity and where students viewed themselves as having not only the ability but also the responsibility to be leaders."

Meaningful on-campus employment of students also supports an institution's retention efforts. In fact, Astin (1993) found that "holding a part-time job on campus is positively associated with attainment of a bachelor's degree and with virtually all areas of self-reported cognitive and affective growth" (p. 388). He noted that this positive impact of on-campus employment is explained by the "concept of involvement: compared to students who spend an equivalent amount of time working off campus, students who are employed on campus are, almost by definition, in more frequent contact with other students and possibly faculty (depending on the type of work)" (p. 388).

Working as peer educators increases students' involvement with the institution and strengthens their connection to it. Peer educators recognize that they are no longer simply students at the university; they are also university employees with the responsibility to represent the institution for which they work in a positive light.

Peer educators provide a cost-effective means to positively impact student success. They can reduce the cost of programming for university college units because they can reduce the number of faculty and professional staff members required to provide a program's services. For example, the University of Rhode Island case study describes how a single professional staff member used peer educators to operate the Academic Enhancement Center that served the entire university campus. Peer educators can also assume responsibilities for activities that do not require the attention of a professional, allowing faculty and professional staff to address areas that require their level of expertise. For example, peer educators working as instructional team members in first-year seminars or learning communities can arrange for guest speakers or can design a scavenger hunt to familiarize students with campus resources, freeing up time for the instructors to focus on other responsibilities.

Gardner (2001) points out another important benefit of the peer educator to institutions of higher education. Peer educator programs provide a means for academicians to be intentional about "recruiting our successors" by providing them "valuable insight into our work" (pp. vii-viii).

The peer educator roles also benefit the students who assume them. Through his research, Light (2001) has determined that "students who get the most out of college, who grow most academically, and who are happiest organize their time to include activities with faculty members, or with several other students, focused around accomplishing substantive academic work" (p. 60). The role of peer educator accomplishes the above. Peer educators often work with a faculty member or a professional staff member to accomplish "substantive academic work," which may take the form of program development, mentoring, tutoring other students, or classroom instruction.

Assuming the role of peer educator also helps students with their own academic development. Whitman (1988) explains that peer educators increase their knowledge of the subject matter through their preparation to teach it. As peer educators, students gain important leadership skills, develop communication skills, learn to work with a diverse population, and apply their knowledge in a variety of situations both in and out of the classroom. In the Victoria University case study that appears in this chapter, the peer educators reported an improved sense of knowledge and confidence in their subjects.

Working as peer educators may also impact students' educational and career choices. Peer educators often discover the personal satisfaction of working in higher education or in teaching. As a result, students may change majors or career paths in response to this discovery.

Summary and Conclusion

University colleges recognize the importance of providing holistic support for student learning both inside and outside the classroom. Though generally housed in academic affairs, university colleges provide programs that address not only the cognitive development of students but also their psychosocial development so that the needs of the whole student are addressed. Through the connection of curricular and cocurricular, enhanced instructional support, and development of students as teachers and learners, university colleges work to increase student learning and personal development in a manner that helps students with the integration and application of their learning. This holistic support for learning provided by the colleges helps support students' academic and personal development, increasing students' opportunities for academic and personal success. The case studies that follow demonstrate a variety of approaches university colleges have used to provide holistic learning support on their campuses. Additionally, the case studies show how university colleges engage faculty, staff, and students in innovative, collaborative efforts that provide students a holistic network of support for learning.

References

Astin, A. W. (1993). *What matters in college? Four critical years revisited*. San Francisco, CA: Jossey-Bass.

Boyer, E. L. (1990). Foreword. In Carnegie Foundation for the Advancement of Teaching, *Campus life: In search of community* (pp. xi–xiii). Lawrenceville, NJ: Princeton University Press.

Eyler, J. S., Giles, D. E., Jr., Stenson, C., & Gray, C. M. (2001). *At a glance: What we know about the effects of service-learning on college students, faculty, institutions, and communities, 1993–2000* (3rd ed.). Nashville, TN: Vanderbilt University.

Gardner, J. (2001). Foreword. In S. L. Hamid (Ed.), *Peer leadership: A primer on program essentials* (Monograph No. 32, pp. v–viii). Columbia, SC: University of South Carolina, National Resource Center for The First-Year Experience and Students in Transition.

Hart, D. (1995). Reach-out advising strategies for first-year students. In M. L. Upcraft & G. L. Kramer (Eds.), *First-year academic advising: Patterns in the present, pathways to the future* (Monograph No. 18, pp. 75–82). Columbia, SC: University of South Carolina, National Resource Center for The Freshman Experience and Students in Transition.

Jacoby, B. (1996). *Service-learning in higher education: Concepts and practices*. San Francisco, CA: Jossey-Bass.

Kuh, G. D. (2007). If we could do one thing. . . In National Survey of Student Engagement, *Experiences that matter: Enhancing student learning and success* (pp. 7–10). Bloomington, IN: Center for Postsecondary Research, Indiana University Bloomington. Retrieved from http://nsse.iub.edu/NSSE_2007_Annual_Report/

Light, R. J. (2001). *Making the most of college: Students speak their minds.* Cambridge, MA: Harvard University Press.

Lynch, C. (2001). The successful operation of a peer leadership program. In S. L. Hamid (Ed.), *Peer leadership: A primer on program essentials* (Monograph No.32, pp. 23–35). Columbia, SC: University of South Carolina, National Resource Center for The First-Year Experience and Students in Transition.

McDaniels, R. M., Carter, J. K., Heinzen, C. J., Candrl, K. I., & Wieberg, A. M. (1994). Paraprofessionals: A dynamic staffing model. *Journal of Career Development, 21*(2), 95–109.

National Leadership Council for Liberal Education and America's Promise. (2007). *College learning for the new global century.* Washington, DC: Association of American Colleges and Universities.

National Resource Center for The First-Year Experience & Students in Transition. (2006). *Preliminary summary of results from the 2006 National Survey on First-Year Seminars.* Retrieved May 11, 2009, from http://sc.edu/fye/research/surveyfindings/surveys/survey06.html

National Survey of Student Engagement (NSSE). (2007). *Experiences that matter: Enhancing student learning and success.* Bloomington, IN: Center for Postsecondary Research, Indiana University Bloomington. Retrieved from http://nsse.iub.edu/NSSE_2007_Annual_Report/

Pascarella, E. T., & Terenzini, P. T. (2005). *How college affects students: A third decade of research.* San Francisco, CA: Jossey-Bass.

Whitman, N. A. (1988). *Peer teaching: To teach is to learn twice* (ASHE-ERIC Higher Education Report No. 4). Washington, DC: Association for the Study of Higher Education.

Chapter 4 Case Studies

Ball State University

Academic Advising and Learning Support Through University College

Michael Haynes & Laura Helms

The Institutional Context

Ball State University is a comprehensive public institution in Muncie, Indiana, with an on-campus enrollment of approximately 17,000 students. Nearly 3,600 students are admitted in the first-year class every fall, and all first-year students are required to live in residence halls unless commuting. The average SAT math and verbal scores for the first-year class are 522 and 515, respectively. Of the total on-campus student population, 55% are female, 5% are age 25 or above, and 8% are ethnic minorities.

University College

Established in 1985, University College at Ball State is a multifaceted support college with a range of administrative and programmatic responsibilities that impact all Ball State students and nearly all faculty. Housed in the division of Academic Affairs, University College is the home of Academic Advising, the Learning Center, Academic Support for Student-Athletes, Academic Systems (i.e., catalog, course schedule, degree audit, automated course transfer system), and support for the core curriculum and interdisciplinary programs.

All students, including graduate students, are eligible to use services in University College. The entire first-year cohort (i.e., approximately 4,500 students) are part of the advising program, and students who are undecided have special services available through University College. Many class-related accommodations for students with disabilities are coordinated through the Learning Center, as are many academic support services for all students.

Academic Advising and Learning Support

The key units of University College at Ball State (i.e., Academic Advising and the Learning Center) work together to provide learning support for all Ball State students from orientation through graduation. The objectives of the academic advising program are to provide students with necessary and useful information in a timely manner; to be accessible, particularly for students in the first year; and to communicate a caring attitude in all work with students throughout the system. Advisors contribute to the development of the student academically, helping the student move toward commitment to an academic plan and develop confidence and independence in working within the University. The Learning Center provides academic support through tutoring, Supplemental Instruction, and focused workshops.

Summer Support: Pre-Matriculation

In the summer before matriculation, all incoming students interact with Academic Advising through the orientation program, and students who are interested also participate in a special academic workshop called Early Start.

The orientation program at Ball State is a two-day event for both families and students. Professional advisors meet with students and their families for one hour on the first day. The emphasis in this meeting is on information (i.e., core curriculum requirements, credit hours for graduation, grading policies, and the basics of building the first schedule). On the second day, each student has a personal meeting with an advisor for 30 minutes to talk about the student's goals and concerns and to build the first academic schedule. These two days with Academic Advising begin the process of helping the student become a focused and independent learner. At the same time that the students are developing their first schedule, the families are receiving an orientation to the Learning Center so that they understand that the students have free and convenient access to focused academic support.

Developed and administered by the Learning Center, the Early Start Program (ESP) provides new students with a short-term academic orientation to the University accomplished through a series of credit workshops held in the summer before fall matriculation. For each individual Early Start week, students live on campus, attend one academic workshop, and participate in a variety of cocurricular activities. Each workshop carries one hour of elective credit applied toward the students' fall class schedules. Workshops are developed by faculty representing all seven academic colleges. The topics cover diverse disciplines but share a common feature of hands-on experience with appropriate academic expectations. Workshop topics include Crime and Chemistry, Television News Production, and Teaching Writing in the Elementary Classroom. For the 2007 program, 242 students registered for one of the workshops. The University provides financial support to keep attendance affordable; students pay only $100 for the entire experience, including room and board, all classroom supplies, recreational activities, and the credit attached to each workshop. Each program year, student and faculty satisfaction with the experience is very high as documented by thorough program evaluations.

The short-term benefits of ESP have been clear to all involved in the program: students (a) enrolled in the fall semester following the program at a higher rate than all confirmed first-year students in the same class, (b) earned higher first-semester GPAs than their peers, and (c) showed higher retention rates into the sophomore year.

Support Through the First Year

All first-year students at Ball State have a professional academic advisor to assist them in academic planning and decision making. As the student moves through the first year, the advisor is aggressive in seeking regular contact to offer special information and help. Advisors develop portfolios of useful materials (e.g., planning guides, time management guides, summaries of academic support opportunities, individual degree audits) that are made available to all students through individual meetings and electronically. A major emphasis for advisors is the importance of using the services of the Learning Center.

The Learning Center provides free individualized and group peer tutoring for all core curriculum courses and other courses perceived as high risk and offers Supplemental Instruction (SI) in selected classes. Learning Center coordinators and graduate assistants hire and train approximately 150 peer tutors and SI leaders. Tutoring and Supplemental Instruction serve as important learning opportunities for students, and the College Reading and Learning Association tutor training certification process offers tutors many opportunities to engage in service-learning and experiential learning projects. During the 2005–2006 academic year, 3,938 students attended 31,950 tutoring and SI sessions.

The first-year advisors are also a significant part of the Ball State learning communities program, Freshman Connections. Certain classes in the core curriculum are linked to residence halls; students who take those classes live in reasonable proximity to each other, which facilitates study groups and other forms of mutual support. Instructors, residence hall directors, and academic advisors form teams who together seek to engage the students in both curricular and cocurricular activities. For the first-year advisors, the Freshman Connections program becomes another means of establishing communications and relationships with other first-term, first-year students.

Making Achievement Possible (MAP) is a survey[1] for all first-year students that asks questions about academic background and goals and then generates a personalized summary for each student of how he or she fits at Ball State, what might need to be changed (e.g., too many time commitments), and what services are available to address the student's particular concerns. A summary of each student's written report is available to his or her academic advisor, which helps the advisor raise pertinent questions about issues of adjustment, academic confidence, and academic goals.

All first-year advisors work with undecided students, and approximately 25% of each matriculating class is unsure of a major or still in some stage of exploration. Virtually every advising conversation involves some aspect of exploration and decision making. Students who are unable to discover an academic path in a reasonable length of time are referred to the University College major/minor coordinator who is responsible for the following pieces of undecided student services:

◇ Meeting individually with undecided students in assessment and planning sessions, which include a four-phase process of individual assessment, feedback, referral to faculty and student contacts in high-interest majors, and academic planning and scheduling. From 2001–2006, the major/minor coordinator completed more than 2,000 undecided student exploration sessions.

◇ Teaching ID 101: The Freshman Seminar for Undecided Students. Through assessment, instruction in decision making, and exposure to University and community resources, undecided students enrolled in this seven-week course establish their preferences, explore major and career options, and prepare a major exploration portfolio with the goal of deciding on a college major by the end of the first semester.

◇ Collaborating with academic departments to identify seniors to serve as resources in program planning and in the Senior Very Informed Person (VIP) program. The VIP program recruits seniors representing every major and many minors to work with exploratory students. The seniors agree to have their academic information and e-mail addresses published in a directory available through their advisors. Undecided students then contact them for information about their academic experiences. A recent addition to the VIP Directory is the inclusion of Senior VIP alumni who can provide a real-world perspective about work life after Ball State.

The coordinator also serves as academic advisor to approximately 100 undecided sophomores.

For many years, Ball State has had an aggressive academic dismissal policy for first-semester first-year students. Fall-semester matriculates must earn a minimum grade point average of 1.0 to continue enrollment into the spring semester. Those first-year students who fail to do so are academically disqualified and must sit out two semesters before they are eligible to re-enroll. The University has followed an appeals process to this policy that offered continued enrollment only to those students who could document severe illness or other situations that adversely affected their academic performance. In general, those students who won appeals failed to succeed in the next semester. In 2006, the University initiated a pilot program, Academic MADE, for students automatically disqualified after their first terms. Named after the popular MTV show, MADE offers enrollment in the next semester to all disqualified first-year students on the condition that they sign an educational agreement, follow a prescribed individual success plan that includes required meetings with academic advisors and Learning Center tutors, and earn a minimum 2.0 GPA for the spring semester. University College staff monitor MADE students' progress weekly; those students who fail to honor their individual plans face immediate dismissal at any point and forfeit paid tuition and fees. Of the 124 students who submitted MADE contracts in December 2006, 112 finished the spring semester, and 76% of these students earned higher spring GPAs than the disqualification averages they had earned in the fall. More than a quarter (27%) earned the required 2.0 GPA to continue enrollment in the following semester.

The Partnership for Academic Commitment to Excellence (PACE) is a program for new students who are on academic probation after their first semester. Students are placed on academic probation if their GPA falls below 2.0 after the first semester. At the conclusion of the fall 2006 semester, 511 first-semester students were placed on academic probation. PACE is an aggressive program that helps students identify what went wrong and develop strategies for getting things back on course. Heavy emphasis is placed on attending Learning Center workshops especially designed for students in academic distress and on seeking focused tutoring in high-risk classes. About 60% of the students in the PACE program are eligible to return to the University the following semester.

Academic Support Beyond the First Year

Students who have completed at least 30 credits and have chosen a major move from the first-year program to departmental advising. To support the faculty in their advising responsibilities, the Advising program has several centers located across campus. Each is staffed with a professional advisor (a coordinator) and an assistant. The centers support faculty advising by offering training sessions for advisors, being available to answer questions and update records, meeting with transfer students who have earned 30 or more credits, and by coordinating the entire graduation process. While supporting faculty advisors, the coordinators also are available to students as a backup advisor, ensuring that a student always has a ready source for specific advising information. Learning Center support is available to all students, and many students use the services throughout their academic tenure at Ball State.

Results and Lessons Learned

When University College was developed in 1985, it was controversial. The primary emphases of University College were working with underprepared and undecided students, and the money to support programming came from adjustments to budgets throughout Academic Affairs. The critical element for initial success was the commitment and stability of the senior administration, particularly the president and the provost. Both were convinced the program would be successful and were unwavering in their support. Of course, the provost brought along the support of the deans, who in turn helped convince the faculty of the importance of the program.

Every program in University College collects data, and over time the programs that University College developed and administered were able to show success. Tutoring, Supplemental Instruction, support programs for students in academic distress—all consistently show clear, positive results. Ball State's retention rate improved, not exclusively because of University College services, but certainly the academic improvement of students using the services was clear. For example, data indicate 2004 Learning Center clients were retained at a higher rate into the sophomore year than their peers (i.e., 82.3 % vs. 76.9%) despite holding weaker academic credentials. In addition, participants in the spring 2007 PACE program earned higher GPAs and moved off probation at a higher rate than their peers who did not participate. Faculty also appreciated the support they received through Advising and through the Learning Center, and it became evident that University College was marketable to prospective students and their families and to legislators. At this point, University College seems very much a part of the identity of the university.

Notes

[1] Originally developed by a team from Ball State's Academic Advising and Learning Center and housing and assessment units, the survey is now available for use on other campuses through Educational Benchmarking, Inc.

Indiana University–Purdue University Indianapolis

A Holistic and Collaborative Approach to Academic Advising

Catherine A. Buyarski

The Institutional Context

Indiana University–Purdue University Indianapolis (IUPUI) is a public, four-year commuter institution located in downtown Indianapolis, Indiana. With more than 28,000 students representing 49 states and 139 countries, IUPUI is the second-largest campus in the Indiana University statewide multiple-campus system. IUPUI is an urban research and academic health sciences campus, with 22 schools and academic units that grant degrees in more than 200 programs from both Indiana University and Purdue University.

In fall 2008, IUPUI enrolled 28,722 students, 19,970 of whom were at the undergraduate level, with 3,040 new beginning students. The University has an enrollment of 17,932 full-time students and 10,840 part-time students. IUPUI has a significant adult (i.e., age 25 and over) student population represented by 13,261 learners. Approximately 1,100 students live on campus. Of those, 64% are first-year students.

More than half (57%) of IUPUI students are female. Total minority enrollment represents almost 16% of the total student population: African American (9.1%), Asian/Pacific Islander (4%), and Hispanic (2.5%). Finally, 44% of undergraduate students are first-generation, defined as neither mother nor father having completed a college degree.

University College

As part of institutional efforts to provide one portal of entry to the multiple degree units and support student success, the IUPUI Faculty Council approved the formation of University College in spring 1997. The founding faculty (representing all degree-granting schools at IUPUI) and the dean were appointed soon thereafter, with the first students entering the College in summer 1998. The founding faculty approved the following mission statement:

> University College is the academic unit at IUPUI, which provides a common gateway to the academic programs available to entering students. University College coordinates existing university resources and develops new initiatives to promote academic excellence and enhance student persistence. It provides a setting where faculty, staff, and students share in the responsibility for making IUPUI a supportive and challenging environment for learning.

All students entering IUPUI are granted admission to University College (either full or dual admission with a degree-granting school). Students remain in University College until they have declared a major and meet the necessary conditions for transfer to a degree-granting school. Approximately 6,500 are enrolled in University College each year.

Programs and services offered by University College focus on assisting students with the development of the knowledge and skills needed for success in the collegiate environment, including academic advising, academic support, first-year seminars, themed learning communities, academic mentoring, new student orientation, and the campus honors program. University College also offers several college readiness programs, which focus on helping area students become college bound.

Academic Advising

The IUPUI University College Office of Academic and Career Development is holistic in its work with students a well as in the nature of the programs it offers. University College functions as an academic unit on the IUPUI campus and therefore all programs, including academic advising, have learning as the focus. The learning outcomes for academic advising encompass both cognitive and psychosocial gains. Advisors function as teachers in that they facilitate learning both in the classroom and through their one-on-one interactions with students.

Mission and Learning Outcomes

The attention to both affective and cognitive student outcomes is articulated in the mission statement for the Office of Academic and Career Development:

> Academic and Career Development facilitates students' academic and career success by providing programs and services that engage students in exploring and committing to educational and career goals, developing and implementing meaningful academic plans, transitioning into degree granting schools, and translating learning to the world of work.

The focus on the academic and career success of the student implies that the student's whole person is considered when engaging in goal setting and planning. Often, a student's personal challenges can affect educational achievement and out-of-class experiences can impact in-class learning. An emphasis on meaning gives purpose and direction for the manner in which these diverse factors are considered in advising conversations.

The mission guides the overall work in the Office of Academic and Career Development, while established learning outcomes point to specific actions advisors must take in their work with students. The establishment of outcomes moves advising out of the realm of student services to become a meaningful forum in which learning occurs. It also forces advisors to become teachers of a curriculum for student learning. The National Academic Advising Association (NACADA, 2006) describes the curriculum of advising as including

> the institution's mission, culture and expectations; the meaning, value, and interrelationship of the institution's curriculum and cocurriculum; modes of thinking, learning, and decision-making; the selection of academic programs and courses; the development of life and career goals; campus/community resources, policies, and procedures; and the transferability of skills and knowledge. (para. 7)

Specific learning outcomes identify "what students will demonstrate, know, value, and do as result of participating in academic advising" (para. 9).

Because of the numerous programs and services offered to a diverse group of students, learning outcomes are established for specific types of advising interactions. Learning outcomes for the advising portion of the New Student Orientation program are set at the knowledge level and include such outcomes as the student's understanding of the components of a degree program, awareness of campus resources, and ability to make future contact with their advisor. In contrast, learning outcomes for students who are meeting with an advisor to discuss academic probation focus on higher-order outcomes, such as the ability to articulate challenges to academic success faced by the student, compare and contrast alternative solutions, and evaluate past techniques for achieving academic success.

Classroom-Based Delivery of Advising Services

All first-year seminar courses and themed learning communities at IUPUI are taught by an instructional team comprised of a faculty member, academic advisor, librarian, and student mentor. The faculty member serves as the course coordinator and primary instructor; the advisor supports students individually and is often the instructor for class sessions focusing on academic skill development; the librarian teaches information literacy; and the student mentor facilitates the development of classroom community and interprets the college experience from a student perspective. The advisor in the first-year seminar course is a student's assigned academic advisor throughout his or her enrollment in University College, and students will meet individually with the advisor at least once during the first semester of enrollment in addition to seeing the advisor in class each week.

By attending class each week, advisors are able to engage in timely advising that addresses student's academic issues in an opportune and relevant manner. Advisors arrive early and stay late at each class session to informally visit with students and ascertain any problems or issues. They make weekly announcements about critical academic dates, deadlines, and resources. By attending class sessions, advisors are able to identify and intervene with students exhibiting high-risk behaviors, such as missing class meetings and turning in assignments late. Overall, through regular interaction, students are taught the importance of working closely with an advisor to achieve college success.

By fall 2010, every student enrolled in a first-year seminar (i.e., currently about 90% of all incoming students with 17 credits or less) will complete a personal development plan, which will serve as the foundation for future academic planning and advising sessions. As each student creates his or her plan, the advisor will facilitate the student's exploration of their strengths and challenges as they relate to collegiate success and majors and careers. The four-year personal development plan outlines not only course sequencing but also participation in powerful pedagogies, including study abroad, undergraduate research, and internships.

Integrated and Collaborative Staffing Structure

As a centralized advising unit, the University College Office of Academic and Career Development is only as good as the connections to degree-granting schools and campus resources that support student success. The most effective tool in establishing these collaborative campus connections has been an innovative staffing structure in which most University College academic advisors work half time in University College and half time in a degree-granting school or campus program.

Advisors are hired jointly by both University College and the degree-granting school; time is divided through either work hours (20 hours in each location) or through work patterns throughout the academic year. For example, an advisor may work primarily in University College during the summer to assist new students in entering IUPUI and more hours in the degree-granting school at the point in which applications for the degree program are evaluated or when seniors are being audited for graduation. Advisors in this role are able to see the big picture of advising from entry to graduation and assist in building smooth transitions from University College to the degree school. They serve as the primary conduit for shared communication such as curriculum updates. In addition to joint advisors with academic programs, a joint advisor is in place with the Office of Residence Life allowing for advising to occur in campus housing.

Given the intense vocational focus of IUPUI students, one of the strongest collaborations has occurred with the IUPUI Career Center. Beginning in 2001, three joint staff members worked half time as advisors and half time as career counselors. In 2004, the Career Center physically moved its location to shared space with academic advising, meaning that students were able to go to one location for both advising and career counseling. Advisors and career counselors met monthly for information sharing and cross-training. In 2007, the University College Academic Advising Center and the IUPUI Career Center were formally merged into one office with truly shared staff, space, and programming.

Strong collaborative relationships have been formed with student services units, including Admissions, Financial Aid, Registrar, Adaptive Educational Services, and International Affairs. In most cases, a specific advisor is assigned to serve as the liaison to the student service and is expected to take a proactive approach in reaching out and sharing information. Further, the Office of Academic and Career Development (OACD) has staff members who serve as lead persons for collaborative programming with new student orientation, themed learning communities, and first-year seminars. These staff members serve as members of the planning committees for these campus programs to ensure that the advising role is supportive of programmatic goals and that the contributions of the advisor are maximized.

Finally, as the largest group of professional advisors on campus, the OACD has taken campus-wide leadership for professional development for faculty and staff advisors. The office has hosted annual advising conferences and a series of workshops on topics including working with at-risk students, using technology to support advising, and serving millennial students. In addition, OACD has served as the leader in establishing a campus advising council to address policy issues as well as a campus organization for academic advisors.

Results and Lessons Learned

The success of the OACD rests in the full integration of the curricular and cocurricular support programs offered by the unit as well as the campus. Through these collaborations a seamless network of support for students is created, and people work in partnership to achieve established goals. OACD has been nationally recognized as an outstanding program by the National Academic Advising Association in 2001, 2002, 2003, 2005, and 2010. Further, an internal self-study indicated that advisors' facilitation of student goals (e.g., helps me set concrete academic goals, encourages me to continue to pursue my goals even when I encounter difficulties, helps me develop alternatives when I have faced obstacles) had a significant positive relationship with scores on items adapted from the Academic Hope Scale (Snyder, Sympson, Ybasco, Borders, Babyak, & Higgins, 1996). In addition, there was a strong positive relationship between scores on hope-related items and cumulative grade point average. These findings suggest that academic advisors in University College, through their holistic focus on facilitating students' goals, are impacting students' levels of academic hope, thereby, indirectly leading to higher levels of student achievement.

Along the way, several lessons have been learned. First, campus networks must be actively built through risk taking, reaching out, and beginning the conversation with others. Potential partners can be identified by looking at established learning outcomes and asking which campus units and individuals can help to make the learning a reality for students. Second, it is important to recognize that relationships with other campus units may be rocky at first and take time to develop. The first person hired into a joint advising position often had difficulty navigating the maze of differing expectations from his or her two reporting lines. Constant communication and negotiation can help in moving through these hurdles. Finally, it is important to be open about the strengths and weaknesses of the advising program. Units should welcome feedback from other campus constituents, particularly in cases where the needs of a specific group of students are not being met. Moreover, they should be the first to recognize and admit limitations while eagerly embracing the opportunity to move forward. When building collaborative partnerships, we cannot be entrenched in our own way of conducting business or worried about protecting egos.

References

National Academic Advising Association (NACADA). (2006). *Concept of academic advising.* Retrieved September 4, 2007, from http://www.nacada.ksu.edu/Clearinghouse/AdvisingIssues/Concept-advising-introduction.htm

Snyder, C. R., Sympson, S. C., Ybasco, F. C., Borders, T. F., Babyak, M. A., & Higgins, R. L. (1996). Development and validation of the State Hope Scale. *Journal of Personality and Social Psychology, 70*, 321–335.

Kennesaw State University

The LINK to Student Leadership Development

Rebecca Casey & Brian Wooten

The Institutional Context

Kennesaw State University (KSU), 30 miles northwest of Atlanta in Kennesaw, Georgia, is a four-year, comprehensive university with expanding undergraduate and graduate programs. Founded by the University System of Georgia's Board of Regents in 1963 as a two-year institution, KSU has grown rapidly and is now the third-largest university in the state. Residential communities opened in 2002, and more than 13% of KSU's undergraduates now live on campus.

KSU's fall 2009 student population included 20,304 undergraduates. Of those students, 76% were enrolled full time, and 14% were first-year students. The majority (59%) were female. While the students had an average age of 24, the median age was 22. The minority population constituted 25% of the total undergraduate population, and 6% of undergraduates were from foreign nations. KSU students can choose from more than 60 undergraduate, master's, and doctoral degree programs and have access to more than 150 student groups and organizations.

University College

Although KSU has a long history of successful first-year experience and transitional programs, the University College (UC) is relatively new, developed and implemented through the recommendations of an advisory body in 2004. As one of 12 founding institutions in the Foundations of Excellence® in the First College Year Self-Study by the Policy Center on the First Year of College (now John N. Gardner Institute for Excellence in Undergraduate Education), KSU formed a task force to examine the first college year. Several significant actions resulted from this project's task force, including the recommendation that a specific organizational structure to house first-year initiatives be developed, which ultimately resulted in the creation of KSU's University College, the seventh and newest college on campus.

KSU's University College was envisioned providing integrated interdisciplinary programs and coursework as well as leadership in undergraduate programs. The most important aspect of the formation of University College was the hiring of 10 new faculty members and the creation of the University College Advisory Council (UCAC), a body appointed to develop a mission and vision statement, create joint-appointment guidelines, and garner campus-wide buy-in for the new College. Much of the group's energy was devoted to the successful implementation of the curriculum requirement for first-year students, which included participation in a first-year seminar or a learning community. Although the College originally consisted of a single academic department, University Studies, a second academic department, First-Year Programs, was added to house all faculty associated with the new curriculum requirement. This department, configured in July 2007, housed two programs (i.e., Learning Communities and KSU 1101) and the faculty who teach in them.

Center for Student Leadership

While president of Kennesaw State University, Betty Siegel focused on building a culture of leadership development on campus, and she began to investigate how to integrate the general education curriculum so that students would have a stronger connection to this philosophy in these courses. In addition, she wanted to create an academic home for all first-year students and a place to house the necessary resources for supporting their success. From this vision came the development of University College with a goal of providing students with a more holistic education by linking rigorous content traditionally associated with academics and active learning traditionally associated with student affairs. To achieve this mission, the Center for Student Leadership (CSL) was proposed, with one of the new UC faculty positions, jointly appointed between the Academic Affairs division and Student Success and Enrollment Services (SSES), to serve as the Center director. Having a tenure-track faculty member as director would ensure a strong connection with academic affairs, while the responsibility of integrating out-of-class experiences would maintain the link to SSES. In 2004, a permanent director was hired and charged with developing a full strategic plan to establish the Center and advance KSU's focus on student leadership development.

Several leadership development programs already existed on campus; however, each targeted a different audience. The Northwest Crescent Leadership Alliance connected five students from KSU with five students from five other institutions in the Northwest Crescent of Georgia. The Presidential Fellows program provided seniors and graduate students the opportunity to personally interact with the University president to discuss leadership after their college experience. The Leaders IN Kennesaw Program (LINK) offered a three-year ethical leadership certificate program. The initial step in planning the Center was to move these programs to CSL.

The development of CSL solidified the intentionality of leadership training and provided opportunities for students to practice leadership skills in concrete ways. The signature program was LINK, which teaches students leadership skills and theory through participation in weekly modules and application of those skills through various service projects. In the first phase of the program, LINK Emerge, students learn basic leadership skills and develop an understanding of how their personality impacts their leadership style. The second phase of the program, LINK Ascend, focuses on skills and theory related to working within a team. Students in this third year of the program, LINK Leads, learn skills that will enable them to take an idea and enact the necessary program to impact various social issues. Each level of leadership development integrates civic engagement activities with leadership education, providing students with opportunities to learn skills and knowledge related to being an ethical leader and apply those skills in a practical way in local, national, and international communities to strengthen their understanding. Upon completion of the three-year program, students are awarded an ethical leadership certificate. In addition, these students become catalysts in building a KSU community focused on leadership.

To encourage more campus-wide involvement in the Center's development, CSL identified the following goals:

◇ Be seen as an institutional resource for students to find information on leadership and ethics
◇ Provide innovative programs that would develop a student's knowledge and skills as an engaged, ethical leader
◇ Garner faculty support and participation in mentoring students
◇ Provide students with opportunities to engage in applied research that would benefit the community

◇ Partner with the various colleges of the University to integrate leadership development specific to their curriculum
◇ Create a culture where leadership was fundamentally connected to engaged activity and where students viewed themselves as having not only the ability but also the responsibility to be leaders

A team of KSU student fellows were given the task of conducting research and creating a comprehensive survey of best practices that would serve as the basis of the Center's initial strategic plan. The team of students worked for one semester, meeting weekly with various members of the University as well as the local community to determine the needs for a leadership center. In addition, the student team facilitated a comprehensive review of institutions and organizations around the world that provided leadership opportunities. The information and research gleaned from these explorations provided the strategic planning team with the information necessary to create the Center.

As the student fellows continued their work, a 32-person committee was formed representing all divisions, units, and members of the University and were charged to think boldly and aggressively about the direction of the new center and create a plan establishing it as a national model for developing civically engaged global leaders. The committee met biweekly for an entire semester and, in 2005, submitted the full strategic plan for the Center for Student Leadership.

Because CSL was a part of University College, the group planned to have civic engagement projects that would connect with KSU's first-year populations. Students within the first level of the LINK program practiced leadership skills initially by serving as orientation leaders and, later, as peer leaders for the first-year seminar. Through these activities, leadership skills were developed and reflection opportunities provided to students. As this program grew, there was a need to add opportunities for students beyond their first year to practice leadership skills and abilities in different environments. CSL developed partnerships with area middle schools and assigned students within the program to visit a specific school twice per week to work with students struggling with their academic assignments. The program followed the same format of other programs with students applying skills and reflecting on what was learned. As students entered their third year of the program, an international dimension was added to the curriculum by including an opportunity to develop an international project. Students articulated an issue and determined an area of the world to build relationships with students in that location. Students then traveled to the country and worked with student leaders from that region on the specific issue chosen. The LINK program continued to expand by providing curricular programs, which targeted specific disciplines, such as the College of Math and Science.

In addition to LINK, other targeted leadership programs were gradually added. These new programs included a Women's Leadership program, outdoor leadership initiative, and other specific programs specifically designed for students in the Arts. To accommodate the program growth, within the past three years, the staff has grown to include eight professionals and five research fellows. In addition, CSL has integrated leadership education into the curricular offerings by adding courses to the Honor's program, learning communities, and first-year seminar.

Results and Lessons Learned

The development of CSL has provided great opportunities for KSU students. The key to its success has been the strong connection between Academic Affairs and Student Affairs divisions. Faculty have supported the leadership initiatives because of the academic focus while students have been more likely to participate due to the active learning components of the programs offered. Achievements include

◇ A significant growth in the number of students applying to the LINK program, increasing from 41 applicants in 2004-2005 to 138 applicants in 2007-2008
◇ More than 365 hours of service to the community provided in 2006 by first-phase LINK students
◇ A decrease in the ratio of LINK leaders to new students at orientation (i.e., from 28 to 1 in summer 2004 to 13 to 1 in summer 2007)
◇ Adoption in 2006 of an team advising approach (i.e., student leader, academic advisor, and KSU1101 instructor) resulting in a significant increase in students reenrollment (i.e., 85% reenrollment rate for team-advised students compared to a 65% rate for comparison groups)
◇ Fall 2007 GPAs of 3.0 or higher for 85% of LINK students with a large percentage (45%) attaining a GPA of 3.5 or higher
◇ Integration of a leadership curriculum into specific KSU 1101 classes and learning communities connecting with more than 200 students in fall 2007
◇ Introduction of an international civic engagement project in phase three of the LINK program resulting in a 2007 collaborative student partnership in Ghana, West Africa, and plans for a 2008 project in Salvador, Brazil
◇ Receipt of an endowment to support CSL's international civic engagement projects
◇ Receipt of a grant from the Center for Excellence in Teaching and Learning (CETL) to employ five students to complete a program assessment of the overall LINK experience, ensuring the program's relevancy, rigor, and retention
◇ Development of new, credited courses, including an honor's leadership course and a foreign study class with the opportunity to go to Oxford University

The success of CSL speaks to the interconnectedness between Academic Affairs and Student Success and Enrollment Services: students, faculty, and staff have collaborated in its development. Members of the initial committee have served as advocates for the Center and continued to educate the academic community on our mission. Through the work of two faculty members, the Center has, in addition, coordinated with the College of the Arts and the College of Science and Math to offer specific programs for those student populations. The leadership skills we hope to build in our students will be based in academic achievement and critical thinking, not a fixed set of behaviors or superficial rhetoric. We look forward to helping KSU students act locally, nationally and globally to promote community and understanding, whatever their direction in life.

University of Rhode Island

Using a Participatory Organizational Development Model to Create a Comprehensive Learning Assistance Center

David Hayes

Institutional Context

The University of Rhode Island (URI) is the flagship of the state's public higher education system and its principle public research institution. It is a land grant, sea grant, and urban grant institution, with a 2007–2008 enrollment of 12,516 undergraduate and 2,564 graduate students. URI's 10 colleges offer 117 baccalaureate, 57 master's, and 33 doctoral degree programs.

In 2007–2008, URI's undergraduate population was approximately 56% female and 88% under the age of 25. The majority (72.2%) of undergraduates identified as Caucasian, 4.8% as African American, 4.8% as Hispanic, 2.3% as Asian, and 0.7% as Native American. Approximately 10% of students did not report identification with any racial/ethnic category.

University College

URI's University College is the college to which all incoming undergraduate students are admitted, regardless of declared major. It is not a degree-granting college; rather, it functions to support students through faculty-based and professional advising; the Academic Enhancement Center; the URI 101 first-year seminar; learning and living/learning communities; coordination of the University's internship, orientation, experiential learning, service-learning, study abroad, and athletics advising programs; and a range of collaborative efforts with degree-granting colleges. Its motto (i.e., We welcome you, we support you, we challenge you.) captures the scope of this work.

While many of its services, including academic enhancement, are extended to all URI students, University College's primary focus is to provide holistic support to students in transition—from orientation through matriculation into a degree-granting college. University College is a function of academic affairs, although its orientation is very much toward the development of the whole student. Some programs support the academic success of specific populations (e.g., athletes, students of color, high-performing students, at-risk students), but its overarching goal is to provide opportunities for growth to students at all levels of academic development. University College also offers hundreds of opportunities annually for undergraduate and graduate students alike to earn academic credit or wages for work in tutoring, counseling, advising, and mentoring as well as program development and management.

Launching the Academic Enrichment Center: Opportunities and Challenges

In 2003–2004, University College introduced the Academic Enhancement Center (AEC). Launched as an expansion of a smaller tutoring initiative (i.e., Learning Assistance Network), the AEC was envisioned as a comprehensive learning assistance center, which would establish collaborative relationships within each of the University's colleges and create peer-driven, supports based on needs identified by students and other stakeholders. University College was an ideal location since it supported the academic transition and development of new students, and the AEC fit perfectly within University College's mission. The Center's proximity to departmental faculty advisors, who conducted advising hours within University College, New Student Programs, Early Alert, and other FYE programming, greatly facilitated outreach, referral, and collaboration.

The Center's motto (i.e., Teaching is Learning) reflects an approach to learning support that is grounded in a participatory pedagogical model (Friere, 1970). From the start, the AEC's goal was to create and sustain a community of peers where students could tap into their collective knowledge and experience to take ownership of one another's learning. Importantly, this philosophy of student's self-leadership was embraced not only in teaching practice, but all aspects of development and administration, including policy development, staff development, and management. This approach was as much a function of necessity as philosophical preference: institutional interest was strong, but in a state university that ranks 50th in the nation in per student spending, funding was very limited. While centers at similar-sized universities often function with a staff of professional specialists and coordinators, URI's initial AEC funding provided for only one professional staff position. To succeed, the Center needed to rely on students not only as tutors, but also to fill organizational and administrative roles typically held by professionals. As a result, the AEC became an organization of, by, and for students.

The process has worked well. With little change to its budget or staff (a second professional position was added in 2007), the AEC has become a partner to all of the University's colleges. Its combined programs now record more than 12,000 student contacts per year. Its participatory staff development techniques, which have earned certification from the College Reading and Learning Association, and programs have been have been presented at national conferences. Its Supplemental Instruction (SI) program has been able to demonstrate a link between program participation and higher course GPAs for three consecutive years.

Adapting Participatory Pedagogy for LAC Development and Tutoring

The participatory pedagogical model embraces the existing knowledge, wisdom, needs, and self-authoring ability of students by involving them directly in curricular development and collaborative teaching. Students and teachers function as knowledgeable co-experts, collaborating to meet the students' needs. Under a participatory organizational model, an organization evolves through a similar integration of cross-hierarchical knowledge. Every interpretation of experience is permitted, and authentic, experiential wisdom is considered valid and valuable. Expertise is by no means devalued, but critical reflection and dialogue help build consensus. Two key assumptions behind this approach at the AEC are that (a) students can identify how they work best and what they require if given an effective process for doing so and (b) they are likely to invest themselves more deeply in their work if it derives from self-identified need.

For educators and program developers who are used to working in more top-down, decision-making models, a participatory approach can feel disempowering. One's knowledge becomes only a part of what is known, and applications for that knowledge sometimes only become clear after work has begun. When it works, though, the results it yields for the program and for the students involved can be very powerful.

At the AEC, all organizational structures and functions have arisen through participatory processes, with definitions and benchmarks of success deriving from research and models of best practice and from immediate experience, student evaluation, staff reflection, and faculty input. All student staff become active agents in the development of organizational expertise. They are encouraged to value research and best practices and to use their experience as students and learning assistants to question those practices and to develop responsive approaches to meeting students' needs.

At the center of the organizational developmental structure is a reflexive staff development process consisting of multiple mechanisms for questioning, sharing, assessing one another's work, developing innovative strategies and techniques, and identifying areas for organizational improvement. The process functions both as a training and development program and as a feedback loop for program assessment. Components allow for multiple forms of engagement and reflective dialogue, and what emerges informs subsequent training, programming, and policy decisions.

During preservice training, program structures, policy overviews, learning theories, and tutoring models are critically examined, with staff using role plays, scenarios, and other collaborative activities to critique program and tutoring theory. Once the semester is underway, an ongoing staff development process facilitates collaborative critical analyses of issues emerging in practice. Monthly training meetings and weekly SI check-ins enable tutors to share experiences, question assumptions, and strategize solutions. A weblog (staff are mandated to post twice per month; many do more) encourages longer, more reflective and varied discussion threads. A peer observation process allows staff to watch one another in practice then debrief, sharing observations and comparing approaches. Semesterly intercultural communication competence workshops enable students to analyze race, ethnicity, culture, gender, disability, and other forms of interpersonal difference that affect their interactions.

For student administrative staff, training also involves several summer meetings in which the prior year is reviewed; revisions to policy, assessment instruments, and other processes and practice are arrived at, and fall training and programming are planned. Once the year is underway, administrative staff meet weekly to evaluate work and progress and plan activities.

The participatory design ensures that training, programming, and policy remain responsive to practice and practice remains responsive to student needs. Issues that are identified in one area (e.g., a weblog discussion) will often inform work in another (e.g., a subsequent workshop). Some issues gain significance over time and across discussions.

Results and Lessons Learned

The level of personal involvement in the growth process can yield multiple learning outcomes. A few years ago, for example, several tutors began questioning the value of teaching specific note-taking methods. They understood the theory behind the methods but felt uncomfortable teaching them because they did not use the methods themselves. The discussion grew to address how high-performing students often took very different approaches to studying. This conversation moved onto the weblog where other staff contributed. Eventually, a group of students developed and implemented an action research project to explore what characterized successful students' work.

When an SI leader in a precalculus course began devising original, index-card based activities to increase students' motivation and engagement with their sessions, she posted her activities on the weblog. Other math practitioners began using, then modifying, the techniques. The SI coordinator, seeing this activity, used the core methodology as a focal point for subsequent training. Staff suggested a handbook of SI facilitation techniques to help the current group but also to initiate an ongoing process of collecting and sharing learned techniques.

As staff involvement has transformed the Center's practice, it has transformed staff members' lives as well. For many, involvement in AEC work has even been a catalyst for changes in career paths or professional goals. More commonly, students who work at the AEC comment that the experience has benefitted their own academic work in that the knowledge they have gained about learning and studying has helped them elevate their own academic performance. They also note that the process of reflecting on the relationship between prescriptive methods and their own practice has been a catalyst for this growth.

While the participatory process can enable significant growth among staff, it can also create struggle for students and the organization. For the Center to function in the absence of sufficient professional staff, professional-level work is required of student staff, regardless of their experience.

For nearly all students, working at the AEC is an education in professional behavioral development. Students are challenged to define their work, to understand how their part supports the whole, and acquire the interpersonal skills and job skills needed to perform effectively. Directing this process requires functioning both as a teacher and as an organizational director to challenge students to work as independently as they can, without losing sight of their developmental needs. The fact that the AEC itself has been a work-in-progress complicates matters. While programming becomes more fixed, responsibilities increasingly defined, and the learning process itself better understood, the need for student staff to perform professional-level work will always be a limitation on organizational growth. Every year, new programs are piloted, each with new goals and responsibilities and requiring ongoing, reflexive modification. Over time, it has become easier to make work and performance expectations explicit to potential staff and to gauge applicants' needs and abilities. It is still not easy, however, to find students who have the critical thinking ability, maturity, and self-confidence to work independently and responsively under these conditions. Many initiatives have faltered or failed to develop due to lack of needed human resources.

Rapid turnover complicates this. Students are hired according to their potential; they are generally very inexperienced at first. Once hired, they work, reflect, and develop experience, insight, and expertise over time. Within a couple of years, many are functioning at a professional level of awareness about their work. Then they graduate, and the process of matching ability to work and developing skills through experience begins anew.

Every graduating class informs organizational growth and improvement. But the limits on experience and historical awareness hampers progress in the long run. Even as the Center learns to streamline administration, develop more effective training, and better define roles, each graduation means a new start.

Of course, these dark clouds have silver linings as well, and learning centers seeking to develop according to a participatory model can find opportunity in the turnover problem. Staff turnover is gradual, so the development of new staff becomes a learning opportunity for all. Again, this highly participatory, collaborative process enables all students to draw from their own strengths, knowledge, and experience, deepening the expertise of veteran staff while challenging new staff members' to build on their existing understanding. Moreover, this constant renewal of ideas ensuring that AEC's approaches remain firmly grounded in the expressed needs and perceptions of the people it serves.

Conclusion

By using a participatory model of organizational development, and a participatory pedagogical approach to tutoring, the AEC has enabled students to identify and build upon their own knowledge, creating models of learning support that are grounded in authentic student experience and needs and becoming a hands-on lab environment where students develop teaching, organizational development and administration, and leadership skills. Importantly, it has done so with a limited budget in an increasingly difficult economic climate. For colleges wanting to develop a learning center on limited resources, a strategy that taps into the organic knowledge of the community to be served rather than relying entirely on the expert knowledge of people in the professional field, a participatory process may also be an inviting cost-efficient approach.

References

Friere, P. (1970). *Pedagogy of the oppressed.* New York, NY: Continuum.

University of Texas at El Paso

Integrating Technology Support Into a First-Year Seminar

Sunay Palsole, Andrea Berta, & Kathy Stein

Institutional Context

The University of Texas at El Paso (UTEP) is a public institution designated doctoral research intensive, with an enrollment of approximately 19,800 students. UTEP is a minority majority institution and among the largest Hispanic-serving institutions in the nation. The demographic closely reflects that of El Paso, with the campus population being more than 70% Hispanic. The majority of students commute and are the first in their families to attend college. A large number also work more than 20 hours a week. Given these situational factors, the University has focused on helping students achieve academic and lifelong success.

University College

In 1999, UTEP's Entering Student Program (ESP) was inaugurated in response to growing concern over the large number of first-year students who ended their first year with GPAs below 2.0 and/or who failed to return to the University for their second year. The program consisted of two courses: (a) UNIV 1301 Seminar in Critical Inquiry for first-year students with fewer than 30 semester credit hours and (b) UNIV 2350 Interdisciplinary Technology in Society for transfer students or those with more than 30 hours semester credit hours. Both courses count towards UTEP's core curriculum. The Seminar in Critical Inquiry is primarily designed to help students acquire study skills while learning content and prepare them for academic life. This case study refers to the support structures created for the Seminar in Critical Inquiry.

Instructors were recruited from all disciplines and colleges and were paid a $1,000 stipend for teaching the course as part of their work load. Training workshops aided instructors in integrating study skills, knowledge of campus resources, and the language of academia with their discipline-based theme to help students make the transition from high school to the University.

The positive impact of the Entering Student Program resulted in an increase in first-year student retention. To support the efforts of the program and to promote an atmosphere at UTEP that encouraged the development of close ties between students and the University campus along with academic success and persistence, UTEP organized the University College in September 2001. The organization of the University College was supported in part by a grant from the Department of Education. Along with the Entering Student Program, University College consisted of the following departments: the Academic Advising Center, Admissions and Recruitment, Financial Aid, New Student Orientation, the Registrar's Office, Student Assessment and Testing, and the Tutoring and Learning Center (TLC). In 2003, Developmental English and Developmental Math joined University College.

Technology Support in the First-Year Seminar

UNIV 1301 Seminar in Critical Inquiry was piloted in 1999 with 785 students. The theme-driven and discipline-based seminar was designed to enhance student engagement within the campus community.

This course is taught by faculty and staff with varied backgrounds, few of whom have formal training in teaching study skills. While the theme-based course content was well-structured, many of the instructors had difficulty integrating the study skills training into their curriculum. Several study skills textbooks were made available, but many instructors were resistant to the idea that these texts could adequately teach students skills that were innate to the instructors or even that such instruction was necessary. To help with the delivery of study skills strategies, UTEP hired a multimedia coordinator to develop online study skill modules as separate entities in themselves. The purpose behind developing the online modules was to create an anywhere/anytime environment for their use and make the task of incorporating study skills easier for the faculty members so they could concentrate on the course content. The development of the modules was written into the original grant that supported the creation of the University College.

The Multimedia Advisory Group was assembled to work with the multimedia coordinator to determine which study skills would most benefit instructors and students and the order in which modules for each skill would be developed. Membership in the Multimedia Advisory Group was extended to staff and faculty in all colleges and offices involved with the first-year experience. The order of module development was the following: time management, lecture note taking, annotation, exam prep (i.e., essay and multiple choice), and financial literacy. The time management and lecture note-taking modules were completed in 2002, the annotation and exam preparation modules in 2003, and the financial literacy module in 2004.

All the modules were designed using Macromedia Flash and were programmed to be user-friendly in online settings. Graphic designers worked along with programmers to ensure that the modules were usable and visually interesting. Modules were interactive and engaged students in tasks such as dragging and dropping icons representing courses or study time into the time management module, or taking part in a game that asked the player to make financial decisions, which if correct, earned the student a game piece. The key element to the modules was a reflection assignment that brought together the results of the activities and students' perceptions of how this would affect their academic lives. New interactive elements were developed periodically to maintain student interest. Data suggested that the students responded well to the engaging elements of the modules and completed tasks that were assigned by instructors.

Because of the need to report data to the granting agency, a database backend was used to track users. This meant that instructors had to be trained how to upload the rosters in the database. As each module became available, faculty were provided with instructional demonstrations and brochures.

Another stated goal of UNIV 1301 is to increase the incoming students' self-awareness concerning their participation in high-risk behaviors. To help instructors facilitate discussions concerning the use of alcohol, interactive CD-ROMs of Alcohol 101 were obtained from the Century Council, a group funded by the nation's distillers to discourage the inappropriate use of alcohol by young people. UTEP's Counseling Center was consulted and provided information to instructors about resources available to students who felt they might have alcohol issues.

UTEP's Counseling Center also provided assistance in meeting the purpose of helping students in goal clarification, assessing their own learning styles, and exploring possible career paths. The Counseling Center offered UNIV 1301 the use of the licensed product DISCOVER, an online interactive career exploration tool. In addition, Career Services personnel are often invited into the classroom to discuss DISCOVER results and other issues concerning career planning.

In the beginning, ESP did not have a dedicated computer lab in which faculty and students could access the modules and commercial software. UTEP's Access to Technology Learning and Services Computer Lab (ATLAS), an open-access computer lab for students, agreed to schedule UNIV 1301 classes. Walk-in students could not be accommodated because of the layout of the lab space. Therefore, the ATLAS Lab needed to be closed to general population students whenever a UNIV 1301 class was scheduled. Class time was frequently lost trying to escort general students out of the lab and waiting for modules or software to load on the lab PCs.

The need for a UNIV 1301 dedicated computer lab became more apparent as time passed. In 2003, ESP and the Tutoring and Learning Center (TLC) joined forces to create the UNIV 1301 lab, which was physically housed in the library as part of TLC. Additional benefits to housing UNIV lab in the TLC were twofold. One benefit was that students had to enter the library in order to use the lab. Far too many students were laying claim to graduating without ever having stepped foot in the library. Second, with the UNIV 1301 lab located in the TLC, instructors were able to tour the TLC facilities with their students and discuss the tutoring and workshop services available to students free of charge.

With the creation of the UNIV 1301 lab, scheduling of classes became easier. Tutors assigned to the lab had the computers set up for specific modules by the time each class arrived, thus allowing more time for work on the modules. Also, the creation of the dedicated UNIV 1301 lab meant that ATLAS was able to return to its original mission as an open-access computer lab for all students.

Both ESP and the TLC contributed funds for equipping the UNIV 1301 lab. Equipment includes 32 PCs, one server, a heavy-duty printer, an LCD projector, and relevant furniture. The room designated as the UNIV 1301 Lab needed to be rewired to update the electrical and network connections.

The TLC commitment to this project included a coordinator to oversee the lab, tutors to support the lab, and front desk personnel to schedule reservations and send e-mail confirmation reminders and handouts to accompany each module. TLC staff also tracked the overall usage of the lab whether it was to complete a module, watch a media presentation, or work on a PowerPoint or FrontPage project. The TLC not only tracked what activities took place in the lab but also when they took place by week throughout the semester. However, many instructors accessed the module online and never used the lab.

Students completed survey instruments after they finished each module. Feedback concerning the modules has been very good. UTEP history is used for the annotation and note-taking modules, and the Bhutanese influence on campus architecture is demonstrated throughout the design of all the modules. The interactive nature of the modules along with the ties in the module content and design to the UTEP campus appeal to the students and personalize their use. Administrative support for the modules has been both strong and intense. Even though not all UNIV 1301 faculty used the UTEP modules regularly, faculty appeared to take comfort from the knowledge that the modules were available. As the program has grown and once the stipend was no longer offered, the Entering Student Program opened more full-time positions. These full-time faculty members are the most consistent users of the lab and of the UTEP modules, indicating that familiarity with the program, the lab, and the modules increases usage of them.

Initially, it was difficult to get instructors to attempt the modules. Faculty often voiced concerns about the perceived difficulty of uploading rosters. In response to this challenge, the modules have been modified and are now available through student self-registration.

Communication with faculty about how to access the UNIV 1301 lab as well as how to use all of the modules and commercial products has been an ongoing challenge. Issues with scheduling as well as identifying the responsibilities of instructors in relation to lab usage require ongoing training every semester. For instance, the multimedia coordinator has no role in scheduling classes into the UNIV 1301 lab, but because he is so strongly identified with the UTEP modules, he still receives calls from instructors wanting to schedule time in the lab.

The Entering Student Program could not have developed the UNIV 1301 modules or established the UNIV 1301 lab in isolation. The synergy of brokered relationships between the ESP, numerous UTEP academic and service departments, and faculty and staff have resulted in better opportunities for student learning than would have been available otherwise.

Results and Lessons Learned

Institutions considering the creation of a computer lab like UTEP's UNIV 1301 lab or the development of modules for lab use should recognize several important points. The institution must commit to hiring an individual with very sophisticated multimedia and programming skills. In addition, a Multimedia Advisory Group should be convened to identify priority areas of service for the lab and modules. This group must be as diverse as possible and reflect the entire university, especially the academic units. Repeated training for the faculty on the use of the institutionally developed modules along with effective communication channels as to how to access the lab and modules should be instituted. Policies for the lab need to be well-considered and intentional and cover all aspects of its usage, including how to provide access to modules to those students who miss class on the day that activity is completed. An entering student program rarely has all of the resources it needs to implement innovations, such as the UNIV lab and the UTEP modules, but with cross-campus cooperation and relationships, goals can be met.

The peer leaders were also very effective at helping faculty understand the technology used in the UNIV Lab. After being trained in the use of the modules in the lab, peer leaders were generally the most effective advocates for the modules with the students.

A model based on the UNIV 1301 lab allows an institution to support the faculty and ease the incorporation of study skills into the classroom. The modules and lab provided the perception that teaching study skills could be easily incorporated into the instructors' repertoire of instructional strategies. Sometimes perception is as important as reality. It should also be understood that opening a lab such as this requires a financial investment on the part of the institution. Building the lab is step one; maintaining the lab with trained staff is an ongoing commitment that needs to be budgeted for from the beginning.

Net-generation students are technologically savvy, and it is important to meet them at their comfort level. Academia has to respond to the changing student population and that means incorporating more technology into the classroom experience. The UNIV 1301 lab and the UTEP modules offer interactive opportunities for students to practice skills that are necessary for their success in higher education and the workplace.

Victoria University (Melbourne, Australia)

The Student Peer Mentoring Program at Victoria University

Gill Best, Darko Hajzler, & Belinda McLennan

The Institutional Context

Victoria University (VU) has grown from its beginnings as a technical college in 1916 to being one of only five multisector universities in Australia. A multisector university is defined as one that incorporates courses for vocational, further, and higher education. Vocational and further education programs are equivalent to courses found in community and technical colleges in the United States. The higher education sector offers traditional undergraduate and postgraduate bachelor's degrees, masters by coursework, and research masters and PhDs.

In 2009, 55,572 students enrolled at VU, with 47,371 onshore, 20,151 in higher education, and 27,190 in vocational and further education. VU is a commuter university. It has 11 campuses located in the central business district and western suburbs of Melbourne, the capital of the state of Victoria. Melbourne's western suburbs are characterized by their lower socioeconomic status population compared with the east of Melbourne, and its cultural diversity has grown rapidly as successive waves of refugees and migrants have settled in the region. In 2007, 40% of VU's Australian students reported the use of a language other than English at home (Messinis, Sheehan, & Miholcic, 2008). Many of the students are the first in their families to attend university "and about 75% of students in the University come from families in the bottom half of Melbourne's socioeconomic distribution" (Messinis et al., p. 6).

The University College

The Victoria University College (VUC) was created in 2007 to maximize access and success for its students. The VUC incorporates courses and staff from each of the vocational, further, and higher education sectors, providing nationally accredited courses in English language, access, preparation, transition (transfer), and further education. In addition, the VUC coordinates and runs nonaccredited institutional programs and initiatives to support students' English language and learning needs. One of these programs is the Student Peer Mentoring Program (SPMP), which is part of Students Supporting Student Learning (S^3L), a wider, new student peer-learning initiative driven by the VUC (McCormack, Best, & Kirkwood, 2009).

The Student Peer Mentoring Program

The SPMP consists of a variety of group-based, face-to-face student peer mentoring programs located within and sometimes across faculties and sectors. One staff member of the VUC has an overall coordination role for the SPMP and is aided in this role by the manager of Counseling Services. The SPMP coordinator in the VUC works collaboratively with staff members to devise, maintain, develop, and assess the programs, including the conduct of student mentor training sessions and student mentor support. The SPMP has evolved through the creative application of evidence-based practice, which in turn has been adapted to meet the characteristics of a culturally and linguistically diverse student population. The SPMP focuses on building connectedness between students, their course of study, the institution, and the students and staff therein.

Each individual SPMP is group-based and exists in order to improve students' experience in a specific course, program of study, or transition. Individual programs vary in their structures and durations. The number of programs occurring at any one time also varies. Supplemental Instruction (i.e., SI, referred to as Peer Assisted Study Sessions or PASS in Australia) is a student peer mentoring model that is likely to increase in the institution after 2010. SPMPs align with Karcher, Kuperminc, Portwood, Sipe, and Taylor's (2006) recommendation that programs focus on both academic and social integration but with differing emphasis depending on the aims, context, and students' needs. Each individual SPMP can be described as being single session, adjunct, integrated, or embedded. Below is a structural taxonomy of student peer mentoring programs coordinated by the VUC. Examples illustrating each type are also included.

Single Session Programs

Single session programs run one time over a few hours outside the formal curriculum. Examples include programs that orient students to a specific University transition, such as articulation or entry into first year. The Chinese Mentor-Guide program, for instance, aims to improve the University transition experiences of students at partner institutions in China who are intending to study at VU in Australia (Best, Hajzler, & Henderson, 2007). The student mentors are Chinese students who have been studying at VU in Australia for six months. The mentors in Australia participate in a live chat on Blackboard with the students in China and exchange practical information and knowledge about studying at VU in Australia. On arrival at the VU campus, the student mentors conduct informal sessions with the new students to help them settle in during their first few weeks in their new environment. The program is supported by a dedicated Blackboard site and a student/teacher workbook with an accompanying DVD in which Chinese students discuss their transition experiences.

Adjunct Programs

Adjunct programs (i.e., Supplemental Instruction in the United States) are connected to specific courses during most of a semester. For example, students enrolled in Accounting for Decision Making opt to attend the sessions outside their normal class time. Pairs of student mentors are recruited and selected based on their prior grade in the course and their performance in mentor training. They facilitate weekly review sessions for 10 weeks with a group of students studying the subject for the first time. Student mentors are also available on Blackboard at specified times during the week for live chats with students about the subject and to respond to posted questions.

Integrated Programs

These semester-long programs form part of the formal curriculum for student mentees, in which student mentors participate on a voluntary basis. An example is student mentors in Paramedics who are trained to provide peer support for lower-division Paramedic students in formal clinical sessions. In Paramedics, two integrated programs have been piloted. One is situated within the higher education sector and the other crosses both the further and higher education sectors. Selected student mentors facilitate discussion and guide mentees during weekly practical clinical classes, to assist them with clinical skills, familiarize students with paramedic equipment, and aid the development of clinical judgment (Best, Hajzler, Ivanov, & Limon, 2008).

Embedded Programs

In embedded programs, both mentors and mentees participate as part of the formal curriculum during most of a semester. Student mentors receive academic credit for their participation. For instance, students of the Graduate Diploma of Teaching English as a Second Language (TESL) choose to do a traditional essay or mentor students in the Certificate 3 English as a Second Language Further Education course. As a mentor, students conduct practical spoken English language and communication skills sessions on 12 occasions across two semesters. Students also write a reflective journal and deliver a presentation about their experiences.

VUC's Integrative Role

The VUC plays a critical role in maintaining an overview and understanding of the breadth and depth of student peer learning across the institution through its Student Peer Mentoring Governance Committee. The VUC's central role is key to the peer program's long-term viability, sustainability, and credibility and guarantees that institutional knowledge of the SPMP and the new, wider S³L initiative are maintained despite inevitable staff and policy changes.

Results and Lessons Learned

Assessment tools vary between individual programs due to their differing aims and requests by teaching staff and the SPMP coordinator to focus on specific issues as a program evolves. However, all the assessment tools focus on the twin elements of social and academic integration to determine how influential the individual programs are on student learning and engagement. Typically, a five-point Likert scale is used, including statements about the mentoring program (e.g., helped my knowledge in the subject, helped my confidence in the subject, increased my friendship networks).

The successes of the SPMP relate to its documented and recognized breadth of impact on student learning. In the Paramedics program in which all students in the specific cohort participate in the mentoring program as mentees, there is no control group with which to compare grades; therefore, assessments focus on the impacts of the program on the students' clinical skills and judgment (Best et al., 2008). In Accounting for Decision Making, the impact of the program on students' academic and social integration has been evaulated. More recently, final grades for participants and nonparticipants have also been compared (Hollingsworth, Sng, & Best, 2008a; 2008b). In the offshore to onshore Chinese Mentor-Guide program, assessments focus on the impact of the program on students' predeparture transition issues (Best et al., 2007). For the dual sector program in which Graduate Diploma TESL work with Further Education students, the benefits of the program to mentors' developing teaching skills and mentees' satisfaction with an extra opportunity to practice English language skills have been assessed (Best, Hajzler, Brogan, Judd, & Fitzsimon, 2006). In addition to assessing the impact of the individual programs, mentor training is also regularly evaluated (Hollingsworth, Sng, & Best, 2008c).

Meeting the learning needs and demands of a culturally and linguistically diverse student population and responding to a complex multisectoral institution have been major challenges. The significant lessons learned have been to create a variety of peer mentoring programs rather than apply a single model. The major strengths of the SPMP are its diversity and adaptability.

The SPMP occurs on five onshore campuses, two offshore campuses, and bridges the further, vocational, and higher education sectors. Staff involvement in a partnership with the VUC has helped to develop a community of practice and increase the program's institutional profile. The receipt of a Vice Chancellor's Award for Enhancing the Student Experience in 2006 and SI/PASS Outstanding New Leader Award in 2009 are institutional and national acknowledgements of the success of the overall program.

Conclusion

The creation of the VUC has provided an enhanced opportunity to broaden and deepen the understanding and scope of student peer learning across the University. This has resulted in improved student learning outcomes and has supported staff in their search for strategies to help them respond to a diverse student population.

References

Best, G., Hajzler, D. J., Brogan, M., Judd, R., & Fitzsimon, I. (2006, December). *Cross-sectorial peer mentoring: A pilot project*. Paper presented at Learning Matters Symposium: Beyond Boundaries, Victoria University, Melbourne.

Best, G., Hajzler, D. J., & Henderson, F. (2007). Communicating with Chinese students offshore to improve their transition and adjustment to Australia: A pilot program. *Journal of Academic Language and Learning, 1*, 78–90.

Best, G., Hajzler, D. J., Ivanov, T., & Limon, J. (2008). Peer mentoring as a strategy to improve paramedic students' clinical skills. *The Australian Journal of Peer Learning, 1*, 13–25.

Hollingsworth, K., Sng, K., & Best, G. (2008a). *Accounting mentoring semester 2, 2007 report*. Unpublished paper, School of Learning Support Services Portfolio of Language and Learning, Victoria University, Melbourne.

Hollingsworth, K., Sng, K., & Best, G. (2008b). *Analysis of the accounting mentor program semester 1, 2008*. Unpublished paper, School of Learning Support Services Portfolio of Language and Learning, Victoria University, Melbourne.

Hollingsworth, K., Sng, K., & Best, G. (2008c). *Review of peer mentoring 2008*. Unpublished paper, School of Learning Support Services Portfolio of Language and Learning, Victoria University, Melbourne.

Karcher, M. J., Kuperminc, G. P., Portwood, S. G., Sipe, C. L., & Taylor, A. S. (2006). Mentoring programs: A framework to inform program development, research, and evaluation. *Journal of Community Psychology, 34*, 709–725.

McCormack, R., Best, G., & Kirkwood, K. (2009). *Students supporting student learning*. Melbourne, Vic: Victoria University.

Messinis, G., Sheehan, P., & Miholcic, Z. (2008, December). *The diversity of the student population at Victoria University*. Update of Report to the Vice-Chancellor, December, Victoria University, Melbourne.

CHAPTER 5

Comprehensive University College Assessment: The Importance of Assessing Students' Needs, Program Processes, and Critical Outcomes

Michele J. Hansen, Scott E. Evenbeck, & Gayle A. Williams

University college (UC) structures often encompass a comprehensive range of programs and services. Innovations such as intrusive and developmental advising, first-year seminars, learning communities, and mentoring may be housed in the UC and are frequently the subject of campus-wide attention when discerning what works in enhancing undergraduate academic success and retention. The high visibility of these initiatives may also entail an elevated level of public accountability, which is sometimes compounded by the newness of the UC structure on many college campuses. As such, UC unit directors, faculty, and administrators must pay increasing attention to assessment planning and implementation, especially when promoting specific policies and programs.

Comprehensive assessment efforts of the university college may also work to serve larger institutional goals or purposes. For example, given its centrality and the comprehensive nature of the university college on many campuses, these structures may be an effective mechanism for ensuring that the assessment of educational experiences for new students is a campus priority. University colleges may also provide an organizational structure that facilitates communication of assessment results and collaborative assessment planning across the campus.

Assessment scholars have advocated for the development of plans with clear purposes closely aligned with valued program goals (e.g., Banta 2002; Swing, 2001, 2004). Further, Banta contends that periodic assessment conducted primarily to satisfy the requirements of external funding agencies or new campus priorities are not likely to make meaningful impacts unless assessment becomes associated with goals and ongoing processes that are valued by program administrators and faculty. Thus, although assessment is often initiated to satisfy external demands, it is critical that assessment findings are actively used by unit directors and faculty to make ongoing program improvements. As such, an effective assessment planning approach should begin with a clearly articulated program theory to help guide the selection of instruments and to increase understanding among researchers and administrators regarding what internal program operations need to be improved when selected measures suggest that desired program outcomes are not achieved (Bickman 1987, 1990). Ideally, this approach expands the assessment focus to include a program theory explication, which is an investigation into the underlying assumptions, history, and context, associated with a particular program. Conceptualizing and clearly defining students' needs, program processes, and intended outcomes can be helpful in enhancing understanding of the program theory and planning subsequent evaluation activities. Clearly articulating students' perceived needs and how program processes lead to intended outcomes may effectively help administrators describe the underpinnings (i.e., program theory) of first-year programs. To that end, this chapter focuses on developing plans that involve a three-phase approach to assessment, including needs assessment, process assessment, and outcome assessment (Posavac & Carey, 2006; Schuh & Upcraft, 2001).

Needs Assessment Methods

Program evaluation and assessment scholars have recommended that a comprehensive assessment plan should include assessments of needs and processes (e.g., Gardiner, 1994; Posavac & Carey, 2006; Schuh & Upcraft, 2001). The measurement of needs is often a prerequisite to effective program development and planning. Information obtained from needs assessments can be used to make decisions about the allocation of program resources and services. Additionally, a comprehensive needs assessment can be the first step toward providing quality learning experiences for all students. Barefoot (2008) argues that "whether students are in their first year, middle years, or final year of college, each has unique needs, both academic and personal, and each will experience a unique transition trajectory" (p. 92). Therefore, she encourages assessment practitioners, faculty, and administrators to recognize the unique needs of students and to refrain from thinking that all students require the same types of interventions to facilitate their successful transitions and enhance their learning outcomes. Although she urges the development of quality relationships and the importance of firsthand knowledge of students' needs, systematic needs assessment is an effective method of taking students' needs into account when developing cocurricular and curricular programs.

Needs assessment data often include entering student surveys, satisfaction surveys, enrollment reports, and nonreturning student surveys as well as qualitative data on student experiences. Cuseo (2001), who writes generously and prolifically on first-year assessment methods and approaches, points out that it is "safe to say that more data are collected on students at college entry than at any other time in the college experience (e.g., student admissions data, placement-test data, CIRP data [ULCA's Cooperative Institutional Research Program]" (p. 4). Although Cuseo and other assessment scholars assert that data collected at college-entry can provide baseline information that can be useful to investigate changes in student development and learning gains when using pre-post designs (i.e., value-added assessment), the vast amounts of data collected from incoming students can also lend insight into students' academic, personal, and social needs.

Such surveys collect a wealth of information regarding incoming students' needs, expectations, commitments, financial resources, educational goals, and intentions. Locally developed instruments as well as national, standardized instruments (e.g., ACT/COMPASS, ACT's Entering Student Survey, the CIRP Freshman Survey, Survey of Entering Student Engagement, and Beginning College Survey of Student Engagement) can be administered to incoming students during new student orientation sessions and other critical points of contact. The data collected via these surveys can enable university college faculty, administrators, advisors, and instructional teams to develop curricula, pedagogical strategies, services, and programs that adequately meet the needs of incoming students. Thus, instructional team members and program administrators can be better equipped to introduce students to the academic culture and help the incoming students achieve their expressed goals. The results from needs assessments can also lend insight into developing services that are needed to help ease the transitions to college for students from diverse backgrounds and groups, such first-generation, veteran, transfer, and international students.

In addition to detecting students' entering needs, university college administrators may want to determine how needs change once students are enrolled in college. Other broad-based college surveys such as the National Survey of Student Engagement (NSSE) and Your First College Year

(YFCY) can be useful in determining who students are and what they need to perform well. For example, NSSE allows students the opportunity to reflect on their educational experience, share how and where they spend their time, and assess their in and out-of classroom experiences. This type of information can be enormously useful for planning and implementing new programs and services. In their investigation of what policies, programs, and practices contributing to student achievement, Kuh, Kinzie, Schuh, and Whitt (2005) found that effective schools learned about students' needs by administrating national and locally developed survey instruments and used this information to "invent, tweak, revise, and discard" programs and practices (p. 125).

Qualitative research methods are also a valuable source of needs assessment data. Conducting focus groups and one-on-one interviews can be enormously helpful for understanding students' perceptions and exploring their academic needs. Content analysis of open-ended comments on surveys can also provide data that increases understanding of students' needs. In a series of one-on-one interviews with first-year students, Light (2001) found that students needed to make links between the academic and the personal, but most importantly, they needed to get involved.

Focus groups, one-on-one interviews, and questionnaires can also be designed to investigate the professional development needs of university college faculty, professional staff, and advisors. For example, when planning retreats and professional development activities, faculty and others can be asked what their needs are in terms of curriculum development, assessment, incorporating diversity into the classroom, designing meaningful cocurricular and service-learning activities, among other topics. Information collected from faculty and others can be used to plan and implement professional development opportunities that are more closely aligned with faculty needs. Taking the time to gather information on the needs of faculty and professional staff members can enhance participation levels, learning outcomes, and satisfaction levels among university college colleagues.

Needs assessments often yield fundamental information to guide ongoing program planning and development. Results can be used to help organize relevant communities of practice within a large institution and assist in the implementation of university college sponsored faculty and staff development activities.

Process Assessment Methods

Once a program has been developed or refined based on needs assessment data, process assessments can be useful to ascertain whether the program was implemented as conceived; served the projected number of students, faculty, or staff and the intended target populations; satisfied recipients, and operated as planned. In other words, once the program is implemented, program tracking and monitoring are essential to ensure attainment of proposed outcomes. Process assessments are particularly useful for helping institutions and university college units develop better information about their programs, courses, and services so that outcome assessment results can be improved. According to Gardiner (1994), conducting studies designed to identify *why* results are (or not) being produced is a fundamental step in any self-improvement effort. Results of outcomes assessments may indicate *whether* or *how much* of a desired outcome produced, but not *why* or *how* the outcome is achieved (Gardiner). Thus, process assessments can be powerful for helping university college units understand what specific activities or components of programs or units are producing or not producing desired educational outcomes. For example, process assessments could reveal that first-year programs that provide opportunities for students to make social and academic connections with other students, advisors, and faculty tend to result in academic performance levels and retention rates that are higher than those of matched control groups.

Process assessments can be used to monitor which students enrolled in first-year programs and to ensure that the intended student populations are being served. They can also be conducted to ascertain which program aspects are making positive impacts on intended outcomes, such as academic performance, retention rates, and learning outcomes so that instructional teams and programs administrators can sustain effective initiatives. On the other hand, process assessments can also reveal ineffective activities, curriculum components, and pedagogical strategies that need to be improved or eliminated. Process assessment methods may include the following: (a) descriptive data analyses to identify characteristics of program participants (e.g., gender, ethnicity, admit status, age, academic preparation); (b) end-of-course or program questionnaires that are designed to assess students satisfaction levels and perceptions of cocurricular and curricular activities, pedagogical strategies, and self-reported learning outcomes; (c) focus groups and personal interviews with students and faculty members to help identify the most effective and ineffective program and course processes; and (d) classroom assessment techniques (Angelo & Cross, 1993), which are employed by faculty to determine what students are learning in the classroom and how well they are learning it. These techniques allow for close observation of students in the process of learning. Qualitative approaches, such as focus groups, interviews, and questionnaires, are most useful for gathering in-depth information about program components and processes. Additionally, quantitative approaches can be employed to investigate what populations are served and if individuals are being served in expected numbers.

Although outcome evaluations can produce critical information about the worth and value of programs (i.e., summative or accountability assessment), process assessments can be valuable for making data-driven improvements (i.e., formative assessment). Based on process assessments, faculty members may learn which pedagogical strategies and course activities have the most impact on student learning and academic performance. As such, information gathered from process assessments may help enhance understanding regarding what activities, assignments, interactions with faculty, and other program aspects helped students adjust to college or were perceived as useful to students.

Outcomes Assessment Methods

Despite the fact that we recognize the necessity of assessment for improvement, assessment for accountability remains an essential approach for ensuring continued funding and upper-administration support of first-year programs housed in UC structures. As Wellman (2001) states eloquently "in the age of consumerism and public transparency, accountability is necessary for preserving the compact between higher education and society" (p. 46). Accordingly, the primary focus of many UC assessment approaches should be the outcomes for students. In planning for assessment of academic units that house first-year programs, it is important to develop specific and measurable program goals that are aligned with the unit's mission, which should explicitly convey what outcomes unit administrators hope to achieve (Carver, 2000). Important measures include retention and persistence, academic performance, learning outcomes, student satisfaction, and student engagement. Outcomes assessment may also involve return on investment estimates to determine if programs are worth the resources that are devoted to them. In sum, outcome assessments are conducted to answer the fundamental questions about the value and worth of first-year programs housed in university colleges such as:

◇ Do programs do what they intend to do?
◇ Are the intended outcomes and goals being achieved?

◇ Is the program, course, or service improving student learning?
◇ Is the program impacting some students more than others?
◇ Can the changes in outcomes be explained by the program, or are they the result of some other factors occurring simultaneously?
◇ Is the program worth what it costs?

In an effort to understand program impacts on a range of student outcomes, UC assessment practitioners can conduct a series of quantitative analyses (e.g., linear regressions, logistic regressions, analyses of covariance). Due to the ethical and administrative difficulties associated with randomized experiments, the general design of many UC outcomes assessments may be quasi-experimental designs with comparison groups (rather than control or nonexperimental groups). Factors, other than the program, that are found to be significant predictors of academic success and retention rates (e.g., high school [H.S.] percentile ranks, H.S. grade point averages, SAT scores, units of H.S. math completed, gender, ethnicity, course load, first-generation status, campus housing) can serve as covariates when making comparisons between participants and nonparticipants (i.e., entered in the first step when using logistical regression procedures to examine program effect on retention rates). In an effort to ascertain which student participants benefit from a program or service, quantitative analyses (e.g., multivariate analyses of variance and logistical regression) can be employed to determine whether the programs are having differential impacts on diverse groups of students (e.g., underprepared or at-risk conditional admits, first-generation students, and underrepresented students).

University colleges' role with regard to student learning and undergraduate general education outcomes may be more general and foundational. As Barefoot and Gardner point out in the foreword to this volume, almost all university colleges have some relationship to general education. The nature of that relationship varies, but collaboration between the university college and other academic units for the delivery of special programs, student support, and faculty development related to general education is common. Within the context of university college's programs, general education learning outcomes may be introduced and students begin to achieve them, but the goal and the ability to measure substantial results over time is often limited due to the fact that students quickly move from university college into the schools that include their major field of study. Thus, the approach toward learning outcomes assessment in the university college may be distinct from other academic units and may involve programmatic collaboration with other schools.

Whether working independently or in collaboration with other units, UC assessment practitioners can employ a variety of methods to assess both indirect and direct student learning outcomes in the context of the first-year of college (i.e., beginning and intermediate levels of learning outcomes associated with general education outcomes). Indirect measures provide evidence that students are probably learning, but the evidence of what they are learning is less clear (Borden & Banta, 1994). Alumni, employer, or student surveys as well as exit interviews with graduates or focus groups are examples of indirect measures of student learning that may provide important information about what students are attaining from first-year experiences housed in UC units. Indirect indicators or criteria may include types of knowledge, skills, behaviors, and attributes. They may be quantitative measures or qualitative judgments and descriptions. It is noteworthy that indirect measures may be employed in process assessments to help enhance understanding of how students perceive particular course or program components.

Direct measures of student learning require students to demonstrate their knowledge and skills. They provide tangible, visible, and self-explanatory evidence of what students have and have not learned as a result of a course, program, or activity (Palomba & Banta, 1999; Suskie, 2004). Examples of direct student learning measures include objective tests, essays, presentations, and classroom assignments. Electronic portfolio systems prevalent on many college campuses allow for the storage and retrieval of these direct student learning assessments. Collecting data on students' learning from the first-year of college and comparing students' learning outcomes at later stages in their college careers is necessary for determining if students' educational experiences are value added. UC administrators and faculty play a fundamental role in understanding which educational experiences and courses contribute to students' attainment of key institutional learning objectives.

Conclusion

University college structures are often unique among academic units at institutions because they may not have extensive curricula, offer degrees, or attempt to prepare students in specific disciplinary perspectives. University colleges' role with regard to student learning and undergraduate general education outcomes may be more focused on beginning and intermediate levels. As a result, the approach toward assessment may be distinctive from other academic units. Some of the features that characterize university colleges' unique approach to assessment include programmatic collaboration with other schools and the relationship to general education outcomes.

The university college model offers a context for assessing all aspects of the first year of college and beyond. Assessment of early academic experiences can be useful in setting the stage for work in the major as well as for the entire undergraduate curriculum. It is critical that university college administrators develop assessment plans that frame the college's strategy, goals, mission, and values. Assessment plans should include a three-phase approach: (a) a needs assessment, (b) process assessment, and (c) outcome assessment. The three-phase approach is an appropriate strategy for addressing university colleges' unique assessment parameters while accommodating the information demands among internal and external stakeholders. Lastly, a firm commitment to conducting process assessments in addition to outcomes assessment may be an effective approach to help to ease the tension between assessment for proving and assessment for improving. Fundamental institutional change and continuous improvement may be more fully realized by sharing critical outcomes and actively discussing the processes that create those outcomes.

References

Angelo, T. A., & Cross, P. K. (1994). *Classroom assessment techniques: A handbook for college teachers* (2nd ed.). San Francisco, CA: Jossey-Bass.

Banta, T. W. (2002). *Building a scholarship of assessment*. San Francisco, CA: Jossey-Bass.

Barefoot, B. O. (2008). Collegiate transitions: The other side of the story. *New Directions for Higher Education, 144,* 89–92.

Bickman, L. (Ed.). (1987). Using program theory in evaluation. *New Directions for Program Evaluation, 33.*

Bickman, L. (Ed.). (1990). Advances in program theory. *New Directions for Program Evaluation, 47.*

Borden, V. M, & Banta, T. W. (Eds.). (1994). *Using performance indicators to guide strategic decision making* (New Directions for Institutional Research No. 82). San Francisco, CA: Jossey-Bass.

Carver, J. (2000). Managing your mission: Advice on where to begin. *About Campus, 4*(6), 19–23.

Cuseo, J. B. (2001). *Assessment of the first-year experience: Six significant questions*. Retrieved April 10, 2009, from http://www.sc.edu/fye/resources/assessment/pdf/Cuseos6Qs-web.pdf

Gardiner, L. F. (1994). Assessment and evaluation: Knowing and judging results. In J. S. Stark & A. M. Thomas (Eds.), *Assessment and program evaluation* (pp. 65–78). Needham Heights, MA: Simon & Schuster.

Kuh, G. D., Kinzie, J., Schuh, J. H., & Whitt, E. J. (2005). *Student success in college: Creating conditions that matter*. San Francisco, CA: Jossey-Bass.

Light, R. J. (2001). *Making the most of college: Students speak their minds*. Cambridge, MA: Harvard University Press.

Palomba, C. A., & Banta, T. W. (1999). Assessment essentials: Planning, implementing, and improving assessment in higher education. San Francisco, CA: Jossey-Bass.

Posavac, E. J., & Carey, R. G. (2006). *Program evaluation methods and case studies* (7th ed.). Englewood Cliffs, NJ: Prentice Hall.

Schuh, J. H., & Upcraft, M. L. (2001). *Assessment practice in student affairs: An applications manual*. San Francisco, CA: Jossey-Bass.

Swing, R. L. (Ed.). (2001). *Proving and Improving: Strategies for Assessing the First Year of College* (Monograph No. 33). Columbia, SC: University of South Carolina, National Resource Center for The First-Year Experience and Students in Transition.

Swing, R. L. (Ed.). (2004). *Proving and improving: Tools and techniques for assessing the first college year, Volume II* (Monograph No. 37). Columbia, SC: University of South Carolina, National Resource Center for The First-Year Experience and Students in Transition.

Suskie, L. (2004). *Assessing student learning: A common sense guide*. Bolton, MA: Anker.

Wellman, J. V. (2001). Assessing state accountability systems. *Change, 33*(2), 46–52.

Chapter 5 Case Studies

Illinois State University

A Case Study in Practical and Effective Assessment: University College Program Review

Amelia V. Noël-Elkins & Mardell A. Wilson

Institutional Context

Illinois State University is a four-year, public institution located in Normal, Illinois, with an average enrollment of approximately 20,000 students. In the fall of 2009, the full-time enrollment was 20,856. Of those, 2,512 were graduate students, 18,334 were undergraduates, and 3,033 were new first-year students, with that number remaining fairly consistent from year to year. Illinois State University is primarily comprised of traditional-age students; of the total undergraduate enrollment, approximately 90% (16,587) are between 18 and 24 years old and 57% (10,143) are female. Undergraduate students list their racial/ethnic designation as White (non-Hispanic), 83% (15,260); Black (non-Hispanic), nearly 6% (1,015); Hispanic, almost 4% (816); with the remaining 7% (1,253) listed as other, undeclared, or nonresident alien. The vast majority of undergraduate students (96%) come from the state of Illinois, with a high proportion (58%) originating from the counties in the Chicagoland area.

University College

In March of 1995, a proposal was submitted to the Academic Senate recommending the creation of a University College "to improve the effectiveness and efficacy of academic support services provided to undergraduates and to provide an academic home for new students and those without declared majors." As a result of this proposal, University College (UC) came into being in the summer of 1996 at Illinois State.

Currently, University College offers a variety of programming addressing the academic and transitional needs of first-year students and students without declared majors. UC is comprised of the following units, programs, and services: Academic Advisement, Instructional and Curricular Services (e.g., Developmental Math, First Year LinC, Transfer Student Seminar); Julia N. Visor Academic Center; Orientation and Transition Services; Testing Services; University Studies major; and TRIO/Student Support Services.

Advisors in University College advise the entire first-year cohort, regardless of whether students have declared a major, as well as all other undeclared students (i.e., an additional 2,500 students). While the primary focus is on first-year and undeclared students, UC services extend beyond these populations. For example, the University Studies major, Developmental Math, Julia N. Visor Academic Center, Testing Services, and TRIO/Student Support Services provide more comprehensive academic support services to all students.

Orientation and Transition Services supports primarily prospective students who have made a commitment to attend Illinois State University and administers the summer orientation program for new first-year students (Preview) as well as the orientation program for transfer students (Transfer Day Program).

Context for Program Review

At Illinois State, the program review process is intended to evaluate academic programs to ensure the quality of those programs and their consistency with the guidelines of the Illinois Board of Higher Education (IBHE). Two essential elements of program review are the documentation of learning outcomes and the identification of actions for improvement. Therefore, the process is intended to assist an academic unit in the identification of strengths as well as weaknesses. The practice is intended to be reasonably public in that it is required by the University's Academic Senate, and it is recommended that the faculty and staff in the unit be highly involved in the self-study. University College was the first nondegree-granting unit at Illinois State required to submit program review documents to the Academic Planning Committee (APC), a subcommittee of the Academic Affairs Committee of the Faculty Senate responsible for the program review process.

Upon submission of the initial report in May 2002, the APC indicated that the report was descriptive of the units within UC but lacked evidence of assessment to authenticate how program objectives were achieved. In April 2004, a response was sent to the APC that included assessment plans and measureable goals for University College. In January 2005, APC again responded to University College asking for a revised program review report due in September 2005. Specifically, the APC asked UC to document its alignment with the strategic plan of the University, reframe short- and long-term goals to be measurable, refine assessment plans so that they did not rely solely on client satisfaction surveys, and articulate the rationale for housing specific units within University College. APC then extended the deadline for submitting the revised materials until September 2006 as a new director of University College was hired in July 2005. In summary, the entire program review process for University College lasted approximately three and a half years, from initial submission of the first report in May 2002 until final approval from APC in October 2006.

Methodology and Process of Program Review

While University College worked with the University Assessment Office (UAO) in preparing the April 2004 response to APC, individual unit coordinators met with the director of UAO beginning spring 2005 to more carefully refine the assessment plans. The director of the UAO emphasized the development of goals with measurable outcomes, suggesting that good assessment practices would affirm the unit's strengths while identifying areas for improvement, eliminating any need for anecdotal justification of their value and/or existence while relying on true evidence-based practice.

In most cases, each unit coordinator met with the director of the UAO at least three times. The first meeting was devoted to explaining the process and purpose of assessment and for reviewing the elements of designing goals with measurable outcomes. In addition, unit coordinators were urged not only to define the goals of the unit but also to consider how those goals complemented the overall goals of University College and how the unit contributed to those goals. Coordinators returned for a second visit with newly crafted goals and outcomes, which were clarified, and discussions began regarding what assessment data would be needed. The third meeting was used to affirm that the goals, outcomes, and assessment measures were aligned. In addition, coordinators brought sample copies of assessment tools, which were discussed and refined. The entire process took only a few weeks and successfully changed the negative and skeptical attitude that many of the staff members had regarding assessment. What replaced the initial skepticism was a sense of eager anticipation to collect evidence to validate the quality of their individual programs and identify areas of weakness upon which improvements could be made.

In developing assessment plans that met the requirements of the APC as well as meeting the effectiveness needs of University College, the comprehensive assessment plans with measurable outcomes provided valuable results to many of the individual units within University College. These results have included substantive ways to improve programming, services, and structures.

Challenges and Successes

The extended submission deadline created by changes in leadership allowed the staff of University College to learn about the value of self-examination and the potential benefits of continuous assessment that reaches beyond the scope of customer satisfaction and addresses the mission and goals of the unit. UC has made a concerted effort to remain loyal to the assessment plans in an effort to provide valid evidence for which to cite successes, base improvements, and work continuously to move units forward. In fact, the units within University College revisit the assessment plans regularly. An example of the effectiveness of the goals, outcomes, and subsequent assessment is the First Year LinC seminar. LinC was developed in 2005 as a three-year pilot. As with many pilot programs, there are successes and failures. However, the assessment plan and goals developed through program review have allowed for the continued refinement of the LinC seminar and syllabus; the result has been a more effective program for first-year students. Evidence of the success of LinC is found in Illinois States' National Survey of Student Engagement (NSSE) results. The University Assessment Office looked at LinC students in comparison to the larger student population. In six different areas, including Enriching Educational Experiences and Student-Faculty Interactions, LinC students performed significantly better than non-LinC students. Without a comprehensive assessment plan, the LinC seminar would likely not have addressed the issues that needed refinement in an effort to be effective for the students and faculty involved in the program. Instead, because of the assessment, it is a program responsive to the feedback of the participants in an effort to achieve the established goals.

Results and Lessons Learned

One of the most important lessons learned was that oftentimes some things are simply outside the realm of one's control. Certainly, the length of time it took to complete the program review process, nearly four years from start to finish, was exceptional and, on the surface, not desirable. However, the length of time and the turnover in personnel proved that an effective assessment plan can be developed despite less than ideal circumstances. Additionally, it demonstrates that the true effectiveness of an assessment plan can be tested, in part, by how it stands up to the challenges and changes that are an inevitable part of higher education administration.

Another lesson learned was that despite initial staff resistance, an effective assessment plan was ultimately achieved, and the purpose of program review was embraced. The staff within University College experienced a difficult time not only learning how to develop an assessment plan, but also valuing its purpose. The difficulty experienced by the staff stemmed from a resistance to the concept of assessment that reflected a general sense of distrust of the process and its goals. Because University College was a fairly new administrative structure and had experienced turnover in leadership, its purpose and organization were not well understood; the staff viewed assessment as a threat to their existence rather than a benefit. While working through that resistance was a difficult process, the final product resulted in more confidence from the staff in the effectiveness and success of their units because there was now evidence to support those assertions.

Critical Elements

The one aspect of the program review process that ultimately made it successful for UC was the fact that the University required it. While nonrequired assessment plans can be effective, an assessment plan imbedded in the program review process, which is highly valued at Illinois State, is one that will continually remain a priority. University College will be required to go through the program review process again in 2013; therefore, it is in the best interest of UC to remain true to the assessment plans, provide regular internal updates, and document the structural and programmatic changes that have occurred as a result of assessment data.

Conclusion

If a UC unit is not a part of an existing program review process, the unit administrator should consider the potential benefits of including the university college in the process. In some cases, an outside consultant might be obtained to guide the unit through the process and make the assessment results public on a regular basis. Though not the same as a required program review, expert consultation can provide a public and objective view of the success of the operation, while validating the need for potential changes.

In addition to providing useful data for programmatic or operational changes, the program review process allowed University College to take the first step in developing an identity. Since its inception at Illinois State, there was no clear understanding of why the various units of University College were housed together in one administrative division. Additionally, those who worked within University College had little identification with it as a whole and, instead, only identified themselves with their own individual unit. There was a clear need to define why the units were together and create buy-in from the staff as to the importance of being connected administratively. Program review required University College to make public statements regarding its identity and its place in the University. The program review process has lead to the development of a strategic plan that will continue to identify University College's valuable contribution to the University structure.

University of Oklahoma

Three Initiatives Making a Difference in Student Success at the University of Oklahoma

Douglas D. Gaffin & Myrna L. Carney

Institutional Context

The University of Oklahoma (OU) is a four-year, doctoral-granting, comprehensive public institution located in Norman, Oklahoma. The University is a residential campus and the fall 2008 enrollment was 30,071, and included 20,736 full-time undergraduates and 3,762 full-time, first-time, first-year students. The undergraduate population was 52.5% female; 12% of the students were over age 25. Undergraduates were 74.4% White, non-Hispanic, 7.2% American Indian or Alaskan Native, 5.8% Asian or Pacific Islander, 5.5% Black, non-Hispanic, 4.2% Hispanic, and 3.0% nonresident aliens.

University College

In 1942, the University of Oklahoma established University College (UC) to address the needs of all first-year students. Since that time it has evolved into a comprehensive, student-success oriented college that includes one-on-one academic advising; the Assessment and Learning Center; Freshman Programs, which coordinates the first-year seminars; and the Center for Student Advancement that directs intervention strategies. UC also runs the Summer Enrollment Program for new students and serves as the administrative authority for the campus ROTC units. Students stay in UC until they have at least 24 credit hours, a declared major, and meet the minimum GPA requirements needed for that major. Exceptions to this transfer policy are students who move directly to the OU Health Science Center upon completing prerequisites for their allied health programs. In all, UC serves approximately 5,500 students.

In this case study, three programs and initiatives are highlighted that are directed at improving student success at the University of Oklahoma: the New Student survey, the Graduation Rates Task Force, and the High School Feedback Report program. Data gleaned from the annual New Student survey has been used to guide many of the student success programs and interventions. The Graduation Rates Task Force is a committee initiated by the president that studies and provides recommendations for improving student persistence and graduation. The High School Feedback Report Program is an outreach effort involving feedback to more than 100 Oklahoma high schools to keep principals and counselors informed of how their students are performing at OU.

New Student Survey

A key to any effective retention effort is informative data. Since 1975, baseline data have been gathered on participation in high school activities, family background, financial need, and various attitudinal items through the New Student survey. Data are correlated with admissions information (e.g., ACT, HSGPA, rank in class, admit date) and first-year performance data (e.g., GPA, credit hours attempted and earned) to detect possible factors that influence student success. Students complete this survey during the summer enrollment program with greater than 90% participation.

Survey information is used in outreach activities and for internal research. The survey gives students the opportunity to provide their student identification number as well as their interest in specific programs, activities, and services. Another item allows students to self-report disabilities. A prominent statement at the top of the survey reminds students that they are free to omit any information they do not wish to provide and that information will used for internal institutional research.

After classes begin, students who express interest in various activities, services, and programs are contacted by e-mail by the responsible department. This program encourages immediate involvement of first-year students in campus life. During the Summer Enrollment Program, University College staff, in collaboration with Disabled Student Services, contact students who state they have a visual, mobility, speech, or learning disability and wish to be notified by the University. This program allows Disabled Student Services to obtain the documentation required to provide services before classes begin in the fall. Data from the New Student survey are also used internally to assess academic preparedness, attitudes, and social backgrounds of first-year students to inform retention programs and services.

The New Student survey continues to be an invaluable tool for generating useful, focused data on the evolving qualities of new students. The survey becomes especially powerful when coupled with admissions data and OU student performance data from institutional research. These numbers are currently being used to detect trends and critical factors related to student success. A logistic regression formula has been developed that accurately predicts first-semester success among first-year students. This forecasting ability opens the lines of communication with admissions officers and helps shape admissions decisions from waitlisted students. Further, this formula is being used to expand the contract program for at-risk students. This new program requires students to sign an agreement as a condition of admission. Contract expectations include enrollment in the Gateway to College Learning Course, use of specific tutoring and Supplemental Instruction services, mandatory advising contacts, and maintenance of a minimum grade point average.

Graduation Rates Task Force

In 2000, the University president initiated a task force to study and provide specific recommendations on how the University can improve the persistence and graduation of students. The Graduation Rates Task Force (GRTF) enjoys considerable impact and success on campus because of the high level of importance given the committee (Hunter, 2006). The vice president for administrative affairs chairs the GRTF and reports directly to the president. Committee members include the provost and administrators, faculty, and staff from across campus. The dean and associate dean of University College are standing members of the GRTF. Because of its central role in the transition of students to and through OU, University College has assumed a major role in providing information and in developing and implementing recommendations for the GRTF.

The partnership of University College with the GRTF has generated several initiatives directed at improving student academic success. In a recent case, University College staff members researched academic resources at several peer universities and the interplay of several factors on the persistence of first-year students at the University. An immediate finding was that OU's application deadline was later than that of other universities that were ahead in national rankings despite attracting students of similar quality. Furthermore, the date that students apply correlates strongly with success in the first year at OU. Poor performance was also noted among students with good ACT/SAT scores but below-average high school grades. Because of these data, the University moved the application deadline forward and changed the automatic admission criteria to incorporate above-average high school performance.

The GRTF also noted that OU lacked a coordinated and centralized center for student learning services and found that many peer universities provided such resources. The committee concluded that while tutoring services existed across campus, students would benefit by having these diverse efforts under a single roof in a new, up-to-date facility and that such a center could improve student retention and graduation. From this charge, UC and the development office worked together to create a proposal that attracted a significant private donation to build a new academic services building (Gaffin, 2007).

The GRTF also researched and changed the 24-hour rule, which required students to earn 24 credit hours and a minimum 2.0 GPA to matriculate to their degree-recommending colleges. Under the new policy, students must have a GPA at least equal to that required for retention in their college. The change curbs the quick and negative consequences of students stopped out of their desired majors with little to no chance of success. To accommodate the increase in retained students, the University provided three new advising lines to University College.

The GRTF also proposed the development of a mandatory course for students on academic probation or notice. This new course helps students regain their bearings and overcome behaviors that limit their academic success. The new venture, called the Center for Student Advancement (CSA) was implemented in the spring of 2003, with the Strategies for Success course initiated in fall 2003. The CSA is under the jurisdiction of University College. The University freed space in an adjacent building to house the center, and the positions of two University College employees were redefined to start the new office.

High School Feedback Report Program

Comprehensive retention efforts involve more than simply making sophomores out of first-year students. Universities need to work with their feeder schools to improve the college readiness of future classes. Because of University College's position at the high school-university junction, UC is poised to inform high school principals and advisors on the preparation of their students for higher education.

Since 1990, University College at the University of Oklahoma has provided annual academic feedback reports to approximately 120 Oklahoma high schools. This initiative is patterned after Astin's (1977) Input-Environment-Outcome (I-E-O) Model with the objective of improving the academic preparedness of first-year students (I-Input) to increase the University's academic success rates that can lead to improved retention and graduation rates (O-Outcome).

This program provides the high schools with feedback for curricular evaluation and more effective advising of prospective students. The annual report compares each high school's first-year and other undergraduate students with all University of Oklahoma students in science and engineering, mathematics, and nonquantitative courses. The report also includes information on how many students place into a remedial mathematics course. Overall OU GPA group summary information is included indicating what percent of the first-year students and all undergraduates have achieved above 3.0 and what percent are not making satisfactory academic progress (i.e., below 2.0 GPA). In addition, the report provides comparative entrance examination ACT data.

This program has been effective in decreasing the numbers of first-year students enrolled in remedial mathematics courses and increasing the number of students who are successful in their first semester. Furthermore, comments from high school administrators attest to the helpfulness of the program. These reports also serve as a vehicle to increase the dialogue that should occur between higher education institutions and high schools for improving student academic achievement.

Results and Lessons Learned

Without the support of key university stakeholders, many good ideas may never be implemented. The GRTF was (and is) crucial to garnering university-wide support for the flurry of recent student success projects at the University of Oklahoma. The new Academic Services Building and Center for Student Advancement are clear evidence of the committee's influence. This is an important lesson for any university looking to make systemic changes in its programs for student success. Committees should include top people with broad knowledge and experience in student retention issues, and must be endowed with the authority to make clear, data-rich recommendations directly to the president.

One of the challenges of such intense retention research is that it inevitably leads to the creation of new programs and initiatives. University College is often identified as the appropriate home for these new programs because of its central place in the student success landscape. The danger is that university colleges can become awash in programs. Because resources are scarce, university colleges need to often step back and assess the big picture of what is working and what is not and be efficient in their efforts. Are all programs still fulfilling their original missions? Can programs be combined? Is it time to jettison a program because it is no longer providing its original purpose or usefulness? This can be sensitive work since real people and real careers are at stake.

At times, it has been difficult to communicate to the rest of the University community what UC is and does. Too many program acronyms and ineffective marketing of UC services has contributed to poor interdepartmental and intercollege communication. There has been a tendency to structure UC thinking among its own internal department lines, but these divisions carry little meaning to students, parents, and those outside the College. University College pressures are different from those of degree-granting colleges, and UC must be sensitive to these differences to effectively partner with other colleges to build consensus and support for UC programs.

Conclusion

Perhaps more than ever, university colleges are in a position to provide guidance to their institutions for improving student retention, persistence, and graduation. It is crucial to develop targeted programs that are data driven. Instruments need to be in place to gather appropriate information on student characteristics and student academic success. Most universities collect these types of data already. The next step is to select the right people, provide them with accurate data, and vet them with the authority to propose significant solutions to the highest administrative levels to improve student success.

References

Astin, A. (1977). *Four critical years: Effects of college on beliefs, attitudes, and knowledge.* San Francisco, CA: Jossey-Bass.

Gaffin, D. D. (2007). Building student success at the University of Oklahoma. E-*Source for College Transitions, 4*(4), 10–12.

Hunter, M. S. (2006). Lessons learned: Achieving institutional change in support of students in transition. *New Directions for Student Services, 114,* 7–15.

Virginia Commonwealth University

Demonstrating Effectiveness and Ensuring Success: Assessing University College

Jon Steingass & Seth Sykes

Institutional Context

Virginia Commonwealth University (VCU) is a public, four-year, urban research university located in the heart of Richmond, the state capital of Virginia. With more than 31,000 graduate and undergraduate students and an FTE of 19,357 undergraduates, VCU holds the distinction as Virginia's largest university. Although primarily a commuter campus with 87% of students residing off campus, 8 out of 10 first-year students live in one of four residence halls designated primarily for this population. VCU admitted 3,850 first-year students in fall 2007, representing a 10% increase in enrollment over the previous academic year. Females comprise the majority (60%) of the student population, and 18% of undergraduates are 25 years or older. With 38% minority enrollment, including 22% African American, 11% Asian, 4% Hispanic, and 1% Native American or Pacific Islander, VCU has the highest percentage of undergraduate students of color among Virginia's state-supported universities except for Historically Black Colleges and Universities. Slightly more than half (52%) of VCU students receive need-based aid funding under Title IV programs, and a little more than one third of all undergraduates at VCU are considered first-generation college students. Finally, 68% of the undergraduate student population attends full time.

University College

Recognizing the need to intensify its efforts for improving student academic performance and increasing student retention, VCU adopted its strategic plan, VCU 2020, in February 2006. The establishment of University College (UC) was a major initiative of this strategic plan. By centralizing academic support services and linking these services to the classroom experience, University College aims to maximize the academic success and persistence of students throughout their collegiate careers.

University College directly addresses the University's retention efforts by providing a central home for the core curriculum and academic support services. UC includes academic advising for all first-year, undeclared, prehealth, and interdisciplinary students, in addition to student athletes. The campus learning, writing, and testing centers; new student programs; first-year seminars; learning communities; summer reading program; academic support courses; and core education program are offered by University College and give students convenient access to a network of resources that enhance their academic success.

In its first full year of operation, University College advisors held 29,986 academic advising sessions with the 3,500 first-year students, 275 student athletes, 80 interdisciplinary studies majors, 800 upper-class undeclared, and 750 upper-level prehealth students. In addition, 9,654 students attended 28,051 hours of tutoring, Supplemental Instruction, and writing center consultations. Three hundred students participated in a yearlong pilot of our new focused inquiry sequence, which replaced English composition, in fall 2007, and serves as the foundation of the University's new core education program.

Comprehensive Assessment

VCU has a longstanding practice of evaluating students' first-year experience using a combination of formative and summative assessments. These assessment measures have played a critical role in determining the impact of various programs and services on student engagement, success, and persistence. In particular, the undergraduate affairs unit of the College of Humanities and Sciences (i.e., the precursor to University College) conducted extensive formative evaluations through student satisfaction surveys, focus groups, informal feedback, and midterm and end-of-semester grades to identify potential problem areas and to improve processes leading to increased effectiveness and enhanced decision making.

The University's Center for Institutional Effectiveness also provides student survey feedback and official institutional data on graduation and retention rates, academic performance, and non-returning student survey feedback. VCU regularly participates in the National Survey of Student Engagement (NSSE) and Cooperative Institutional Research Program (CIRP) and formerly administered the Student Satisfaction Inventory. These results are used in making data-driven decisions. For example, based on the past three NSSE benchmark reports, first-year students expressed lower levels of engagement in virtually every cluster compared to national norms and comparable institutions. Consequently, VCU recognized the need to intensify its efforts to increase student achievement and improve student persistence through the formation of University College.

UC continues the tradition of assessing students' first-year experience, and assesses itself at several levels. The University College Academic and Student Affairs Advisory Committee, chaired by the dean of University College, provides oversight to the evaluation process. Formative evaluations are conducted continuously to identify and correct potential problem areas. Summative evaluations assess the overall impact of programs and services on students' academic performance and persistence through graduation.

Over the next five years, the University projects that the number of first-year students will steadily increase whereas the quality of students accepted to VCU, as measured by SAT scores and high school GPA, is unlikely to change appreciably. At the same time, University College is expected to document continuous improvements in student engagement, academic success, and retention. The benchmarks below provide a basis for measuring the impact of University College.

Formative Assessment Measures

University College incorporates four major formative assessment measures to help determine if it is on track for contributing to the overall campus retention efforts. The extent to which the midyear targets are met provide important information for increasing overall effectiveness. Based on the information provided, adjustments can be made to improve the chances for meeting our year-end retention goals. These formative measures include

◇ *First-semester retention rate.* The percentage of first-year students who return for their spring semester helps determine if University College is meeting year-end retention goals.
◇ *First-semester academic standing.* Based on five-year data trends, a strong relationship exists between students' first-semester academic performance and the likelihood of those students returning for a second year.
◇ *Number of credit hours earned during first semester.* According to institutional data, a strong relationship exists between the number of credit hours a first-year student earns each semester and persistence at the institution.

◇ *Number of students and frequency of times they use academic support programs.* According to data collected by the undergraduate affairs unit of the College of Humanities and Sciences, students who meet with an advisor at least twice each semester are more successful academically and persist at higher rates than students who meet with an advisor less frequently. Moreover, students who attend at least seven Supplemental Instruction sessions receive final course grades that are a half-letter grade higher than those who do not. Similar results are observed in students who access tutoring and writing center services.

Examples of midyear adjustments implemented include expanding outreach efforts to increase the numbers of students using academic support services, targeting specific student population groups for more intensive academic support, and analyzing the data to determine what changes are necessary for the following year.

Summative Assessment Measures

The University is required to submit retention and graduation projections to the State Council of Higher Education for Virginia. A portion of state funding is dependent on the extent to which these projections are met. University College has been charged with leading and monitoring first-year retention efforts to ensure gradual increases in the percentage of students who successfully persist through their sophomore year. Year-end evaluations assess the overall impact of University College programs and services on students' academic performance and persistence. These summative assessment measures include

◇ The percentage of students who return for their second year
◇ The percentage of first-year students who end their first college year in good academic standing
◇ The number of students served by the programs and services offered in University College
◇ The percentage of students who are satisfied with the services they received through University College
◇ The percentage of students who achieve the specified learning outcomes by the end of their first year of college

These benchmarks for measuring the effectiveness of University College as a whole have also become the means by which each professional UC staff member evaluates his or her own effectiveness.

The academic advising program is the cornerstone of University College with each full-time advisor assigned approximately 180 first-year students. Because a one-size-fits-all approach to advising is not the most effective way to serve our diverse students in the wide array of academic programs offered at VCU, University College requires each advisor to determine the best advising approach for his or her students. Advisors are entrusted to create an advising plan that addresses five distinct areas.

Fall semester advising structure. Advisors determine how they will advise students in the fall. For example, each advisor decides how many FYE course sections they will teach each year and how they will advise those students, both in and out of classroom, based on a standard curriculum. For the advisees who are not enrolled in the FYE course, advisors outline in detail a plan to advise them.

Spring semester advising structure. Advisors also identify how they will advise students in the spring. For example, they describe the type of students who need more intrusive advising and the specific strategies used to encourage students to participate in such advising interactions.

Advising learning outcomes. One advantage of University College is that it provides a common learning experience for all students, regardless of the major. The advising plan of each advisor provides information on how he or she addresses and evaluates the advising learning outcomes for every student on his or her caseload. Examples of advising learning outcomes include understanding the degree requirements for the major and demonstrating awareness of University resources and support services.

Outreach. Advisors identify strategies to connect with advisees, particularly those most resistant to advising. This component addresses the extent to which advisors incorporate technology and the types of technology to be used (e.g., Facebook, e-mail), as well as a projection of when they will begin developing and cultivating relationships with their more resistant advisees.

Assessment. Finally, advisors establish advising target goals, related to the University's retention goals and unit objectives. These targets are based on historical data and patterns of students in majors they advise and include

- First-semester retention rate
- Percentage of students in good academic standing after fall semester
- Percentage of students earning 12 or more credit hours during fall semester
- Percentage of students who meet with the advisor individually at least twice per semester
- Average number of advising sessions held per student each semester
- Percentage of first-year students who return for the fall of the second year
- Percentage of first-year students who end the spring semester in good academic standing
- Percentage of advisees who rate the quality of advising as good or excellent in the spring satisfaction survey
- Percentage of students who earn at least 20 credit hours by the end of the first year
- Percentage of advisees who master all advising learning outcomes

After completing an advising plan, each University College advisor meets with his or her supervisor to discuss it in more detail. During this conversation, the supervisor ascertains whether the target goals, established by the advisor, will contribute to the overall effectiveness of University College. By so doing, the supervisor also ensures that each individual advisor will be assessed with the same measures as University College as a whole.

Results and Lessons Learned

In its strategic plan, VCU 2020, Virginia Commonwealth University made a major commitment to become a learning-centered research university that engages its students, retains them from year to year, and assures their graduation. An important initiative in achieving these goals is the creation and implementation of University College. From matriculation to graduation, demonstrating the value of University College programs and services in students' undergraduate success and persistence is as essential for newly formed university colleges as it is for long-established ones.

A comprehensive assessment plan has been essential to show campus stakeholders, particularly those who are the most dubious about the very nature of a university college, that VCU is producing a return on its investment. University College had a comprehensive assessment plan in place before it opened its doors. The benchmark measures were clearly identified and communicated to University College staff members to serve as targets for setting goals and objectives of this new unit. Through formative assessment, directors and individual advisors had feedback available to determine if they were on target for meeting their individual and unit goals. Some of the feedback prompted some changes to the delivery of services and helped to enhance the effectiveness of individual and group programs. All of the units and staff members within each unit cooperated to provide students with the programs and services that are necessary to enhance students' success and improve student persistence, particularly during the first year of college. A well-designed assessment program also helps identify problem areas, leads to enhanced decision making, and maximizes the impact of programs and services offered by University College.

During its first year of operation, a significant amount of time and effort was spent on communicating the potential benefits of University College to various campus stakeholders—from the Board of Visitors, vice presidents, and academic deans to the faculty senate and student government association. Not only was it imperative to clearly articulate the purpose and objectives of University College, but it was also critical to provide assessment data as soon as it became available. Of particular interest to various individuals was the number of students served and whether this corresponded to an increase in student success and persistence. By the end of University College's inaugural year, the University recorded the highest percentage of first-year students who ended their first year in college in good academic standing (76%) and the highest percentage of students who returned for their sophomore year (over 82%). In addition, the number of students receiving various academic support services increased by 55%, and student survey feedback indicated satisfaction with UC services. This information was (and continues to be) communicated through formal presentations, press releases, web site updates, and informal communications as soon as it became available. In this era of increasing institutional accountability, it is imperative for University College to implement a vigorous assessment program to ensure continuous improvement and to demonstrate its contributions to student success and persistence.

Wright State University

Institutional Self-Study as a Context for Collaboration in First-Year Programs

Edwin Mayes

Institutional Context

Wright State University–Dayton (WSU) campus was founded in 1964 and granted full university status in 1967 as the 12th state-assisted university in Ohio. WSU was developed to provide access to higher learning to the city of Dayton and the surrounding counties. Today, 54% of our student body derives from the aforementioned counties, and 93% of the students are from the state of Ohio. Wright State is an open-admission, four-year public institution serving approximately 17,000 students each year, with 3,000 students living in campus housing.

With a fall 2006 enrollment of full-time undergraduate enrollment of 10,850, approximately 40% of the 4,468 first-year students were first-generation students (i.e., students whose parents have not earned a college degree); and 15% were minorities (i.e., 80% African American, 11% Asian, 7% Hispanic, and 2% Native American). Eighteen percent of the students were age 25 and over. Wright State is among the 161 schools from 12 states listed as "Best in the Midwest" in the Princeton Review's 2008 *Best Colleges: Region by Region.*

University College

The University Division was initially created in 1970 to address a 75% first-year attrition rate. Growth in the number of students served in University Division and the changing needs of the student population were addressed by WSU's strategic plan in the late 1990s. In 1999, University Division was transformed into University College with a mission refocused on giving first-year students an academic home that would provide direction, services, and opportunities to assist in their timely movement into their chosen majors. In 2002, University College led the way in the development of the First-Year Coordinating and Advisory Council (FYCAC). The FYCAC is a president's award-winning collaborative council developed to support the objectives of the first-year experience. This council is comprised of individuals from academic affairs and student affairs including University College, undergraduate admissions, campus recreation, career services, disability services, residence services, student activities and the Student Union. In 2006, the FYCAC was reconstituted to include faculty who teach primarily first-year students. The reconstitution of the FYCAC was essential in moving the first-year experience forward as an institutional self-study (described in greater detail below). The Council found that faculty, specifically general education faculty, were not aware of first-year experience programming or the needs of first-year student population. Including faculty in the programming process and developing initiatives to improve faculty/student relationships were necessary.

UC's nationally recognized first-year experience program serves 3,613 first-year students but continues to work with sophomores, juniors, and seniors as they transition into their major of choice. University College houses the following programs and services: Learning Communities, Academic Advising, Testing Services, Student Academic Success Center (i.e., Tutoring Services, Math Learning Center, University Writing Center, and Developmental Education), and Phoenix and PASS programs for students on probation.

Institutional Self-Study

In the fall of 2005, Wright State University began an institution-wide self-study process using the Policy Center on the First Year of College's (now the John N. Gardner Institute for Excellence in Undergraduate Education) Foundations of Excellence (FOE) dimensions as guides to determine the institution's level of excellence in the first-year experience for all first-year students. These dimensions included philosophy, organization, faculty, learning, transitions, all students, diversity, roles and purposes, and improvement. Assisted generously by the Policy Center and a seasoned advisor and consultant, WSU began the process of completing the comprehensive self-study using the Current Practice Inventory (CPI), FOE surveys, and other source documents as tools to determine and document the current status of the first year of college and to begin implementing change based upon the findings.

To complete the self-study properly required institution-wide involvement beginning with an FOE task force that was widely representative of the campus and appointed by the provost. This task force consisted of 20 faculty, including the president of the faculty and chief negotiator of the faculty union; 26 staff, including the chairs of the Unclassified and Classified Staff Councils; and 10 students, including the president of the student government. Staff support was provided by University College. A subcommittee was developed for each of the nine dimensions and cochaired by a staff member and a faculty member and consisted of five to eight members.

The following are recommended actions that were developed by the dimension subcommittees and examples of institutional responses to date:

◇ Develop an overarching first-year philosophy statement that melds the four current stated goals of the first-year experience with the three stated goals of general education
- The Philosophy Dimension Subcommittee developed an overarching first-year and general education philosophy statement that combined the seven goals and shared the draft with the campus community for review.

◇ Enhance communication with faculty and staff about the goals of the first-year experience
- The heightened campus energy and interest in FYE facilitated sharing more about what has been developed in the FYE program.
- Work was started on a FYE handbook for faculty and staff, a FYE brochure, and an enhanced web presence specific to the FYE program.
- The faculty president began using Facultyline, the faculty newsletter, to promote the FOE project, educate faculty about the importance of FOE, and encourage greater faculty involvement.
- Expand the FYE structure to include greater involvement of academic units across the campus
- The First-Year Coordinating and Advisory Council (FYCAC) was reconstituted to include faculty from across the university.

◇ Enhance faculty involvement in FYE
- Opportunities were promoted for general education faculty members to share in the development of courses and programs dedicated to first-year student success.

◇ Enhance reward system for faculty who work with first-year students
- A campus-wide $200,000 Request for Proposal (RFP) was launched to improve teaching and learning and enhance the participation of units across campus in FYE. This program has been very successful involving other departments across campus in the FYE program. Many faculty and staff have taken the opportunity to develop RFPs to foster

programs that benefit first-year students over the last two years. Due to budget constraints the program was suspended in 2008.

◇ Enhance student course completion and success in the top five courses taken by all first-year students. Focus particularly on at-risk or barrier/gateway courses

◇ Ensure appropriate placement of students in courses based upon skills levels, particularly for students who register late

◇ Expand FYE beyond fall quarter and include all first-year students (e.g., part-time, transfer, adult), no matter which term they enter the University

  • FYE was expanded to include more part-time, transfer, adult, and online students, as well as students who enter the University in the winter or spring terms. Additional efforts to expand the program include developing a study abroad program for first-year students as well as service-learning initiatives through the first year.

◇ Strengthen connections with feeder high schools and with parents of first-year students

  • The *So You Want To Go To College* guidebook is published and distributed to high school students and parents. Various other initiatives are currently under way, including the publication of an e-newsletter and summer institutes that bring English and math high school teachers together with their University counterparts to bridge students' achievement gaps.

◇ Enhance institutional support in general for FYE and student success

The positive relationship with the former provost, now president of the University, has contributed to moving UC's course of action forward. University College has been successful in hiring a coordinator dedicated to the development of service-learning and civic engagement opportunities for first-year students. In fall 2007, 37 course sections (i.e., 14 staff-led and 23 peer-led sections) were offered to students within the Learning Community Program to experience a service opportunity either through the common reading project (i.e., 28 sections connected to *An Inconvenient Truth*) or through other activities with community partners (i.e., 9 sections). A new course was also developed dedicated to service in the Wright State community and exploring the importance of service as a lifelong learning opportunity.

Another success has been the development of a first-year seminar cotaught by University College peer instructors and the Center for International Education to introduce and prepare students for study abroad opportunities.

Results and Lessons Learned

A critical element in the success of the self-study was the initial involvement of the vice president of curriculum and instruction and the dean of University College. Beginning the process at this level of administration aided in the collaboration with the provost and other University officials, including the president of the faculty. In addition, having a combination of faculty and staff on each subcommittee allowed for both stakeholders to share knowledge and opinions about each dimension, including developing awareness of activities and programs that existed across campus.

A challenge for the future is the state's new directive to bring increased collaboration between the institutions within the state to ensure affordable, high-quality educational opportunities for all Ohioans. Since 93% of WSU's students are Ohio residents, it will be important for Wright State University to take a leading role in this new directive and reach out to institutions in the area to foster this collaborative effort. Collaborative initiatives with community colleges in southern Ohio have already been implemented to develop seamless connections for students to easily transfer to Wright State and to have a first-year experience at the community colleges that mirrors the experience at WSU. The University System 10-year plan will set benchmarks and a timeline for all institutions to advance the opportunities for the citizens of Ohio, and Wright State University has accepted this challenge.

CHAPTER 6

Resource Management in the University College

Maggy Smith & Scott E. Evenbeck

As the center for collaboration and cooperation on campus, the university college (UC) is the unit that provides leadership for and guides development of programs for the support of entering students and their success. Often the university college's operating budget includes tuition revenue, fee-based income (e.g., activities fees, placement testing fees), and other institutional and external allocations. Important university college resource needs were identified in the results of the survey of 58 institutions discussed in chapter 1. For example, physical space (e.g., classrooms, lounges), the virtual environment (e.g., technology, equipment), personnel (e.g., faculty, staff, and student salaries), and programming were identified as important resource needs by survey respondents. This chapter discusses the resource development and management choices facing the university college's administration and leadership. In particular, the chapter addresses resource needs, such as physical space, the virtual environment, personnel, and sources of income for the university college.

Balancing the Physical and Virtual Environment

As higher education becomes an increasingly hybrid environment, occupying both physical and virtual spaces, addressing the needs of students, faculty, and staff is even more critical in shaping how they see the campus. In the case of students, their experience of both the physical and virtual environments impacts their interest in attending, persisting in, and graduating from a given institution. Like all units on campus, the balance of physical and virtual environments is critical, and the interface between them has significant implications for teaching, learning, and service delivery in the university college.

Physical Space

The nature of the informal and formal physical learning spaces, as well as space that houses personnel who are serving students, demonstrate the dedication of the university college to student success. These spaces include everything from the grounds of a campus; the contiguous location of related university college services; social space for first-year students to congregate study, socialize, or relax; classrooms and computer labs; and residence halls that house living-learning communities for first-year students. These spaces and facilities are important not only to prospective and entering students but to continuing students, as well. Studying, working, and socializing in a pleasant home away from home encourages students to stay in school, get involved, and return for subsequent semesters. While not all of the physical spaces described above will be under the direct control of the university college, UC administrators have a vested interest in working with campus partners to ensure that the physical environment supports student learning and success.

In addition to physical space for student academic use, university colleges often need space to house enrollment management departments. Many university colleges have invested in physical space to establish one-stop enrollment service centers for entering and continuing students. A one-stop center brings together a set of functions and services that facilitates the enrollment of all students. This collection of services often includes all or most of the following: admissions, financial aid and scholarships, the bursar, the registrar and registration activities, and academic advising services. These service functions are integrated and located in close proximity to one another to reduce the runaround that students sometimes report characterizes their interactions with an institution. Such centers are ideally situated in the heart of the campus, easy to access, and in visible locations for campus visitors.

A one-stop center such as this might integrate the physical and the virtual environments into a single service area as it does on The University of Texas at El Paso (UTEP) campus where a state-of-the-art facility offers students the flexibility of computer-based services with enrollment advisors available to offer help with standard questions and problems. A student who visits UTEP's Enrollment Services Center can receive basic academic advising, select classes, enroll in classes, make schedule changes, pay university bills, turn in admissions applications, submit financial aid forms, and review placement test results—accomplishing eight processes in one location rather than completing those processes in eight different locations. Students with detailed questions or very specific needs are referred to the department for counseling by an expert. Much as UTEP does, many campuses with one-stop centers have staff cross-trained within the constituent units so that staffing in different functional areas can be adjusted during peak times. For example, when the demands for financial aid assistance are high, demands in other areas might be low, allowing for the cross-trained staff to facilitate traffic through financial aid processes.

The funding implications for such a service can span the gamut from a major investment of new funds to a simple reallocation of existing funds. For example, because a one-stop center replaces individual department offices, reassigning staff from primary departments (e.g., financial aid) to the one-stop center is a budget-neutral expense. The initial investment of creating space and essential infrastructure (e.g., computers, printers, other materials) can be a substantial one, however. These costs might be funded through grants and/or donor contributions as discussed later in this chapter.

Virtual Environment

The vastly increased dependence on technology across the range of institutional and educational programs in higher education creates a conundrum in serving students and in providing them with the virtual environment that they expect. Students and parents alike want easy, rapid access to information and processes. Often, at the same time, however, they demand contact with staff or administrators who can provide individualized attention to student questions and demands. One-stop centers for student services are structures that can deliver both high-touch and high-tech solutions to student needs.

Whatever the overriding mission and functional components of the university college, everyone in student- and academic-serving units must attend to technology and to the virtual environment. Any number of issues arise that impact the university college's resource needs. It is not a small issue to ensure that web-based information is current and reliably operational 24 hours a day and that the virtual environment matches with absolute accuracy the physical environment. For example, as students explore our campuses either in person on the physical campus or through the virtual environment on the web, they must find welcoming environments where they can get their questions answered, move into the institution, get settled in their classes, and graduate with few glitches. Yet, Adelman (2006) notes that the lack of transparency for prospective students in finding information they need for the first year of college is a concern.

Many institutions have moved well beyond information and enrollment services online. They are aggressively placing academic courses and programs online so that students around the world have choices. Wong (2006) predicts that "The classroom of the future isn't on a college campus. It's in the virtual world of 'Second Life'" (para. 1).

University College Personnel

Perhaps equally or more important than the balance between the physical and virtual environments to the success of a university college is the investment in personnel. Funding for university college personnel includes a wide variety of models for students, faculty, staff, and administrators. Some models are a direct replication of the traditional academic model while others are entrepreneurial, flexible, and creative.

University College Faculty

Frequently, faculty teaching courses that reside in the university college are either jointly appointed between their academic discipline and the university college or are on loan, so to speak, to teach a course for the college. On some campuses, the university college employs full-time faculty; occasionally even tenure-track faculty are assigned to or hired by the college. One such model exists at Kennesaw State University in Georgia where their university college instructors are tenure-track faculty. Yet, the most common model is one of shared faculty or full-time lecturers. Historically, faculty have spent the majority of their time in their departments carrying out research, teaching, and service roles in their disciplines. Thus, the university college becomes the place where they collaborate with colleagues outside their disciplines to support entering students' transition to and success in college.

The shared-faculty model has a number of advantages. Most importantly, from a funding perspective, it allows an institution to redistribute teaching loads and expertise rather than hiring additional faculty who will be teaching only first-year courses. Faculty are engaged with entering students and can expose the students to college majors and areas of expertise the students may not have considered. This serves as a good opportunity for recruitment into major fields of study. In addition, students meet faculty whom they may encounter in their future courses. Faculty from different disciplines teaching courses at a range of levels provide opportunities for a varied first-year curriculum and bring a rich perspective to the classroom that does not become rote or stale. The most significant challenge from a funding perspective is to be certain that the first-year courses are considered part of the faculty workload.

The provision of resources and attention to reward structures are important in supporting the faculty's involvement with the university college. University college administrators may want to consider one or more of the following strategies for encouraging faculty involvement:

◇ Providing summer stipends for course development
◇ Creating a funding model to buy out faculty time to support their engagement with new initiatives for entering students

    ◇ Offering competitive professional development grants. Oftentimes, the return on the relatively small marginal cost of such enhancement for faculty pays huge dividends in enhanced teaching and learning for the entering students.

    ◇ Providing funded opportunities for first-year faculty to collaborate on learning community curricula

Chapter 3 offers additional information about faculty appointments and faculty development.

University College Staff

Unlike faculty models, university college employees are generally full- or part-time employees working only for the UC departments. Staff, ranging from admissions counselors to orientation staff to academic advisors and support staff, are at the front lines in the university college in serving entering students. Within the college, positions may be shared to facilitate service delivery. For example, a financial aid counselor might divide his or her time between the Office of Financial Aid and a one-stop shop as described above. Once staff are cross-trained in university college processes, they can be shared during individual department's peak demand times. The university college maximizes resources in this way.

Oftentimes program development is derailed for budgetary reasons; however, a cost analysis of staff positions often demonstrates that creative solutions to student needs can be implemented without incurring additional costs. At UTEP, for example, advisors were moved into the first-year seminar classrooms and out of the Academic Advising Center for part of their workweek so that entering students would receive rich and regular contact with their advisors without having to make appointments. This redefinition of the advisor role was not more expensive; instead, it redirected the use of existing resources to more effective contexts for serving entering students.

In addition to new models for professional staff roles, experienced students can add much needed resources to first-year programs. These student roles are being redefined in university colleges to fit a more student-centered culture that also provide students with the opportunity for meaningful work, provide the university college with additional resources, and offer new students the helpful assistance of experienced students. Successful students who are in at least their second year of college are working as peer leaders in the classroom alongside faculty teaching first-year students and serving as peer advisors providing students with useful academic guidance, as peer tutors assisting in academic assistance centers, and in a number of other roles. Because student staff are less expensive than professional staff, they offer a cost-effective mechanism for enhancing support to new students.

Unlike traditional academic colleges, the staff in the university college comprise most of the college budget. Given the resources devoted to staffing, UC administrators will want to protect that investment through staff development opportunities. In fact, staff development may represent a marginal investment with the potential to yield significant returns in serving students. This is especially true when staff development efforts focus on improving service delivery. For example, staff may be asked to engage in an appreciative inquiry process where they visualize and develop plans for achieving larger goals rather than focusing on solving specific problems (Cooperrider & Whitney, 2005). Through individual and group sharing, reflection, and planning, staff are engaged in creating a collective future built on the strengths and positive aspects of the organization.

Individual staff development efforts are also important. Many campuses have tuition remission plans for staff. Encouraging university college staff to continue their own education acknowledges the potential of the staff while investing in the future of the college. It also models for staff the kind of approach to take with students.

Sources of Income for the University College

In addition to institutional sources of funds (e.g., tuition revenue, student course and/or activity fees, redistributed campus funds), university colleges make cases for external funding from federal and state granting agencies, private foundations, and donors. Yet, external funds secured to launch a university college or new initiatives within the university college are unstable revenue sources. For this reason, assessment during the soft-money years of such entrepreneurial efforts is critical and often results in the commitment of ongoing institutional funding. The collaborative working relationships among university college departments and with other units on campus may also lead to resource sharing.

Institutional Sources

Often, when a university college is formed, the recurring operating budget is created through the consolidation of the budgets of formerly independent departments brought together to form the college (e.g., orientation, academic advising, academic support departments, developmental education). Since the university college is the institution's structural way of serving entering students on a campus, it may be helpful to think of and describe funds that are made available to the university college as pooled resources for the campus to meet the common goal of supporting entering students. Sometimes, a portion of the fee income from the courses the students take is redirected to such support. Other times, a fee is assessed on students, such as a fee for orientation programs. A one-time entering student fee imposed on first-year UTEP students covers costs for orientation, testing, and some portion of the university college operations.

External Sources

In addition to institutional sources of funding, university colleges search for and depend on external sources of funding, such as federal and state grants, private foundations, and donors.

Federal and state grants. As the need to address a less traditional student body increases and as the means of delivering higher education diversifies (e.g., online courses, dual credit, early college high schools), external agencies are funding those efforts to increase higher education opportunities for all. While a large infusion of external funds provides the opportunity for the university college to grow and develop robust programming more quickly, the college must also simultaneously prepare for the grant's conclusion and for the institution's ultimate responsibility to assume the program's funding. The size of the grant, the duration of the funding, and the nature of those things funded all contribute to the college's strategies for assuming fiscal responsibility at the grant's end. For example, UTEP's University College received several large grants, one from a private foundation and, ultimately, two from the U.S. Department of Education that enabled the institution to ramp up efforts to serve first-year students much more aggressively than it would have done otherwise. For example, a $2.5 million grant from the U.S. Department of Education supported the development of UTEP's Entering Student Program. This grant funded a number of activities and personnel over a five-year period. During that time, the University began to factor these personnel and infrastructure costs into its budget planning. When the grant expired, the program was institutionalized, and the university college funded the personnel and other programming costs.

Some grants fund one-time needs to create infrastructure, such as building or renovating facilities; purchasing supplies such as computers, hardware, and software; and paying for professional and program development (e.g., consulting fees, travel to conferences). While these leave an institution with long-term maintenance, they do not require permanent institutional budgetary growth.

A number of different kinds of grants, especially federally funded programs, are renewable. Upward Bound, Talent Search, Educational Opportunity Centers, Student Support Services Program, and McNair Scholars are time-tested, effective programs serving low-income and first-generation students. On many campuses, a primary activity of the university college is a TRIO program. States also have developed funding initiatives used to support entering students (e.g., New York). Often these resources are provided for low-income or underprepared students. Many university colleges have been successful in obtaining U.S. Department of Education Title III or Title V grants and/or private foundation support to pilot efforts with entering students.

Donor support. Donor support is a more elusive, but nonetheless valuable, source for external funds. Since units for entering students do not have alumni, it is not common to have the alumni donor base as a viable option for entering student programming support. However, other strategies for developing potential donors are available. On one campus, for example, the president made first-year programming efforts the primary focus of his annual appeal to the community.

Recommendations

University college leadership and administration have the opportunity to develop and manage resources in an entrepreneurial environment where program development on behalf of new students is valued. While there is no one-size-fits-all university college model, a number of strategies are essential. Assessment must be a top priority for the college so that as budget decisions on the campus are made, the university college can show the value it brings to the students' experience. In addition, a student-centered culture must be maintained. The following recommendations pertain to any university college model:

Make assessment a priority. Building the case for resources comes best from assessment. The university college can make the case inside and outside the institution for support, as they are able to demonstrate impact from policies and practices in place to serve students. If retention increases, if satisfaction increases, if student success increases, if more students seek a college education, the university college can make a case for its effectiveness and its sustainability.

Focus on faculty. Though faculty culture varies across campuses and disciplines, attention to faculty governance and faculty input and ownership of programs is essential. Faculty control the culture of the campus, and having authentic faculty ownership and oversight of academic policies and practices for entering students is essential. While not all the work has to be the work of the faculty, the university college must have the faculty voice front and center in its work.

Consider forming an advisory board. The university college may have an advisory board from inside and/or outside the campus. Such boards can provide valuable insights in reviewing the work of the unit. In some cases, they can be the venue for launching fund-raising programs.

Focus on the positive. Too often, an academic or administrative unit can become besieged with a catalog of barriers to success and then become too focused on fixing each barrier as it arises. It is certainly the case that work with entering students will never be perfect. There are too many changes in the culture and too many missed steps with students, which can and must be corrected one at a time as they are identified, but overarching attention to barriers and challenges can be debilitating in getting on with the work of serving entering students in the university college. Rather than reacting to each barrier, university college administrators must create proactive processes that continue to refine the work of the college on behalf of all students.

Similarly, campuses are able to give detailed catalogues of what is not possible, and those iterations are laundry lists of budget items or resource items that are not in place. Backing off a structural change that will make positive impact on student success until everything is in place in terms of resources that might be needed is shortsighted. With constant change in culture and in expectations of entering students, the litany of resources needed at one point in time is likely to be very different five years in the future. Electronic resources, for example, are rapidly replacing printed materials. Many campuses would have declared, for example, that the printed campus bulletin was a permanent fixture of the institution 15 years ago. Yet, many campuses have long since printed their last bulletins. A focus on what a campus does not have in terms of resources is energy misspent. Instead, the university college should use what is in place, gathering the resources that are present, and, then, building on its strengths.

Appreciative inquiry is one approach that provides a systematic way of building on strengths in support of the mission. The Foundations of Excellence project (2009), an aspirational plan that involves a careful review process for improvement in the first year, is another strategy for examining and capitalizing on current program strengths.

Share funded opportunities campus-wide. An aspiration for the university college might be to provide funding on the margin—to identify and support those campus priorities that drive student success, but that are not clearly the responsibility of other campus units. For example, there may be faculty development grants to expand the scholarship of teaching and learning for students in entering classes. Or there might be funding for retreats for faculty and staff across campus to attend to student success. Outside experts or fellow practitioners from other campuses could visit the institution to identify strategies to enhance student success. In this way, the university college might be a beacon for the campus in its commitment to student success by articulating issues and identifying, often limited, resources to move toward campus aspirations for student success. These kinds of activities can infuse the campus with new ways of doing business.

Keep the students and their learning first. The university college is about serving entering students. The test of the unit's effectiveness is fundamentally about the students and their learning. Everything—the programs, services, and courses of the university college—has to be measured with that standard. A unit will lose its way if it does not keep students and their learning at the center. A university college should be the place where the campus comes together to make real the statement widely attributed to William Butler Yeats: "Education is not the filling of a pail but the lighting of a fire."

Conclusion

Enhancing the academic achievement and persistence of the students admitted to and matriculated on a campus to increase their chances of graduating is often the raison d'être for the university college. The provision of resources to meet that objective—enhancing academic achievement and persistence resulting in graduation—will receive increased attention as low-income, first-generation, and racially and ethnically diverse students come increasingly to characterize the entering students of our campuses. At the same time, maintaining a diligent focus on the development and management of resource needs and sources of income is critical for the university college leadership and administration.

References

Adelman, C. (2006, October 27). How to design a web site that welcomes prospective applicants. *The Chronicle of Higher Education,* p. B26.

Cooperrider, D. L., & Whitney, D. (2005). *Appreciative inquiry: A positive revolution in change.* San Francisco, CA: Berrett-Koehler.

Foundations of Excellence. (2009). *Home web page.* Retrieved June, 26, 2009 from, http://www.fyfoundations.org

Wong, G. (2006, November 14). *Educators explore 'Second Life' online.* Retrieved June 26, 2009, from http://www.cnn.com/2006/TECH/11/13/second.life.university/index.html

CHAPTER 7

The University College: A Context for Student Success and Institutional Change

Scott E. Evenbeck, Maggy Smith, & Dorothy Ward

The hallmark of the university college is to be a change agent on behalf of entering students. It is the locus of creativity on a campus, providing leadership and vision and a home for experimenting with new ideas and programs. University college faculty and staff often collaborate on program development that brings the whole campus into conversations about the future of the institution and its students. In addition to facilitating collaborations supporting student success, these administrative structures have moved institutions forward in significant ways by attending to the curriculum and the cocurriculum, taking a holistic approach to learning, and stressing assessment and improvement. This chapter addresses the university college in its role as organizational change agent and offers some concluding observations about the issues moving to the forefront of university college work.

University College as a Change Agent

University college leadership champions continuous reflection and change for students, especially for students entering higher education, which often ripples through the entire institution. As the locus of transformation for a campus, the university college model establishes a community of practice and institutional context to enhance student success. Frequently team-oriented, the university college personnel—students, faculty, staff, and administration—are passionate about developing contexts for student success and institutional transformation, both pedagogical and programmatic. The work of the university college as it plays out in physical space, best practices, and policies helps students build on their strengths, focuses on assets rather than deficits, and brings to life a talent-development model for entering students. By attending to student academic achievement and persistence, the university college often pioneers early warning, mandatory attendance, administrative withdrawal, contact systems for students, and other policies and practices to enhance student success. In providing these contexts and then in living out the aspiration of an environment of continuous learning and improvement, the university college model becomes an important change agent for a campus as its practices and policies are frequently adopted beyond the entering students' programs to serve all students.

The university college becomes a change agent through its support of and advocacy for entering students. While academic departments focus on their majors and on their graduate students, the university college provides faculty, many of whom joined the academy because they were committed to both research and teaching, a structure for working with others across campus to help ensure the success of entering students as well as the success of continuing students entering the major. As faculty work with advisors, student affairs professionals, and peer educators to support student success, they gain insights into the contributions each brings to support students. In fact, all participants gain an understanding of the importance of one another's roles on campus and the possibilities for collaboration. Faculty learn that advisors are also teachers. Advisors and faculty see the power of peer mentoring as student mentors work with entering students. Upper-level student mentors also bring the peer support approach to their respective academic departments, extending and expanding a climate focused on student learning through engagement in research and internships in their majors. Student affairs professionals learn about what goes on in the classroom, and faculty learn about what goes on in the cocurricular lives of their students. This growth of understanding, then, extends beyond the university college and positively impacts students campus-wide.

While the university college is designed as a campus unit committed to continuous change on behalf of support for entering students, there are many unintended and very positive consequences that extend well beyond the entering students served by the university college. Positive impacts include extension of a climate of continuous learning and improvement across campus. For example, faculty implement pedagogies first used in learning communities and first-year seminars organized by the university college in their other courses, thus improving the learning experience for all students.

The Ongoing and Future Work of the University College

Postsecondary education exists in a dynamic environment with persistent calls for accountability and demands for substantial increases in the number of baccalaureate graduates. Since most attrition happens in the first years of study, it is imperative that campuses attend to students having a more successful transition to college study. As the structure for a campus to do this work, the university college must attend to several issues as identified below.

Bringing Successful Habits to Campus

Generally speaking, new college students do not bring habits conducive to academic success to campus as they begin their study. For example, the amount of reading reported for high school students continues to decrease. As Scherer (2005) points out, "Young people ages 15–24 spend an average of eight and one-half minutes a day reading for enjoyment" (p. 7). Even many young adults who do read often do not have the skills necessary to decode complex material. In an informal survey of teachers in the high school where he taught, Tovani (2005) asked what skills "students most needed to improve their comprehension of assigned readings. The number one response was that students don't know how to determine what is important in the text" (p. 48). Americans, in general, are not reading as much as past generations. Gioia (2004) explains that "literary reading in America is not only declining rapidly among all groups, but the rate of decline has accelerated, especially among the young" (p. vii). Even newspaper reading is declining around the country, resulting in major newspapers struggling financially due to reduced subscriptions. *The Detroit News*, for example, is now published only three days a week, the *Christian Science Monitor* has moved to a weekly edition, the *Seattle Post-Intelligencer* has moved to a web-only publication, and the *Rocky Mountain News* in Denver has folded. This alarming trend has implications for higher education. The National Endowment for the Arts (2007) explains that as people "read less, their reading skills worsen, especially among teenagers and young males" (p.12).

However, current research points out that students' use of social networking and text messaging has increased both their reading and writing habits, but in nonconventional modes (Lunsford, 2009). While students are entering college spending less time in traditional reading activities, the academy continues largely to stress words printed on the physical page. A focus on traditional academic discourse remains important; however, Baxter Magolda (2006) suggests that "it is [also] important to bridge possible gaps between languages of the disciplines and languages that reflect current student experience" (p. 2).

The use of newspapers in the classroom and common reading programs are two ways that university colleges work to bridge the gap. Often the university college is the organizing unit for common reading programs for entering students during the summer, during welcome weeks, or in first-year seminars (Laufgraben, 2006; Evenbeck & Ross, 2007). Students are asked to read the book before new student orientation and then to spend time on it during orientation activities or to use it as a primary source for the first-year seminar or general education courses.

Using Technology—In and Out of the Classroom

Students' social worlds are increasingly centered on digital technologies. They use texting and other forms of instant communication and social networking to be in touch with one another. Campuses are finding more platforms for using these student-friendly technologies for both social and academic engagement, often in the context of the university college. Many campuses are using blogs, Twitter, and Facebook to maintain communication with and among students. As one faculty member pointed out:

> It's amazingly rewarding to meet my students in their technolog[ical] world by using podcasts, videocasts, and active learning methods in the classroom. It keeps me on my toes, and students love to see that as an experienced faculty I care enough to try new learning techniques. (K. Thedwall, personal communication, June 25, 2009)

Yet, validating entering students' current modes of communication while impressing upon students the need to expand beyond those modes and messages is a challenge for those serving them. The communication skills students use and prefer are frequently not those needed for success in the university or in their future employment. The university college gives faculty a structure for working together to develop strategies to expose students to new ways of communicating and to use those communication strategies for integration and application of knowledge.

Classroom management programs, such as Blackboard, are transforming the teaching and learning environment, making it much more interactive and allowing students and faculty to exchange assignments and notes easily in electronic formats. These formats provide forums for class-based electronic discussions, chat rooms, and grading, all dedicated to a single class section.

Balancing Challenge and Support for Entering Students

The most essential reference tool for anyone managing a campus first-year experience is entitled *Challenging and Supporting the First-Year Student* (Upcraft, Gardner, & Barefoot, 2005). In describing the first college year, Upcraft et al. draw heavily on Nevitt Sanford's recommendations for supporting learning and development among college students, proposing that

> . . . In order for students to succeed, they must be both challenged (provided with educational experiences that foster learning and personal development) and supported (provided with a campus climate that helps students learn and develop). When a proper balance is maintained between challenge and support, students are positioned to succeed in college. When that

balance is not maintained, students are more likely to fail. Likewise, institutions are more likely to succeed in helping first-year students make a successful transition to college if they provide challenging educational experiences accompanied by effective support services and programs. (p. xii)

Particularly in an era of increasing racial/ethnic diversity in higher education and greater numbers of low-income and first-generation students entering college, it is imperative that the university college model be a place where the role of high expectations, coupled with support, is stressed.

Schilling and Schilling (1999) note that students come to campus with expectations that college will be more difficult than high school. When those students arrive on campus, they are told to allocate three hours of study per hour in the classroom. So a student taking a full load of 12 credit hours is urged to set aside about 36 hours a week to study. Yet, students in their first semesters generally report that they did not have to work as hard as they expected to (or were told they would need to) when they began college (Schilling & Schilling).

Paradoxically, students who find college to be too easy may not do very well. A follow-up analysis of the 2009 National Survey of Student Engagement (NSSE) results for IUPUI revealed that first-year students' perceptions of the level of challenge in their courses was significantly and positively related to their first-year grades and persistence to the second year of college. That is, students who perceived their courses to be academically challenging were more likely to have higher grade point averages and to persist to the second year than were students who did not perceive their courses to be challenging. This result is consistent with the recommendation made more than two decades ago by the Study Group on the Conditions of Excellence in Higher Education (1984), which recommended that faculty, colleges, and universities set high expectations for student performance in order to enhance learning and student success.

Schilling and Schilling (1999) note, "The economies of time use that students put in place during their first year are the very same economies that structure their allocation of time in the last semester of their senior year" (p. 8). If they are not challenged in the first year and required to develop good time management and study habits, then they are likely to struggle once they enter more challenging, upper-division courses. A university college can become the leader in helping students develop successful study habits and time management skills. Many university colleges offer workshops or other programs where students can learn about resources on campus and develop improved study skills. The peer leadership programs, described in chapter 4, are another resource for helping students develop strong academic skills. Some students may mistakenly believe the best way to study is through individual memorization sessions. Treisman (1992) discovered that while minority, blue-collar, and rural students spent many hours studying alone, they rarely studied with their classmates. He explains that these students "were getting *A*s in 'Study Skills,' and *F*s" in the class (p. 367). Peer leaders can help students discover early in their college years the value of group study.

Increasing New Student Diversity: The Changing Profile

The population of students entering postsecondary education is increasingly diverse in a number of ways. Students are more likely to be members of minority populations. They are more likely to bring dual credit, advanced placement credit, early college high school credits, or credits from the military, and they are more likely to be transferring from other institutions. Borden (2004) used the term *student swirl* in describing the demographic shift in higher education from students who enroll in a single institution to a population that moves among multiple institutions. The university college structure is a likely entry point, and sometimes temporary home, for such swirling students. Programs and policies will have to attend to these dimensions of diversity and the new profile of students entering college in order to ensure their success. For example, the university college can provide special orientation sessions or programs supplementing orientation, including bridge programs as well as special sections of the first-year seminar and cocurricular programs offered in conjunction with student life units, to support these new college populations.

Involving Parents and Families

The parents and families of new college students need to be invited to be more involved in students' college experiences. Administrators frequently focus on helicopter parents, those parents who hover over their students and are often intrusive—even if well intentioned—in the college adaptation process. On the other hand, many low-income and first-generation college students do not have family members and friends who can serve as role models or guides in the college transition process. Research suggests that interventions with precollege students are effective to the extent that parents are supportive of the students' involvement. For example, Maimer (2004) reports that parental involvement is an effective tool and has been shown "to explain academic achievement" (p. 73). She further explains that "parents, no matter what their income or education level, can contribute to their child's education through involvement in and discussions about school" (p. 75). In its role as campus change agent, the university college can be the leader for enhancing parental understanding of and support for their students' academic success through programming that engages students' support systems. Students should be invited to campus with their parents. Parents may well be invited to work with one another in programming for the parents of precollege students. Campus visits, supplemented by exposure to research and even on-campus enrollment for precollege students, will enhance students' later success in college and their parents' understanding of and involvement in their academic success.

Focusing on the Big Picture

Through its mission to serve entering students, the university college can be the unit where the campus addresses big questions of enhancing student success. The university college, in collaboration with institutional research, is a place where administrators, faculty, and staff command the concepts of the changing realities of postsecondary education. These professionals are the persons and units serving the entering students, the first on campus working directly with the new students, and often the ones entrusted with helping students make the transition to successful study. The university college may be the unit collaborating with the P–12 sector in enhancing student preparation for and expectations of college. Even when not offering the classes, the university college is intensely involved with the general education curriculum in which new students are most often engaged. The university college organizes first-year seminars, learning communities, and academic support programs for these students and often provides academic advising, as well.

It is important that the university college be intentional and reflective in doing this work—not apart from, but grounded in, connections with the schools and departments also serving students. Expanding dual credit coming from high schools is an emerging issue for many campuses. How can the university college study what is going on and help both students and departments make the transition to more dual credit? How might the university college foster more bridge programs for entering students and use of summer for students in general? The university college and its programming are not separate from the rest of the student experience but exist an important juncture in the students' lives. How can the university college be connected both with what comes before and set the stage for success as students move into their majors and on to graduation? The answers to these questions must be determined by the context of the institution and the community that it serves.

A Final Word

Kurt Lewin, the founder of experimental social psychology, stated that behavior is a function of the person and the environment (Lewin, Heider, & Heider, 1936). His seminal research, for example, showed how contexts (i.e., in his case, autocracy versus democracy as operationalized in a laboratory) resulted in very different behaviors on the part of the subjects in his experiments. For too long, higher education has attributed students' behavior only to the student, to his or her motivation or ability, and has ignored context. The university college, as the place where students enter the campus, must be the primary site for providing contexts that will enhance student success by the sorts of innovative programs and policies articulated in the chapters and case studies here. The diverse students coming to college in the second decade of the new century and beyond require more, not less, attention; and society is mandating that higher education meet its expectations for such support of students. The university college model can and should be a primary means of meeting these expectations.

References

Baxter Magolda, M. B. (2006, January). Self-authorship and identity in college: An interview with Marcia B. Baxter Magolda. *Journal of College and Character, 7*(1), 1–2. Retrieved from http://www.collegevalues.org/pdfs/Baxter%20Magolda.pdf

Borden, V. M. H. (2004, March-April). Accommodating student swirl: When traditional students are no longer the tradition. *Change, 36*(2), 10–17.

Evenbeck, S. E., & Ross, F. E. (2007, January 15). *The development and assessment of an integrated general education curriculum in the first college year.* Institute on General Education and Assessment, Association of American Colleges and Universities, New Orleans, LA.

Gioia, D. (2004). Preface. In *Reading at risk: A survey of literary reading in America* (Research Report 46). Washington, DC: National Endowment for the Arts.

Laufgraben, J. L. (2006). *Common reading programs: Going beyond the book* (Monograph No. 44). Columbia, SC: University of South Carolina, National Resource Center for The First-Year Experience and Students in Transition.

Lewin, K., Heider, F., & Heider, G. M. (1936). *Principles of topological psychology.* New York, NY: McGraw-Hill.

Lunsford, A. (2009, November 12). *Issues in new media writing.* Presentation at The University of Texas at El Paso.

Maimer, P. J. (2004, April 24). *Making the square peg fit the round hole: Social and cultural capital in pre-college programs.* Paper presented at the 16th National Symposium on Doctoral Research in Social Work. Retrieved from https://kb.osu.edu/dspace/bitstream/1811/37359/1/16_Maimer_paper.pdf

National Endowment for the Arts. (2007). *To read or not to read* (Research Report 47). Washington, DC: National Endowment for the Arts.

Scherer, M. (2005, October). Required reading. *Educational Leadership, 63*(2), 7.

Schilling, K. M., & Schilling, K. L. (1999, May/June). Increasing expectations for student effort. *About Campus, 4*(2), 4–10.

Study Group on the Conditions of Excellence in Higher Education. (1984). *Involvement in learning: Realizing the potential of higher education.* Washington, DC: National Institute of Education, U.S. Department of Education.

Tovani, C. (2005, October). The power of purposeful reading. *Educational Leadership, 63*(2), 48–51.

Treisman, U. (1992). Studying students studying calculus: A look at the lives of minority mathematics students in college. *The College Mathematics Journal, 23*(5), 362–372.

Upcraft, M. L., Gardner, J. N., & Barefoot, B. O. (Eds.). (2005). *Challenging and supporting the first-year student: A handbook for improving the first year of college.* San Francisco, CA: Jossey-Bass.

Appendix A

Responding Institutions

Abilene Christian University	Abilene, TX
Appalachian State University	Boone, NC
Arizona State University, West Campus	Phoenix, AZ
Augusta State University	Augusta, GA
Aurora University	Aurora, IL
Ball State University	Muncie, IN
Bridgewater State College	Bridgewater, MA
City University of New York Medgar Evers College	Brooklyn, NY
Columbus State University	Columbus, GA
Dartmouth College	Hanover, NH
Denison University	Granville, OH
DePaul University	Chicago, IL
East Carolina University	Greenville, NC
Edward Waters College	Jacksonville, FL
Fayetteville State University	Fayetteville, NC
Ferris State University	Big Rapids, MI
Hudson Valley Community College	Troy, NY
Illinois State University	Normal, IL
Indiana University, Bloomington	Bloomington, IN
Indiana University-Purdue University Indianapolis	Indianapolis, IN
Jackson State University	Jackson, MS
Kennesaw State University	Kennesaw, GA
Montana State University	Bozeman, MT
New Mexico Junior College	Hobbs, NM
Nicholls State University	Thibodaux, LA
North Carolina State University	Raleigh, NC
Northeastern State University	Tahlequah, OK
Northwestern State University	Natchitoches, LA
Pennsylvania State University	University Park, PA

Prairie View A&M University	Prairie View, TX
Slippery Rock University	Slippery Rock, PA
Saint Peters College	Jersey City, NJ
State University of New York Buffalo State College	Buffalo, NY
Sullivan County Community College	Loch Sheldrake, NY
Texas A&M University, College Station	College Station, TX
Texas A&M University, Kingsville	Kingsville, TX
Texas State University San Marcos	San Marcos, TX
University of Akron	Akron, OH
University of Alaska Fairbanks	Fairbanks, AK
University of Arizona	Tucson, AZ
University of Central Arkansas	Conway, AR
University of Central Florida	Orlando, FL
University of Houston	Houston, TX
University of Houston, Downtown	Houston, TX
University of Louisiana, Monroe	Monroe, LA
University of Maryland	College Park, MD
University of Memphis	Memphis, TN
University of Montana	Missoula, MT
University of New Mexico	Albuquerque, NM
University of North Carolina, Charlotte	Charlotte, NC
University of Oklahoma	Norman, OK
University of Rhode Island	Kingston, RI
University of Texas, El Paso	El Paso, TX
University of Texas, San Antonio	San Antonio, TX
Virginia Commonwealth University	Richmond, VA
Wilkes University	Wilkes-Barre, PA
Winthrop University	Rock Hill, SC
Wright State University	Dayton, OH

Appendix B

University College Survey

This survey is part of a research project to document the ways that colleges and universities organize and administer policies, programs, and services to new undergraduate students. Aggregated results will be reported in a monograph to be published in 2007 by the National Resource Center for The First-Year Experience and Students in Transition. This research is conducted with the support of the Policy Center on the First Year of College and the Association of Deans and Directors of University Colleges and Undergraduate Studies. Your responses will not be individually identified.

Institution Name: ____

1. Please provide the name of the administrative unit that organizes and administers policies, programs, and services to new undergraduate students or comment below.

   ____

   ____

   ____

2. Please provide the title of the unit's leader.

   ____

   ____

   ____

3. Compared to others on campus with the same position title, which best describes this unit head's range of resources, responsibility, and status?
   ❑ Generally lower than the same title in other campus units
   ❑ About equal to the same title in other campus units
   ❑ Generally higher than same title in other campus units
   Please elaborate (optional).

   ____

   ____

   ____

4. Does this unit serve as an official "academic home" for students?
    ❑ Yes
    ❑ Yes, for some specific types of students
    ❑ Not for any
    ❑ Don't know

5. Does this unit award any degrees?
    ❑ Yes
    ❑ No

6. Does this unit have tenure/tenure-track faculty lines?
    ❑ Yes
    ❑ No
    ❑ N/A

7. Please select the response that best describes the unit's service to each of the following categories of students.

	Serves all	Serves most	Serves some	Serves none	Don't know/ NA
First-year students (freshmen)					
Students who *have not* yet declared a major					
Students who *have* declared a major					
New transfer students					
Students on academic probation					
Honors students					
Provisionally admitted student					
International students					
Specify other types of students served.					

8. Please select the response that best describes this unit's connection with each of the following services.

	Primary campus responsibility	Responsibility shared with other units	Very limited responsibility	No responsibility	Don't know/NA
Academic advising services					
Academic support for student athletes					
Academic support/learning center					
Admissions functions					
Assessment/institutional effectiveness studies					
Bursar functions					
Career exploration/planning services					
Developmental mathematics courses					
Developmental reading courses					
Developmental writing courses					
English as a second language courses					
Faculty development programming					
Faculty/student mentoring program					
Financial aid services					
First-year (freshman) seminar/ FYE courses					
General education courses					
Honors program(s)					
Instructional technology services					
Interdisciplinary studies degree(s)					
Learning communities					
Mathematics tutoring/support services					
New student orientation					
Online courses					
Parent/family support program					

continued on p. 170

	Primary campus responsibility	Responsibility shared with other units	Very limited responsibility	No responsibility	Don't know/NA
P-16 college readiness programs					
Peer advising					
Placement testing					
Registrar functions					
Service-learning					
Stop-out program					
Student leadership development					
Student life/student affairs					
Study skills workshops/instruction					
Supplemental Instruction					
TRIO Programs (e.g., Upward Bound, Student Support Service)					
Tutoring/mentoring					
Writing tutoring/support services					

9. Please identify other programs, services, and activities of the unit that are not included above.

____

____

____

10. To what degree does this unit collaborate with the following organizations on services and programs for students?

	High	Moderate	Low	Don't know/ NA
Other postsecondary institutions				
Area K-12 schools				
Neighborhood organizations/community centers				
Local businesses				

11. Approximately how many faculty/staff report to this unit in each of the following categories?
    (Use head count and include full and part-time employees.)

    Second-level administrators (e.g., assistant/associate dean/vice president)   _____________

    Third-level administrators (e.g., directors, coordinators)   _____________

    Tenured/tenure-track faculty   _____________

    Other faculty (nontenure-track)   _____________

    Clerical/support staff   _____________

    Other professional staff   _____________

    Student employees   _____________

12. Approximately what is the annual operating budget for this unit?
    ❑ Salary   _____________
    ❑ Nonsalary   _____________

13. Which best describes this unit's physical setting(s)?
    ❑ Primary/only occupant of a dedicated campus building
    ❑ Majority of facilities are located in a single building shared with other campus units
    ❑ Facilities are located in multiple buildings shared with other campus units
    ❑ This unit is not assigned specific physical space on campus.

14. Please describe other features of the facilities occupied by this unit (e.g., ease of student access,
    prominence on campus, number of buildings, square footage).

    ____

    ____

    ____

15. Please describe other major resources of the unit (e.g., number of computer labs, special
    equipment).

    ____

    ____

    ____

16. Please briefly describe the unit's mission. If the unit's mission statement is available online,
    please provide the URL.

    ____

    ____

    ____

continued on p. 172

17. Please provide a brief history of the unit. When was it founded? How has it changed over time? What was the impetus for establishing the unit?

____

____

____

Survey completed by: _______________________________________

Name: ____

E-mail address: ____

Phone: (____) ____

Appendix C
Resources for University College Work

Association of American Colleges and Universities (AAC&U). This organization is the hub for attention to liberal and general education. As such, it is of key importance to the success of entering students (see www.aacu.org).

Association of Deans and Directors of University Colleges and Undergraduate Studies (AD&D). This association, with a home office at Ball State University, is the network for deans and directors of units serving entering students (see www.bsu.edu/web/adandd). At annual gatherings, those responsible for serving entering students use an open meeting format to address issues of importance in enhancing service to students.

John N. Gardner Institute for Excellence in Undergraduate Education (formerly the Policy Center on the First Year of College). This center, located in Brevard, North Carolina, developed the Foundations of Excellence Project, an aspirational model for enhancing student success in the first year (see www.firstyear.org).

Institute for Higher Education Policy (IHEP). This group provides national leadership in the articulation of policies and practices associated with increasing access to and success in higher education among underrepresented student populations (see www.ihep.org).

Lumina Foundation for Education. This organization has the mission of helping people gain access to and experience success in education beyond high school. The web site, publications, and funded projects are central to the call to enhance student access and success (see www.luminafoundation.org).

National Academic Advising Association (NACADA). This association provides a wealth of resources for serving all students, with particular attention to entering students in many cases (see www.nacada.ksu.edu).

National Orientation Directors Association (NODA). This organization focuses on programs and initiatives designed to orient students to college and help them make a successful transition to a new academic environment (see www.nodaweb.org).

National Resource Center for The First-Year Experience and Students in Transition. This center, located at the University of South Carolina, has for many years been the locus for faculty and staff attention to entering students. The Annual Conference on The First-Year Experience, complemented by other conferences, publications, and services, is at the center of work for enhancing the success of entering students(see www.sc.edu/fye).

About the Contributors

Julie Alexander-Hamilton is the associate vice president for assessment administration at the John N. Gardner Institute for Excellence in Undergraduate Education. She actively engages with colleges and universities as they prepare for and conduct an intensive self-study of the first year of college and/or the transfer student experience. She oversees various operational, technological, and data activities associated with supporting participating institutions. Alexander-Hamilton has authored and co-authored several publications, including a 2009 *About Campus* article, "Beyond Retention: A Comprehensive Approach to the First College Year." She holds a master's degree in college student development and a baccalaureate degree in psychology from Appalachian State University.

Scott E. Evenbeck is professor of psychology and dean of University College at Indiana University–Purdue University Indianapolis (IUPUI). He joined the faculty at IUPUI in psychology in 1972, after completing his PhD in psychology at the University of North Carolina at Chapel Hill. Evenbeck has been involved for many years in the design and assessment of general education, including the development, ongoing implementation, and assessment of IUPUI's outcomes for student learning. He has also played a major role in various P-16 initiatives to support student academic achievement and in retention initiatives for Indiana higher education. He has given more than 100 presentations on serving entering students and written many articles and chapters on enhancing student academic achievement and persistence. He represented IUPUI in the Association of American Colleges and Universities (AAC&U) Greater Expectations project and has served as a task force advisor in the Foundations of Excellence in the First College Year. Evenbeck also serves as a resource faculty member at the Summer Quality Academy, as faculty for the Summer Institute on Learning Communities with the Washington Center for Improving the Quality of Undergraduate Education, on accreditation teams for three regional associations, and as a consultant to several campuses in the BEAMS project. He is a former member of the Advisory Board for the National Resource Center for The First-Year Experience and Students in Transition.

Michele J. Hansen, is the director of assessment for University College at Indiana University–Purdue University Indianapolis (IUPUI), where she is responsible for conducting outcome assessments and program evaluations of first-year programs including learning communities. She holds appointed faculty positions with University College and is an adjunct associate professor with the Department of Psychology at IUPUI. Hansen's primary research interests are in the areas of learning outcomes assessment and program evaluation methods, using social psychology theory to understand the effectiveness of interventions to enhance retention and academic success of undergraduate students, survey research methods, and incremental and fundamental change implementation. She has maintained an active professional profile that includes participation in national organizations such as the Association for Institutional Research (AIR), conference presentations, and publications in journals such as *New Directions in Institutional Research* and the *Journal of Learning Communities Research*. She received her baccalaureate degree in psychology from Michigan State University and her master's and doctoral degrees in social psychology from Loyola University Chicago.

Barbara Jackson is a professor of anthropology and associate dean emerita of University College at Indiana University–Purdue University Indianapolis (IUPUI). Her work as an anthropologist was centered on religion, social change, and gender in Native North American and Central Mexican cultures. She spent her entire professional career at IUPUI, where she was privileged to participate, as both a faculty member and administrator, in the founding and development of its Department of Anthropology, Women's Studies Program, and University College. She received her baccalaureate degree in anthropology from Hunter College and her master's and doctoral degrees from the University of Minnesota.

Frank E. Ross is the associate provost for student success at the University of North Texas at Dallas (UNTD). As the chief student affairs officer, he is responsible for developing initiatives to support student success and retention, including development of a comprehensive first-year experience. Previously, Ross was the assistant vice chancellor for student life and learning at Indiana University–Purdue University Indianapolis (IUPUI), where he worked with both University College and student affairs. Ross is editor for the *Journal of Learning Communities Research* and is also involved with planning for the annual National Learning Communities Conference. Ross is involved with the research division for the National Association of Student Personnel Administrators (NASPA) and has research interests in student success, learning communities, and enhancing civic engagement among first-year college students. Ross earned his PhD in higher education at Indiana University and completed master's programs at both Ball State University and Western Kentucky University.

Maggy Smith is a professor of English at the University of Texas at El Paso (UTEP) where she has been a faculty member and an administrator since 1987 with the exception of a brief tenure as vice president for Academic Affairs (2008-2009) at St. Mary-of-the-Woods College in Terre Haute, Indiana. As founding dean of UTEP's University College, Smith collaborated broadly with campus constituencies in both academic affairs and student affairs to guide UTEP's work in achieving student success. She led the efforts to create a first-year seminar, learning communities, a student leadership institute, and other programs to enhance the success and satisfaction of entering students, including integrating enrollment service departments into the entering student focus. In addition to working collaboratively with educational entities in El Paso, Smith was instrumental in developing a close working relationship with the El Paso Community College. The author of several large grant programs, a consultant for undergraduate education nationally and internationally, Smith has authored articles and conference presentations on topics related to the first year of college. She received both her bachelor's and master's degrees from the State University of New York at Fredonia and a PhD in Communication and Rhetoric from Rensselaer Polytechnic Institute.

Randy L. Swing is the executive director of the Association for Institutional Research (AIR), a professional association of more than 4,200 institutional members. Prior to joining AIR, Swing served as codirector and senior scholar at the Policy Center on the First Year of College and as a fellow in the National Resource Center for The First-Year Experience and Students in Transition at the University of South Carolina. He has worked with numerous research teams in Japan and served as an advisor to the Quality Assurance Agency of Scotland. He has authored articles, chapters, monographs, and books, including *Achieving and Sustaining Excellence in the First College Year* (2006) and *Proving and Improving: Tools and Techniques for Assessing the First College Year* (2004). He is a frequent speaker at national and international conferences on institutional change, assessment, retention, and undergraduate student success. He serves on the editorial and review boards for the *Journal of General Education*, *The Journal on Excellence in College Teaching*, and *Innovative Higher Education*. For two decades prior to 1999, he held various leadership positions at Appalachian State University in assessment, advising, Upward Bound, and Freshman Seminar. He holds a PhD in higher education from the University of Georgia, master's and educational specialist degrees from Appalachian State University, and a baccalaureate degree in psychology from the University of North Carolina-Charlotte.

Dorothy Ward is director of the Entering Student Program at The University of Texas at El Paso (UTEP). In this role, she collaborates with key University staff and administrators to develop and coordinate academically centered initiatives that strive to improve the success and retention of entering student. The Entering Student Program received the Texas Higher Education Coordinating Board 2003 Star Award, recognizing it as an outstanding program in Texas. Ward has received two of UTEP's most prestigious awards: the 2000 Outstanding Advocate for Entering Students Award and the 2001 Distinguished Achievement Award for Teaching Excellence. In 2004, she received the Outstanding First-Year Student Advocate Award from the National Resource Center for The First-Year Experience and Students in Transition. Ward has served as a consultant for first-year programming and has been an invited keynote speaker at three regional conferences addressing learning communities. Ward earned her PhD in English at the University of North Texas.

Gayle Williams is the assistant dean of University College at Indiana University–Purdue Indianapolis(IUPUI) and has participated in the development, management, and assessment of academic support programs for entering students, including first-year seminars, themed learning communities, structured learning assistance, critical inquiry, and a summer bridge program. In addition, she oversees the campus orientation program and manages the Bepko Learning Center, which houses support initiatives including Supplemental Instruction, Structured Learning Assistance, and a resource desk. Williams has been the retention coordinator for IUPUI since 2001.